"Patrick Henry is a giant of ecumenical imagination, and just the sort of giant you'd hope to encounter on a walk through the theological woods—well read, thoughtful, humble, and wise. St. Ignatius taught us to find God in all things, and Henry certainly does—from philosophy to music, literature to TV shows, loss to profound joy. It is a delight to follow along through his eight decades of encounters with the grace of a God who is not stingily either/or but generously both/and."

— **Cameron Bellm**
author of *A Consoling Embrace: Prayers for a Time of Pandemic*

"'Be someone on whom nothing is lost'—Henry James's admonition to the writer—is something Patrick Henry must have read in the cradle. In a long and distinguished career he has not ceased from spiritual exploration, always 'pressing forward,' and this inventive book, notable for its wide range of reference, radiantly shows an openness to the necessity and vitality of change and new patterns in these giddy times, while honoring the *cantus firmus* of invaluable traditions. His clear, aphoristic prose is a joy to read. 'Fully alive' indeed."

— **Michael Dennis Browne**
poet and librettist

embedded in a life. onships, education, pop culture, Henry eals new truths as it ography that teaches the reader while also encouraging her to reflect more deeply on her own story."

— **Kristel Clayville**
senior fellow, MacLean Center for Clinical Medical Ethics,
University of Chicago

"'This is my first (and last?) foray into the field of American religion.' That's how Patrick Henry self-identified decades back for a journal bio. We should all rejoice his prediction was mistaken. His newest book is the perfect antidote to our American age of spiritual discontent, his faith the right prescription for today: one shorn of doctrinal triumphalism, stamped with intellectual honesty and rigor, ever open to discovering religious wisdom in many crevices and byways. Reading this beautifully written spiritual autobiography instantly brought to mind W. H. Auden's observation that 'a Christian is never something one is, only something one can pray to become.' For religious seekers on their way to becoming, no matter what their particular label, *Flashes of Grace* shows the way forward."

—**Barry D. Cytron**
rabbi and former director of the Collegeville Institute
Multi-Religious Fellows Program

"*Flashes of Grace* is a fascinating book. Written with the swoop and dip of lively conversation and ranging through a lifetime of opinions and experiences, it is a portrait of a deeply sincere Christian fully open to being astonished and illuminated by a changing world. Since Patrick is a scholar and a teacher, his personal musings are infused with the history of religion. I learned so much from this book! Its good-spirited honesty cheered me up."

— **Norman Fischer**
author of *The World Could Be Otherwise:
Imagination and the Bodhisattva Path*

"Patrick Henry, in his latest book, makes some brave forays into questions of faith, history, orthodoxy, ecumenism, and hope. His style, at the same time erudite and accessible, always honest, and with an occasional whimsical touch, invites us to test old boundaries and certainties and to do so with a sense of joy and adventure. One could easily imagine this book serving as a pungent and provocative catalyst for discussion groups, whether in or beyond formal religious communities."

— **James Gertmenian**
senior minister emeritus,
Plymouth Congregational Church, Minneapolis

"*Flashes of Grace* offers thirty-three glimpses of wisdom gained from a lifetime of listening. The book's insights are drawn from the well of memory and poured with just the right mix of humility, honesty, and irony. The preacher's impossible job—speaking plainly of that which is inscrutable—is made slightly less intimidating by the story that unfolds in this collection of encounters with grace."

— **Timothy Hart-Andersen**
senior pastor, Westminster Presbyterian Church, Minneapolis

"Patrick Henry's *Flashes of Grace* is a contemplative ordering of the often-disordered fragments of divine wisdom lodged in him throughout his long life. Without letting go of the traditions and education that ground him, he explores an expanding universe of science, religion, and social change that expose and enhance, challenge and confirm his deeply held Christian faith. His teachers along the way are as likely to be a Star Trek captain or his own small daughters as Thomas Aquinas or Albert Einstein. Ultimately, it is grace he navigates by and grace he invites us to encounter with him."

— **Michael N. McGregor**
author of *Pure Act: The Uncommon Life of Robert Lax*

"Patrick Henry is one of the wisest people I know, so I am not surprised he has written so beautifully on grace. This artful book shows there is hope in unexpected places and that our troubled age is not the last word on the future. Drawing readers in with skillful stories, his book is like a drink of cool water in a dry land."

— **Linda A. Mercadante**
author of *Belief without Borders:*
Inside the Minds of the Spiritual but not Religious

"This thoughtful and thought-provoking book, rich in reference to theologians, historians, biblical scholars, philosophers, and social critics—including those critical of religion—is for anyone who wants to understand what a Christian faith can mean in the present day. If you're a seeker and a doubter with a liberal and ecumenical bent, this book helps you understand that you're not alone. The author demonstrates that people like you have long been a valuable part of the Christian tradition."

— **Kathleen Norris**
author of *Dakota: A Spiritual Geography*

"*Flashes of Grace* propels the Christian theological tradition forward into new terrain. With references both ancient and contemporary (and to the 24th century—when he reflects on *Star Trek: The Next Generation*), Henry draws us into the depths of his question 'Why am I Christian?' through telling stories of his encounters with God's grace—stories that open our imaginations to create fresh theological ideas for future generations. With fluency in the Christian tradition(s) and provocations to take the Christian faith into territories yet to be discovered—to 'explore strange new worlds'—he challenges readers to examine their own narratives."

— **Ann M. Pederson**
Augustana University

"Sadly, it's unusual to encounter a book on Christian faith that simply conveys the 'unbearable lightness' of that faith—not with the dire fixed jollity of the sales rep, but with the wit, realism, and loving wonder that speaks of a lifetime's delighted discovery, as a woman married for forty years might speak of a partner or a child. Patrick Henry draws on an immense range of learning—as well as offering theological reflections on *Star Trek: The Next Generation*—to chart for us a territory where we can explore in confidence, expecting at every turn the completely unexpected and completely committed grace of God in Christ."

— **Rowan Williams**
author of *Being Christian*

FLASHES OF GRACE

FLASHES *of* GRACE

33 *Encounters with God*

Patrick Henry

WILLIAM B. EERDMANS PUBLISHING COMPANY
GRAND RAPIDS, MICHIGAN

Wm. B. Eerdmans Publishing Co.
4035 Park East Court SE, Grand Rapids, Michigan 49546
www.eerdmans.com

27 26 25 24 23 22 21   1 2 3 4 5 6 7

ISBN 978-0-8028-7864-9

Library of Congress Cataloging-in-Publication Data

Names: Henry, Patrick, 1939– author.
Title: Flashes of grace : 33 encounters with God / Patrick Henry.
Description: Grand Rapids, Michigan : Williams B. Eerdmans Pub-
    lishing Company, [2021] | Includes bibliographical references. |
    Summary: "Reflections on encountering grace and finding God
    in the world through the mystery of memory"—Provided by
    publisher.
Identifiers: LCCN 2020033821 | ISBN 9780802878649 (paperback)
Subjects: LCSH: Grace (Theology)
Classification: LCC BT761.3 .H565 2021 | DDC 231.7—dc23
LC record available at https://lccn.loc.gov/2020033821

TO THE NEXT GENERATION

Stephan and Sundance, Miranda and Micah,
Christina and David, Juliet and Kim,
Brendan and Sara

AND THE GENERATION AFTER THAT

Patrick, Henry, Nolan, Aiden,
Joplin, Andrew, Annabel,
Natalie, Acadia

Contents

Foreword

There's barely a thinking person in the Western world who has not heard, and, at some time in their life, not felt, the profound weight of Socrates's famous observation: "The unexamined life is not worth living." At the same time, it is the few and far between who have ever much examined it, either theirs or someone else's. What a pity.

This book is a truthful, glowing, authentic exposé not only of the truth to be found in that kind of examination but also of the price to be paid for doing it. It is a confrontation with the self and so it is a model for the rest of us.

But first, let's consider what this book is not. It is not a narration of events. It is the dissection of the events that shape us all, really.

Living, growing, and dying—the standard dimensions of every person's journey—are not really the outlines and events that explain a person to themselves, let alone to anybody else. They are simply the categories of time we have constructed to find a reasonable way to explain why what happened in a person's life, did. But that is to say little or nothing at all about what shaped the attitudes or the enmities or the tangle of misconceptions that still struggle for control in each of us, no matter how much we try to ignore them, no matter how deeply we would like to forget them.

This book is also not an autobiography. Not in the normal sense of the word. It is, instead, the x-ray of a soul. It is a grainy picture of light and dark that sheds shards of light on all the byways that

were missed as we lazed through life, all the off-roads we took that
upended us. It shows them, in the end, to be a very straight line—
however crooked it seemed to be at the taking—to the meaning
of the present moment. It retraces the map of the heart from the
present to the past in a way that makes the present—the reader's
as well as the writer's—translucent. It brings into focus the ideas
that drove us, the ideas that let us down, the ideas that, left over
at the bottom of the heap, turned out to be the real, the loving,
the living self.

The truth is that there is a world of difference between the standard autobiography—with its skeletal outline of birth, background,
education, relationships, and aspirations—and the soul-stretching
understandings that come with putting our own lives under the
microscope of time. Most of all, only the most perceptive, only the
most honest of us, is really willing to tell the world what we saw
and rejected, what we wanted but never got, what we were faced
with and failed, what we gave our heart to and then took it back
as we grew from one love to the other and how they each shaped
us. Or not.

You're lucky, whoever you are, to be reading this book. It is
written by one of the most self-critical and intellectually astute
people you may ever come to know. More, it is written for the
sake of understanding, not for the joy of retelling old stories, or
for the opportunity to justify the uncomfortable parts of life, or
to redeem our most irredeemable part. And, most of all, this one
is written for you, to help you understand yourself as you watch
understanding emerge in this honest, authentic surgery of the
soul—by someone just like you and I. This journey through ideas,
written straight from the heart of the other, will enable you to filter
out the big pieces of life and light your own way to the meaning of
it by paying attention to the smallest parts of it. To the parts of it
that we all take for granted: the way we were taught religion, for
instance, and the way it affected us as we grew.

This book stands as a profound look into the mirror of a soul who has been brave enough, wise enough, honest enough to follow the path expected of him up to the beginning of his real self and how he dealt with each idea along the way. Some elements and ideas on this soul's journey confirmed what he had always known. Some tore him away from his roots and gave him new life.

The life that came out of a life so acutely dissected comes from the kind of honesty that will give you, too, a way to look at your own self and all its twists and turns. It will pull you like a mountain climber's rope up the North Face of your soul. It will stop you in the process of falling. It will show you that every path is eventually the right path.

How do I know this? Because I have known Patrick Henry for over forty years. What I thought about him the first time we ever exchanged ideas in public, to our most enlightened and enlightening conversations since, I think still: Here is a man of great intelligence, wit, and insight who is not afraid to look every idea about religion, God, humanity, and creation straight in the eye and learn from every one of them.

I have never talked to anyone anywhere about the role and place and effect of God in a liberal, scientific, changing world of robots and spacecraft and present theological mixtures called ecumenism and the spiritual impact of the fall of boundaries around the world so much as I have with Patrick. At the same time, I have never felt the presence of God more than in those conversations with Patrick while we questioned everything we'd ever been taught.

Patrick has spent his life learning religion at the knee of his pastor father, carried that faith into his own call to teach religion, and then as adulthood demanded answers to the questions of his youth, he returned to the well of faith to question every bit of it. Then, finally, he found his way to the home of the one true self and the unnameable, undefinable God who created it, inhabits it, and leaves us to find it and define it for ourselves.

This is a book for believers. It is as well a book for those unbelievers who have come to see that unbelief is also important to belief. It is a book for those who are afraid to believe such things anymore and are often more right than wrong about it. This is a book for those who have come to believe in something—but who don't understand how it is that what they can't believe is itself a spiritual experience.

This book lets in the sun. It shows us that our one life is about the one statement the God of Scripture answers when Moses asks, "Who shall I say sent me?" And the voice of God answers, "Tell them that I am who am sent you. And that will be enough."

Perhaps the best thing that could happen to believers, to unbelievers, to seekers, and to those perpetually contented with where they have come at this moment, would be to gather in groups, to read this book, to talk about it—and then to watch their own inner life grow in the lightening hot rays of a living Spirit.

Socrates would be proud.

— Joan Chittister

Acknowledgments

My computer files tell me that this book was more than ten years in the making. It has been through many iterations.

At various stages various friends read it and offered comments, always making it better: Andy Anderson, Mary Bednarowski, Geno Beniek, Barb Carlson, Jerry Carlson, Howard Crook, Mary Jane Crook, Tom Darnall, Garvin Davenport, Paul Dorsher, Dan Finn, Judy Foster, Roland Froyen, Jim Gertmenian, Grant Grissom, George Ham, Clark Hendley, Walt Herbert, Barry Hudock, Alison Killeen, Liza Knapp, Kathy Langer, Martha Meek, Diane Millis, Erin Moore, Kathleen Norris, Ann Pederson, Julia Rendon, Judith Rock, Dolores Schuh, CHM, Donna Stoering, Ric Studer, Demaris Wehr, Rowan Williams.

I am grateful, too, for comments and encouragement I received from my colleagues in Studium, the research program at Saint Benedict's Monastery in St. Joseph, Minnesota, directed by Ann Marie Biermaier, OSB.

The librarians at the College of Saint Benedict and Saint John's University were very helpful sleuths, as I'm sure they and their colleagues throughout the country and world have been for many others as well, when the coronavirus pandemic foreclosed physical access to their holdings.

Paul D'Andrea and Leanne Loy deserve special thanks for their interventions at critical points. Paul: "It's really about grace." Leanne: "What you really want to do is tell a story." Their "reallys" made all the difference.

Joan Chittister, a good friend for nearly half a century, and who is one of the busiest people on the planet, gave me the extraordinary gift of the foreword.

Chris Fortunato, agent and friend, kept with me through the long slog.

The folks at Eerdmans are an author's dream come true: senior acquisitions editor Andrew Knapp, who suggested a reworking that injected new life and energy; editorial administrator Amy Kent, who helped me navigate the author questionnaire; editor-in-chief James Ernest, who said of the book, "We don't have anything else like it—no one does!"; project editor Laurel Draper, who kept everything moving in sync; copyeditor Victoria Jones, who often knew better than I did what I was trying to say and has a foolproof detector for anything imprecise or sloppy; director of marketing and publicity Laura Bardolph Hubers, and her colleagues Alexis Cutler and Michael Debowski, who have warmed my heart by their enthusiasm for getting the word out.

My late parents deserve thanks for what I initially thought was a curse but turned out to be a blessing. They kept all the letters (there are hundreds) I wrote to them in my undergraduate and graduate years. These texts, whether handwritten or typed, have been essential to my "rereading all the sources."

My wife, Pat Welter, is my best editor. When my prose gets murky, she shows how to dispel the fog. When it's good, she says so.

The book is dedicated to our kids and their spouses, who are doing good work, and our grandkids, who delight us. I hope *Flashes of Grace* offers them some useful clues for navigating their twenty-first century.

Off the Plane, into the Airport

"Anything more to throw away?" The flight attendant cruises the aisle as the pilot starts the descent to Minneapolis–Saint Paul.

She's asking for empty pretzel packages and used plastic cups, but at the beginning of my eighth decade, and returning from Florida where my younger daughter has recently had a pancreas transplant, I hear something else—about life and vulnerability and death and medical miracles and loss and gain and holding on and letting go. About living in time. Deciding what to throw away means also deciding what to keep.

"Will the person who left an item behind please return to the Rosetta Stone on Concourse G?" This is what I hear as soon as I'm off the plane and in the airport.

The *Rosetta Stone*! I know, of course, that it's a kiosk selling a program for quick learning of another language, but in the ruminative frame of mind activated by the flight attendant's question, I hear something else: I should try my hand at code breaking.

For much of my life, I thought of the world as a jigsaw puzzle. Its challenge to me was to put the pieces together. Now the world presents itself more as a text in an unfamiliar language, needing translation and interpretation.

The convergence of "Anything more to throw away?" and "Please return to the Rosetta Stone" fixes my attention. What to keep and what to throw away, and what are the keys to unlocking mysteries—these are my questions, from my earliest years all the way to now, my ninth decade.

My story is one of encounters with God's grace.

I don't start with a theory about God's grace that I then go looking for examples of. I readily acknowledge that not everyone sees even grace itself, much less the grace of God, where I see it.

I don't know how to say what the grace of God is. What I can say is what it's like for me.

Perspectives change, depending on where I am in space and time. The way I conceive of what is required, what is available, and what is forbidden, is not fixed. In the face of change, it is humility and reflection and flexibility that keep me free and nimble, alert to both the challenge and the reassurance of God's grace—grace that is reflected and refracted in countless ways. I prefer deep and skeptical to shallow and sure.

Taking a long view, telling my story now is an exercise of what one of my college mentors, George A. Buttrick, called "the rewriting grace."

It's about the mystery of memory.

My memories crisscross, overlap, go off on tangents. They circle, they spiral, they go full speed ahead. They reinforce each other, trip over one another, sometimes even cancel each other out.

My memory is full of faces and voices. I have myriad dialogue partners, many dead, some still alive. Through face-to-face talk or through what they have written, they have shaped who I am, including who I am as a Christian. In many decades of reading and thinking, literature has been for me one of theology's richest sources, theology one of the keys to literature's meaning.

I am not hiding behind these conversation partners. They are companions on the journey. They have helped me become the person who has these memories, this story to tell.

Centuries, years, months, days—they happen in sequence, in order, one after the other. But in my memory they twist and turn, double back, go through the looking-glass. They ricochet. Syncopate. They're linked, networked, webbed. Memory makes mincemeat of the calendar. To tell my story chronologically would be to get it wrong. I regularly slip in and out of time warps.

Sometimes a memory shows directly how I felt. Other times the showing is implicit in the way I tell it—the verbs and the adjectives, the style, the tone. It comes naturally to me to toggle between the analytic and the anecdotal, between incidents and influences. But whether the memory comes across head-on or at an angle, it's me you're meeting.

Part One

How I Became the Source of This Story

Grace in Formation

"Why are you Christian?"

An unexpected question, though fair enough.

It's 2001. I'm being interviewed by Sister Mary Margaret (Meg) Funk, OSB, executive director of Monastic Interreligious Dialogue.[1] The occasion is a book I had recently edited, *Benedict's Dharma: Buddhists Reflect on the Rule of Saint Benedict*. How the book came to be, I will say more about when that memory surfaces in encounter 19.

"Why are you Christian?"

I Was Born into It

I suppose I could conjure a theologically sophisticated response, but honesty is the best policy. "The quick answer is what it would be for most (though certainly not all) Christians: I was born into it."

I recall conversations with people of other traditions when it has struck me that if I were they, they're what I'd be. They, too, were likely born into what they are.

"Why are you Christian?" Here's how it started.

I grew up in the church—for a while, quite literally. From the time I am twelve we live in a parsonage on the church grounds. It never feels 100 percent home. My parents periodically remind my sister and me that because the house really belongs to the church, it has to be kept in good order lest a congregation member stop by unannounced. (Nowadays the norm is for pastors to own their own homes, which makes both economic and psychological sense.)

My father was conversant with the Bible, Beethoven, and baseball. His sermons were illustrated by quotations from T. S. Eliot's poetry and remarks by his good friend (whom he baptized), Hall of Fame pitcher Dizzy Dean. He read Faulkner and Camus and understood, even shared, their questionings. He could talk to anybody. He didn't interpret another's story before carefully listening to it. I marveled at (and suppose I was puzzled by) his close friendship with his barber, who had little formal education.

He was suspicious of shop talk. When he chaired the Dallas Pastors Association he abandoned the tradition of "theological" speakers, opting instead for the different kind of theological musings—no less serious and substantial—that a baseball player or clothing store owner could offer.

My dad once cut through my smugness when, after I approvingly repeated a seatmate's comment (made while looking out an airplane window) about "all those people down there, knee-deep in the little messes they call their lives," he replied, "Yes, but that's all they've got, and many of them are doing the very best they can with it."

It took me a while to catch up with my father's nuanced, nontriumphalist way of being Christian.

As a white, well-educated, middle-class, Protestant, American male, coming of age in the can-do Texas of the Eisenhower 1950s—the mix was exuberance, hyperbole, hospitality—I was programmed to take charge, set agendas, explain the world, and know what was best for everybody. I was overloaded with entitlements. My family wasn't exactly part of the ruling structure, but we knew the people who determined what happened. I'm pretty sure I was in my mid-twenties at the earliest before anybody ever really challenged me on anything.

In such a context, God-talk can work as much ill as good. The entire culture surrounding me was saturated with Christian institutions and Christian chatter to such an extent that it hardly occurred to me there were alternatives.

My fourth-grade public school teacher began each day's class with a reading from the New Testament. In retrospect I—as a Christian—find that practice objectionable, but at the time I didn't give it a second thought.

On Being a PK (Preacher's Kid)

The "Christian" culture I grew up in, which seemed utterly natural to me, appears in historical perspective to have been an anomaly, a time warp of its own. Sociologists marvel at the 1950s as the apogee of religious identity and participation in America.

The size of my dad's congregation was growing, church budgets expanding. I think he was a bit skeptical of this success, and not surprised when the tide turned. I wish I'd absorbed some of his suspicion earlier. I was surer of my Christian identity than he was of his—or rather, I was too sure that I knew precisely what Christian identity meant.

There is great pressure on a minister's family to be exemplary, an icon. I was a model child. This did not require an act of will, or even of decision. I simply absorbed, internalized the expectation, and was not unhappy with it. I loved being good. I don't recall ever letting "damn" or "hell," much less anything worse, cross my lips. I don't recall ever even thinking them. My father did, on occasion, counter my prudence—"I'm a preacher's kid, and everybody's watching me"—with one of his favorite aphorisms: "Don't worry what other people are thinking about you. They aren't."

I wish my parents had made clearer to me the complexity of the lives of congregation members. I don't mean details, but I do mean letting my sister and me know they weren't all "nice" people. I once overheard my parents talking about a couple in the church who were publicly "exemplary" but behind the scenes were doing everything they could to sow discord. Had I not eavesdropped, I'd never have known. Maybe our parents were trying to protect us from how messy the world can be.

One of the family ideals was an aphorism of Will Rogers's, repeated often by one of my grandfathers (also a pastor, as was my other one too): "I never met a man I didn't like."[2] There was probably a time when I thought this a distillation of the gospel. If I didn't like somebody, I counted it my fault. Not liking somebody is something Jesus wouldn't do.

Thinking I already knew it all—a condition to which religious people are peculiarly susceptible—it wasn't easy to learn, whether from the past, the experience of others, or even from my own life. The precondition for any learning is listening without interrupting.

My initial privilege—white, to be sure, but lots of other kinds too—has been reinforced by a string of academic degrees. This means I've been carefully trained to be an interrupter. It's a professional hazard for academics that we think it's our job to understand people (whether alive or dead) better than they understand themselves, and we don't often enough shut up and just listen. My claim to know what somebody else "really" means is frequently arrogant and often wrong.

Learning to Shut Up

I've had to unlearn in order to learn.

In therapy in later years, the fruitless times are when I, as someone accustomed to acing exams, come in to "report" what "happened" during the week. "She said this, I said that, I was clearly right, so there."

The electric sessions are the ones when I feel stuck and can't "explain" anything. I have to keep working my way out of the head trip. I can't deny that things are out of whack, but I'm incapable of saying why, or what to do about it.

In 1987 one of my therapists, the late Leighton (Lee) Whitaker, writes to me. "Therapists, like everyone else really, can work with only what the client offers, sometimes just the tip of the iceberg, until the person—hopefully—becomes more open."

Then he goes on. "We seldom encounter that most productive of attitudes: 'I've been going through this quite intriguing and I guess quite meaningful dilemma that I'm determined to understand and to learn from. I'm having what I hope to turn into a highly creative crisis.'"

When I'm tongue-tied, something happens. Understanding dawns. Sorting through inherited stuff, especially fears of loneliness and abandonment (and acknowledging that sometimes things are a lot worse than I think they are), I give up control—and find freedom and spontaneity. I do an about-face. I come to see that my effort to control, which I thought was extreme freedom, is in fact extreme bondage. The crisis becomes creative.

Further, I learn the truth of what one of my former students, Gary Greenberg, a psychotherapist, told me. There are only two significant moments in therapy, he says: the time you spend in the waiting room before the session (I'm not sure what he means by this, but it sounds ironic enough to be profound), and when you say goodbye. That final meeting is a moment where fright and truth and peace and floods of tears and love all fuse. I would hate to go through it again. I wouldn't have missed it for the world.

Still, my therapist has gently but relentlessly alerted me that memory doesn't follow a syllabus. My control defenses can redeploy at any time. It's tempting to resist the unlearning that has set me free.

Getting All Theological

Now I'm back with Sister Meg. I suggest to her that there's another, even more interesting question: "Why am I still Christian?"

"It's because I find Trinity and Incarnation compelling: God is community and God is for us. This is the core, and it doesn't require exclusivisms that rule out, for example, Buddhism. A Buddhist friend reminded me that the ultimate Buddhist confession is, 'I know nothing.' This is very different from saying, 'I don't know anything,' and would serve very well, I think, as an enlightened Christian confession."

Nearly twenty years earlier, in 1980, when I am engaged in a conversation about "What does it mean to confess faith in God today?" at the Collegeville Institute for Ecumenical and Cultural Research (where in 1984 I would become executive director), I am preparing the way for what I will say to Sister Meg in 2001. "I am certain that now we see in a mirror dimly, as Saint Paul says. All our seeing is an act of interpretation, what we see is subject to the uncertainty inherent in all history, and our seeing itself is distorted by our prejudices and hidden agendas. God's truth cannot be formulated in neat propositions." Yes, "I know nothing" is a good starting point. My theology is not so much arrived at as sidled up to.

I think it fortunate that Christianity does not any longer hold the same sway it did when I was growing up. In my college years I had a brief period of mental rebellion against what I had inherited—spring of sophomore year, "living the cliché," so to speak—but this paved the way not for abandonment but for a retrieval of the profound view of life that finds in personal and communal experience the title of one of my father's sermons, "More than meets the eye."

"Retrieval" is not quite the right word. It is more like a journey along a Möbius strip, where you end up at the same place but on the other side. In college you can fall off the deep end—or you can find yourself turned inside out.

My Father's Death

Now, my father's "both/and" spirituality, which I am grateful to him for planting in me, wasn't a bulwark against his lifelong depression. He died from suicide six years into retirement from forty-one years as pastor to the same congregation. As was the way in those days, his psychological condition had been effectively masked from my sister and me.

It's May 17, 1983. My mother calls to tell me my dad had closed the garage door and turned on the engine. I fly to Dallas. I walk into my parents' house. Many family friends are there.

Dr. James Bledsoe, our dentist, comes up to me, puts his arm around me, and says, not "God meant this for good," which would distance him from me and would be despair masquerading as hope, but "It's a son-of-a-bitch, isn't it?"—words that imply meaninglessness but actually bring us together, hope masquerading as despair.

Prior to this moment I would have hesitated to classify those words as a prayer, though I am half expecting, even half hoping, to hear them. Years before, I heard the story of how, when the Bledsoes' teenage son died in a skiing accident, my father went immediately to their house, put his arm around Jim's shoulder, and said, "It's a son-of-a-bitch, isn't it?"

This day when my father has died, when access to his meaning for me is blocked by my bafflement at his desperate act, Jim Bledsoe, by completing this "prayer circle," blesses me with my father's wisdom. When I wonder how it happened that my father's death—the death of a pastor, no less—didn't drastically shake my faith, I suspect the answer has something to do with "It's a son-of-a-bitch, isn't it?" My father's suicide wasn't shattering because I didn't have to believe it wasn't.

Maybe something from more than two decades earlier prepared me, at least a little bit.

It's 1960. I've just arrived in England to start my study at Oxford. In a conversation on the transatlantic crossing I hear about a new venture in London called Samaritans. Chad Varah, rector of Saint Stephen's Church, decides that the alarming rate of suicide in the city calls for action, and the church should do something. He establishes the phone number of his church as a twenty-four-hour watch point. Word gets around that anyone in despair can call this number, and there will be a sympathetic ear at the other end. By the time I show up at Saint Stephen's, the phone is handling over a thousand calls a year.

Besides two assistant rectors, a psychiatric social worker, and a social worker, there are 150 volunteers, the "Samaritans," willing to go at a moment's notice to anyone in their neighborhood.

I give the church my name as a possible Samaritan in Oxford. Before long I have a client, a man very far removed from the academic realms I inhabit. I befriend him and stretch beyond the language I'm familiar with to help him find something to live for. Eventually I am assigned another, this one a student. Dealing with him, I learn that academic jargon by itself is inadequate. As far as I know, neither of my clients dies from suicide.

One day a week I go to London, where I observe in the Saint Stephen's vestry the sort of problems that are presented and the way the staff handles them. I of course have no idea that one day, years later, I will wish my father had called so I could try to persuade him to keep living.

But that doesn't happen.

So, in a way Jim Bledsoe becomes a Samaritan for me. He keeps me from isolation, which would be the supreme flight from reality. He fashions out of the darkness a source of light, a light that he can know for me until I can trust it for myself. "It's a son-of-a-bitch, isn't it?" lays the groundwork for a place where, eventually, grace will give me back my father—where darkness moves from center to periphery, light from periphery to center. That place is a baseball diamond. The memory will surface further on, in encounter 27.

"Why are you still Christian?"

If I'd thrown the whole thing over, friends might have thought, "Of course. His dad died at his own hand, two marriages didn't work out. That's enough." But my father's suicide and my own two divorces constitute about average trauma these days, not enough to either excuse anything or warrant pity. President John F. Kennedy put it succinctly: "Life is unfair."

I have an automatic shock-proof cheap grace detector. I am neither consoled nor edified when someone dumps isolated Bible verses or happy faces on me.

I remind Christians who too easily invoke the grace of God that it was Job's "comforters," feeding him all the "correct" theological answers, who felt the sting of God's rebuke. They were sure they knew what God wanted. They counseled Job, repeatedly and repetitively, to give it up: "Agree with God, and be at peace." Their speeches are full of "How can you?" and "You should!" while Job over and over again asks, "Why?"

At the end of the story the tables are turned. Those who thought they were honoring God hear these words from the Lord: "My wrath is kindled against you . . . ; for you have not spoken of me what is right, as my servant Job has." Then the Lord adds the most stinging rebuke of all: "My servant Job shall pray for you" (Job 42:7–8).

Explorer, Not Colonizer

In my early years I thought my calling as a Christian was to bring God into a world where God isn't. Thanks to the way my story has unfolded, especially with my father's influence, I know my Christian calling is to find what God is up to in the world where God already is—in the past and in my own time.

I often—though by no means always—find God at work in places called "Christian," but also in places where Christ, and even God, aren't explicitly acknowledged, whether in the past or in my immediate surroundings.

As a Christian I'm an explorer, not a colonizer.

"Santa Claus" seems an odd additional answer to why I am still Christian. Most kids around age six or seven begin to realize he isn't real.

But I find profound theological wisdom in what is arguably the most famous editorial of all time.

Francis P. Church, in the *New York Sun* on September 21, 1897, responds to the question "Is there a Santa Claus?" posed by eight-year-old Virginia O'Hanlon (who grows up to be a New York City public school teacher and principal).

Church in a single sentence captures what is for me a starting point and goal of theology: "Nobody can conceive or imagine all the wonders there are unseen and unseeable in the world." My encounters with the grace of God are a lifetime's voyage of conceiving and imagining more and more of those wonders—exploring strange new worlds.

Music and Prayer

It's January 18, 1998. I'm speaking at a Christian unity hymnfest at Saint John's Abbey Church.

> I looked over Jordan, and what did I see, comin' for to carry me home?
> A band of angels comin' after me, comin' for to carry me home.

A song, by the way, I hear sung two decades later by the seventy-seven-year-old Joan Baez as the concluding number of the encores to her "Farewell Tour" concert in Minneapolis.

"Over Jordan, the other side, angels," I say, and note how much talk like this there is on television and in magazines. I expect it in the tabloids I surreptitiously scan as I wait in the supermarket checkout line, but angel talk is now respectable. At this time, I continue, "one of the highest-rated TV shows says we're touched by them." The question is no longer how many angels can dance on the head of a pin but how many angel books can fit on a shelf at Barnes & Noble. "The popular TV series *The X-Files* insists that 'the truth is *out there*,' and another show, *The Visitor*, brings the past from the future to try to fix an ailing present. Here, there, now, then—lines are blurred, boundaries fluid."

I've never forgotten entirely that there's more than I can see and measure. I've kept saying the Nicene Creed, which credits God as Maker of all things visible *and invisible*, even when practical, everyday thinking relegates *the invisible* to the illusory. But I doubt creeds could by themselves have shielded the ineffable from the onslaughts of skepticism. It is music that has been the vehicle for hope that is the evidence of things not seen.

The great example of this, of course, is the spirituals, with their double meaning. When they appear to be about the future, the spirituals are really about—or also about—resistance and hope in the present. The "other side" is the other side of *now*, where the God of justice presides. The Rev. Dr. Martin Luther King Jr. injected divine power into our common life when he wove images from the spirituals into his great orations.

A story told by Julius Lester in his autobiography, *Lovesong*, demonstrates how music is a kind of spiritual wormhole.

"I am eight or nine years old," he writes. He's playing a simplified arrangement of a Bach fugue. "The lines of music move away from and back to each other, never merging or separating, like windblown ribbons on the tail of a kite." Then the breakthrough: "I forget that I am playing, and I slip through the lines to the other side of the music, where I understand all that was, is and will be." But it can't be held on to. "When the music ends, I return to this side and cannot remember what I understood."[3]

Lester is certain that he went through the music to the other side—he *knows* he was there. But he is unable to say anything specific about what he found. Nearly all mystics say this, and even Saint Paul, who was transported to the third heaven, says he saw things that can't be uttered (2 Cor. 12:2–4).

The boundary I face is the one I see when I look over Jordan to the ultimate other side. I hope there will be that band of angels.

I hope the chariot will swing low. Christians are sharply divided, however, on ways of expressing this hope.

It's later in 1998. At the Collegeville Institute we are engaged in an inquiry on prayer in the ecumenical movement. We think that even if Christians can't gather at a common table, we could at least pray together, but it turns out it isn't so easy.

We find out just how difficult when we set ourselves the task of fashioning an ecumenical funeral service. The hypothetical recently deceased is given the unisex name Jo(e)—and we find that, try as hard as we can, we cannot get Jo(e) buried. There are many points of contention, none so sharp as whether to pray for the dead and to the dead. Traditions are at odds on this question. Some participants even find themselves, at a deep level of feeling, at odds with their own traditions.

I suspect that the solution to our dilemma, or at least the best we could do, would be a funeral hymnfest. The music would take us where our words by themselves refuse to go. Hymns might get Jo(e) buried. I think this not theoretically but because of a true story.

A friend of mine, Michael Vertin, as Catholic as they come, grew up in western Minnesota, the son of a funeral director. The town is small enough that the funeral home served everybody, including evangelical Christians whose music was as foreign to a young Minnesota Catholic as heavy metal would be to someone whose dial, like mine, is set to Minnesota Public Radio.

Michael hung around his dad's business and learned *all* the hymns, not only "Salve Regina" but also "Bringing in the Sheaves." I thought I, growing up in Protestant Texas, knew the gospel hymn repertoire, but my Catholic friend from rural Minnesota taught me ones I'd never heard. He could bury Jo(e) because he has helped to bury everybody.

Many times I've sung the refrain, "When the roll is called up yonder, I'll be there." It's presumptuous to make such a claim. I hope I'll be there, but I don't know. It's enough for me now to sing this, and a hundred other songs, with those who, like me, have an abiding hope but see through a glass darkly.

When we sing hymns together, do we go through the notes to the other side of the music? Maybe not, probably not. Still, there's wisdom in a tongue-twist I once heard from a priest, who prayed "for all those who've gone to their rest in the rise of hoping again."

But you never know. I look over Jordan, and what do I see? I listen over Jordan, and what do I hear? I can't tell you for sure, because I don't know for sure, but I suspect the deepest unity of Christians is our common expectation that God will surprise us.

Starting with Christmas

Christian belief in God is much odder than is often assumed. It starts with Christmas—the aforementioned editorial's "unseen and unseeable."

I see crèches in front yards, sing "O Little Town of Bethlehem," sit as a proud grandparent watching grandkids play Mary or a shepherd—or a donkey—in the pageant. The Christmas story is so familiar that I am shielded from its assault on everything that makes sense.

God a human being? As Saint John Chrysostom in the fourth century is reputed to have put it: "The miracle strikes me senseless. The Ancient of Days has become a child, he who sits on a high and lofty throne is placed in a manger."[4] This was an affront to ancient intellects. It should be to ours. A student of mine, Margaret Coulling Miller, once wrote on an exam, "If God had wanted to appeal directly to our minds, Mary would have written a book instead of bearing a child."

And if Christmas is shocking, it is also reassuring. If God became an infant—vulnerable, dependent—that infant also carries the same hope and expectation we sense in any child. My father preached a Christmas sermon called "The Baby Grew Up." His point was not only that the Mary who rejoiced on Christmas grieved on Good Friday, but that the doctrine of the Incarnation— God became fully human while remaining fully divine—means God knows our story from the inside.

The 1990 Grammy Song of the Year, Julie Gold's "From a Distance," made popular by Bette Midler, can be interpreted many ways, but the point of its refrain, "God is watching us from a distance," is not the message of Christmas. I think, on hearing the song, "No, God is watching us through the eyes of a baby, up very close and very personal." Because God has been here and still is, I value where and when I am. God's thoughts may be too high for me, but my life is not too low for God. I can, and certainly do, mess up all the time, but apologizing for being human is not acceptable. I have neither the pride nor the terror of being on my own.

When I give and receive gifts during the Christmas season, other words of Saint John Chrysostom (genuinely his) remind me that the shock, reassurance, and challenge of Christmas affect the way I deal with the whole world: "God has made certain things common, as the sun, air, earth, and water, the heaven, the sea, the light, the stars; whose benefits are dispensed equally to all. . . . But when one attempts to possess himself of anything, to make it his own, then contention is introduced, as if nature herself were indignant, that when God brings us together in every way, we are eager to divide and separate ourselves by appropriating things, and by using those cold words 'mine and yours.'"[5]

Still Christian

"Why are you Christian?" I am asked.

I'm Christian because I was born into it.

I'm Christian because I'm freed from the illusion of control and from the conviction that life has to be fair. Divested of this illusion and this conviction, I have at least a chance of obeying what I consider Jesus's toughest command: "Do not be anxious" (Matt. 6:25 RSV).

And I am Christian because there are things I do not understand that exist nonetheless. In such a world, the Christian tradition—as I have been fortunate to receive it, to inhabit it, and to pass it on—provides clues for tracing and decoding the unseen and unseeable wonders. The Christian tradition is my Rosetta Stone.

I'm still Christian thanks to the fine-tuning my dad and many other teachers—some dead, some living—have given me. As my memories gather round, mix and mingle, shout and whisper, tumble and trip and run, I detect signals of God's grace—seldom easy, never cheap, sometimes challenging, occasionally consoling, nearly always surprising. It's my story.

IN A WORD

I encounter God's intimidating grace when I shut up, quit interrupting, unlearn, and in consequence see more than meets the eye and see it through more eyes than just my own.

intimidating

Grace in Perspective

If my Christian identity originated in the time warp of mid-twentieth-century Texas, it was given perspective in a moment that took me back to the age of the pharaohs.

Heron on the Nile

It is Monday, July 9, 2000, in Kom Ombo, Egypt. Through the window of our room on the boat I see a heron glide past, flying from the left that I can't see but am headed toward, to the right that I equally can't see but have already been to.

I think of the nobleman who, fourteen centuries ago, reminded King Edwin of Northumbria that life is mysterious and transitory. A sparrow flies through a window at one end of a warm banquet hall and out the other end, where all is cold and dark. Life is like this, the nobleman says. "At birth we emerge from the unknown, and for a brief while we are here on this earth, with a fair amount of comfort and happiness. But then we fly out the window at the other end, into the cold and dark and unknown future."[1]

I didn't remember the story in quite this detail, but I remembered its gist, right then and there, on the boat.

A small skiff carrying two fishermen moves into the reeds on the other side of the river. Our tour guide has told us that the life of these dwellers along the Nile is, in its essentials, indistinguishable from that of their ancestors five thousand years ago. Pharaoh Narmer of the First Dynasty, sailing on his royal barge, likely saw what I am seeing now. To this twentieth-century American, who has jetted to Egypt and whose grandparents reminisced about horse and buggy, this continuity across millennia adds an unfamiliar dimension to "remembering."

Conversation at lunch has been about the big questions that an encounter with antiquity raises—change, progress, what we know and don't know, patterns of thought and behavior—in short, what it all means. This afternoon's epiphany—a heron on the hot Nile reminding me of King Edwin in his cold castle—gets me thinking about the territory of my Christian identity.

And I wonder: seeing the impressive evidence of religions long gone, that for their adherents were as much alive as mine is for me, how would I feel if I knew my tradition would go the way of those? Would I be confident that the truth the tradition carries would survive?

It's on the banks of the Nile that the seed of *Flashes of Grace* is planted.

Rereading All the Sources

More immediately, though, in a memory ricochet, I recall a conversation with Sir Henry Chadwick, who had been one of my teachers at Oxford. He knew as much as anyone about Christian identity across the centuries.

It's 1994. "What are you working on now?" "Oxford University Press has been after me for years to do an updated and expanded edition of *The Early Church*. I have finally said yes." This book of Chadwick's, first published in 1967, is a true classic—learned, trustworthy, winsomely written.

"How," I ask, "do you revise something you wrote so long ago and that has become the standard against which other treatments of the subject are judged?" I expect something like what most scholars would say—adding recent works to the bibliography and refashioning some portions about which he has changed his mind in the intervening years. He has plenty of laurels to rest on.

"I'm rereading all the sources."

I'm thunderstruck.

He says this without the slightest bombast or self-congratulation. It expresses the humility of the truly exceptional scholar who acknowledges the unending mystery and depth of the world. His revised edition is going to be what all the sources— Chadwick is one of a handful of experts who could state *all* and mean it—say to him now in his eighth-going-on-ninth decade.

No one would fault him for doing a lot less, but I know that doing anything less would never occur to him. In 2001, at age eighty-one, he will tell us what the sources tell him: Oxford University Press will publish *The Church in Ancient Society: From Galilee to Gregory the Great.*

It's a couple of years after his new book appeared. At the Collegeville Institute we are having a discussion about scholarship itself—what it means to us who do it, and what it means about us who do it.

What I say is shaped by that earlier conversation with Sir Henry. "Why did I become a scholar in the first place?" I wonder. "People sometimes caricature me as out of touch, pointy-headed, a master of more and more about less and less"—the whole litany of academic put-downs. "But my intention is to be a listener, careful but adventurous, curious, expert but not condescending, alert to the question lurking in every answer. These times require of me courage and compassion as well as learning"—a whole identity, in fact—"a me who has reassembled parts of myself that get too easily dispersed—the researcher, the teacher, the practitioner, and the integral member of a community."

Sir Henry's disarming and overwhelming "I'm rereading all the sources" sets a high standard.

And it acknowledges how memory and time, change and

growth, cannot be stopped. I can reread what I knew (not just *thought* I knew, but *knew*), and discover new meaning in it, or at least a new perspective. Center and periphery can switch places. I can even decide I got it wrong, as will be revealed repeatedly in this story. Christian identity, whether my own or that of people who have been dead for centuries, is fluid, not fixed once and for all in the living, or in the interpretation of the past.

With his openness to surprise, to fresh insight, to what he could learn from other perspectives, Chadwick would understand how that heron on the Nile, six years after our conversation, is for me an impetus to take a fresh look at—to reread—my experience.

On Being Surprised

Surprise is at the heart of my Christian identity.

The way I understand it is shaped by my encounter with Saint John Henry Newman (1801–90), who reveals an experience of unanticipated, even unwanted, but finally welcomed surprise. Newman is a towering theological and historical scholar, whose intellectual and religious journey (recorded in collected works that total thirty-one volumes) riveted the attention of his contemporaries. Originally an Anglican priest, he converted to Catholicism, eventually becoming a cardinal of the church—but he never stopped asking questions.

It is 1841. Newman is in great spiritual turmoil. Writing some quarter-century later, he vividly remembers his quandary then: "How was I any more to have absolute confidence in myself? How was I to have confidence in my present confidence? How was I to be sure that I should always think as I thought now?"[2] At this point in his life, age forty, the very notion that he might have to change his mind is abhorrent.

Just four years later, in 1845, Newman turns 180 degrees. "In a higher world, it is otherwise, but here below, to live is to change, and to be perfect is to have changed often."[3]

I don't recall ever being quite so panicky as Newman at the thought of change, though his way of putting it makes it very real to me. While I might have named "perfection" as what I was aspiring to when I was younger, I don't readily adopt Newman's term. It's when I meet one of Newman's contemporaries, Matthew Arnold (1822–88), that I find a definition of perfection I embrace: "not a having and a resting, but a growing and becoming."[4]

Earlier, I'd not have dreamed that Matthew Arnold would become a hero of mine.

It's mid-September 1956. I arrived at Harvard a week ago.

"Most of what now passes with us for religion and philosophy will be replaced by poetry."[5] What am I to make of these words of Arnold's that stare out at me from the test I'm taking to qualify for an honors General Education course?

"Tommyrot," I think, prudishly avoiding the more pungent "bullshit" and clumsily attempting faux-British.

Nine pages later I've disproved Arnold, or so I think. I've marshaled theological writers I'm familiar with, doing a lot more asserting—Christian chatter—than arguing.

It's now a few days later. My name is not in the list of those chosen for the honors course. Two hundred twenty-four others of the three hundred who took the test aren't there either. I suppose they—used to coming out on top as I am—are equally disappointed, but still . . .

Remembering ahead, in my senior year I will toy with the idea of writing an honors thesis on Matthew Arnold (not to bury him but to praise him). For now, though, I see him as a foe, not a friend. On the day of that test in 1956 I didn't even suspect that I ought not to have confidence in my present confidence.

Change, which causes Newman to shudder, he subsequently recognizes as the way the world really is. He switches from fearing change is a poison that kills religion to recognizing it as religion's lifeblood. Newman's about-face between 1841 and 1845 registers a radical transformation, a turnaround that both instructs and reassures me.

Seeing the Old Afresh

Two contemporary women transpose Newman's and Arnold's insight into more familiar terms. In a supreme irony, Kathleen Norris, whom I know personally, and Anne Lamott, whom I know from her books and her Facebook posts, are helped to see the old afresh by a book from 1843, Søren Kierkegaard's *Fear and Trembling*.

These days the dour Dane's relentless probing of Abraham's near sacrifice of his son Isaac probably generates revulsion more often than conversion.[6] Lamott, however, says that when she was assigned the book her sophomore year in college, "my life changed forever."[7] Norris recalls the impact of "the pale yellow, well-worn paperback" she bought at a used bookstore while still in high school.[8]

Lamott distinguishes between Kierkegaard's leap of faith and her own staggers and lurches. By naming and illustrating the dipping and darting and soaring of faith, the glides, Möbius strips, U-turns, stumbles, pirouettes—and even the tsunamis and eddies, hurricanes and breezes—of faith, Lamott and Norris attract a huge following. What they describe is what I know.

What they do is this: they show what faith is like, they don't pretend to tell what it is—a distinction similar to the one I draw between saying what God's grace is like, which I do, and saying what it is, which I don't. Lamott and Norris validate the wisdom their readers already have but may never have known was theology.

Lamott as a young girl is all of us, "bursting with hope and secrets and fear"[9]—Saint Augustine didn't say it any better. Norris, blurting an answer to a from-left-field question following a talk she gave, admits to the common surprise (one I've experienced countless times) of saying "things I hadn't fully realized were true until I'd said them."[10]

The life stories of Lamott and Norris are case studies for the effectiveness of hands-off evangelism. They help me understand my aversion to Christians who think it a Christian duty to hammer away at someone until they become Christian.

Lamott's father, the son of Presbyterian missionaries, couldn't stand Christianity.[11] His antipathy rubbed off on her. But in her early thirties she began "stopping in at St. Andrew"—a small, mostly Black church in Marin County, California—"from time to time, standing in the doorway to listen to the songs," and "always left before the sermon."[12] Nobody pressured her. When, one year into sobriety, she was toying with the idea of being baptized but said to the minister that she thought she "wasn't good enough yet," he replied, "You're putting the cart before the horse. So—honey? Come on *down*."[13]

Norris's story demonstrates the wisdom of the Presbyterians in Lemmon, South Dakota, who stayed off her case for eleven years while she attended sporadically and came to terms, gradually, with her religious inheritance.[14] Their patience, and the unconcern for her "weighty doubts and intellectual frustrations over Christianity"[15] shown by the Benedictine monks she was coming to know, were the precondition for discovering how to refresh the vocabulary of faith even for those, like me, who never left.

The way these two authors help shape my Christian identity is by bringing theology down to earth.

Norris challenges our reach for "higher consciousness" by engaging in "a search for lower consciousness."[16] Lamott refuses to fly above the fray when, talking about grief and its uncanny ability to blindside us, she says that "if you are lucky and brave, you will be willing to bear disillusion."[17] Norris and Lamott are earthy and full of genuine joy, not happy faces. They repeatedly startle me with something unexpected, or by coming at something familiar but at a slant.

"The Common Thing"

Lamott and Norris are long past and far distant from my time-warp visit to the age of the pharaohs. But the heron ties all the memories together.

I owe a debt to that heron on the Nile. What it means to me is captured in a poem by the late Mary Oliver, "Heron Rises from the Dark, Summer Pond."[18] She begins, marveling at how "always it is a surprise" when the heavy bird "rises into the air and is gone," but by the end of the poem Oliver is amazed that "it isn't a miracle, but the common thing." And that, of course—its being "the common thing," like theology for Lamott and Norris and me—is the biggest surprise of all.

IN A WORD

I encounter the daring grace of God when I'm not having and resting, but growing and becoming—eager for change, not fearful of it.

daring

Grace in Balance

My story begins with formation in Texas. It gets some perspective from a heron on the Nile. It achieves a measure of balance thanks to a thinker from the nineteenth century via baseball great Yogi Berra.

Berra said—or is at least credited with saying—"When you come to a fork in the road, take it."

John Stuart Mill (1806–73) and Yogi Berra (1925–2015) have probably never appeared in the same sentence before, but in my remembering they converge. Mill came to a fork in the road and took it.

I'd not have predicted that Mill would be a guide. I'd have predicted that he wouldn't. He was certainly a skeptic (though a huge fan of Jesus).

But when, in a college course, I encounter him through a pair of his essays, he turns out to connect me with my father's both/ and Christianity that has so far not quite gotten through to me. Mill, who finds that his father isn't nuanced enough, upends me by persuading me that *I'm* not nuanced enough.

Mill's father, James, was a lifelong devotee of Jeremy Bentham (1748–1832), the founder of Utilitarianism (the moral worth of an action is directly proportional to its contribution to happiness). The son is brought up to be a true believer. But John Stuart Mill finds Bentham's view too narrow, or rather, incomplete. He discovers in the poet Samuel Taylor Coleridge (1772–1834) the necessary balance.

"Is It True?" and "What Does It Mean?"

I find Mill's essays on Bentham and Coleridge rich in detail and color. The gist of his argument is this: "In the main, Bentham was a Progressive philosopher, Coleridge a Conservative one." Neither is an ideologue: "The writings of both contain severe lessons to their own side, on many of the errors and faults they are addicted to." But each has an angle: "To Bentham it was given to discern more particularly those truths with which existing doctrines and institutions were at variance; to Coleridge, the neglected truths which lay in them."[1] Bentham and Coleridge offer guidance on what to throw away and what to keep.

It is this discovery of both/and that sets Mill on a journey he characterizes in his *Autobiography* as "the successive phases of [a] mind which was always pressing forward, equally ready to learn and to unlearn either from its own thoughts or from those of others."[2] I'm no Mill, but I like to think my mind is always "pressing forward" in just the way he says his does—"equally ready to learn and to unlearn."

I count myself fortunate to be an inheritor of Mill's stereoscopic intellectual vision, which depends on making the virtues of both Bentham and Coleridge my own—to ask of anything I encounter both "Is it true?" and "What does it mean?"—to ask them simultaneously, so that the answer to the one question does not prejudice the answer to the other; to be able to look both as from without and as from within. To come to a fork in the road and take it.

This is not unlike "to live is to change, and to be perfect is to have changed often," the breakthrough made by John Henry Newman mentioned in the previous encounter. Newman is Mill's senior by five years, and in some ways his polar opposite.

Two things Bentham gets right, Mill says. First is "the method of detail—of treating wholes by separating them into their parts, abstractions by resolving them into things—classes and generalities by distinguishing them into the individuals of which they are made up; and breaking every question into pieces before attempting to solve it." Second is suspicion of "abstractions [which] are not realities *per se*, but an abridged mode of expressing facts."[3]

Bentham's suspicion of abstractions is planted in me when I am an undergraduate. It comes to fruition through six subsequent decades of my study of religion.

I'm convinced that Christianity is an abstraction, as are Judaism and Islam and Buddhism and Hinduism and all the rest, including the unaffiliated, what are today classified as "Nones." These abstractions are at best an "abridged mode of expressing facts." They aid analysis but hinder understanding.

The reality is people: Christians and Jews and Muslims and Buddhists and Hindus and the unaffiliated. The traditions exist only as they are lived, and they are lived by people, all of whom put their own spin on what they have received. People praying and eating and singing and serving and lighting candles and bringing up children—these are what the traditions really are. As a student of mine, Nancy Niemczyk, once wrote, "Ultimately it's not intellectuals who form living cultures, it's grandmothers."

Mill believes Bentham gets two things wrong.

First is his contempt for other thinkers and blindness to their distinctiveness from one another. "Every inquirer," Mill notes, "is either young or old, rich or poor, sickly or healthy, married or unmarried, meditative or active, a poet or a logician, an ancient or a modern, a man or a woman. . . . Every circumstance which gives a character to the life of a human being, carries with it its peculiar biases; its peculiar facilities for perceiving some things, and for missing or forgetting others."[4]

Bentham's other fault is his stunted imagination. "He had never been made alive to the unseen influences which were acting on himself, nor consequently on his fellow-creatures."[5]

What Coleridge gets right, Mill says, is balancing Bentham's question about received opinion, "Is it true?," with another question, "What is the meaning of it?"—that is, "by what apparent facts it was at first suggested, and by what appearances it has ever since been rendered continually credible—has seemed, to a succession of persons, to be a faithful interpretation of their experience."[6]

"The Common Feelings and Common Destiny of Human Beings"

Mill's mature appreciation of the both/and of Bentham and Coleridge is given depth and staying power by his encounter with the poetry of William Wordsworth.

Mill is suffering from what we today call depression. "At first I hoped that the cloud would pass away of itself; but it did not. . . . I carried it with me into all companies, into all occupations. Hardly anything had power to cause me even a few minutes' oblivion of it. For some months the cloud seemed to grow thicker and thicker." He sees no way out: "There seemed no power in nature sufficient to begin the formation of my character anew."[7]

I suspect my father could have said much the same.

What Wordsworth's poetry does for Mill is open up "the common feelings and common destiny of human beings."[8] Mill begins to feel himself part of the human community again.

It wasn't Wordsworth who did this for me, but his friend John Keats.

An "interior life" is something I used to think I didn't have. Literature intrigued me but also baffled me, because it presented people as being way more than what appeared on the surface. Through intellectual analysis I could diagram relationships but not delve into them. I was so dense that I wrote an undergraduate paper saying that poets would have chosen to write prose if they really knew what they were trying to say. To write a poem was to throw in the towel.

In my junior year, breakthrough happens. My rationalist illusion—delusion—that poetry is unfulfilled prose is demolished when my study of Romantic poets arrives at Keats's "Ode to Autumn." At the end of the poem, "gathering swallows twitter in the skies," and the floodgates of tears are opened. (I'm glad I was reading it in the late 1950s. Had I come across it today, I'm afraid the image of birds sending tweets would have provoked a guffaw.) Wordsworth's "thoughts that do often lie too deep for tears"[9] are, for me, turned inside out by Keats into tears that lie too deep for thoughts.

I "begin to feel myself part of the human community," perhaps "again," but, more likely, "for the first time." Head and heart are no longer at odds.

The Grand Practice of Arguing with God

There are many Christians today, and probably have been from the beginning, for whom the sort of balance I strive for is the antithesis of faithful belief. They take their cue from the Jesus of "Let your word be 'Yes, Yes' or 'No, No'" (Matt. 5:37), either/or, period. I cast my lot with the dairyman Tevye in the musical *Fiddler on the Roof*, whose theological ruminations are shaped by "on the one hand . . . but on the other hand . . . but on the *other* hand . . ."

Tevye frequently looks quizzically—sometimes reproachfully— heavenward, and questions God why so much that is puzzling and then damaging and then destructive is happening to him and his family and his people. It is impossible to doubt Tevye's deep faith in God. One reason I do not doubt it is his willingness to argue with God, even to accuse God.

One of my students, a young Jewish woman, recounts to me the exhilarating experience she has as she reads the book of Job carefully and gets madder and madder at God. For a while she is afraid she is endangering her faith by letting her feelings run so free, but then comes the breakthrough to genuine understanding—she is coming to know the God of Jewish experience, the God who deals so closely with people that they can talk back, the God who challenges them to stand up and be counted.

She is discovering that her faith is grounded beneath both her affirmations and her doubts, in the God with whom we have to do. It could be said of God what I once wrote about another student in a letter of recommendation: "She is unpredictable, but she can be counted on."

From my students, particularly the Jewish ones, I learn the truth I heard in the 1950s spoken by Anna Leonowens in *The King and I* (in encounter 19 I will say how Broadway musicals were my *Sesame Street* and *Mister Rogers' Neighborhood*): "It's a very ancient saying / But a true and honest thought / That if you become a teacher / By your pupils you'll be taught."

I'm taught by my students that my doubts are part of my worship, that my believing includes my doubting, that God deals with me as I am (and this includes as I believe, not as I think I ought to believe), that clear-eyed honesty is the only sure ground for joy. The grand practice of arguing with God is rooted not in despair but in trust and hope and faith. Maybe you can have "Alleluia" without "How long, O Lord?," but an alleluia that pretends that "How long?" is an affront to God is itself a true affront to God.

The New Testament, even with its "yes yes" and "no no," is not simply a set of prescriptions without shade or context. Students in my introductory courses who were previously unfamiliar with the Bible were often struck by how the people closest to Jesus frequently don't understand what he is saying. It is not simply that different disciples see and understand different things. Particular ones perceive differently at different times. Jesus, the Jewish carpenter, regularly has to play Tevye, the Jewish dairyman, to his disciples.

My appropriation of faith is shaped by Bentham's suspicion of tradition and Coleridge's wariness of upending everything and Tevye's "on all the other hands." I believe Peter, and even Paul, would find this familiar. They would see it as expressing the common feelings and common destiny of human beings—human beings made in the image of God, an image they saw fleshed out in Jesus.

The disciples, time and again when they come to a fork in the road, take it.

IN A WORD

I encounter God's mind-boggling grace when I come to a fork in the road—"Is it true?" and "What is the meaning of it?"—and take it.

mind-boggling

Part Two

REORIENTING

Grace in Dimensions

Formation, perspective, and balance in my Christian identity come into clear focus in my images of God in time and space, which have been fundamentally reoriented in the years since my youth.

I am certainly no cosmologist, but what people in that line of work have accomplished in the last hundred years or so is at least as discombobulating to widely held assumptions as was Copernicus's demonstrating that the earth is not the center of the solar system. Being taught by scientists who know how the universe is actually put together—and by a literary genius who turns their findings into story—I have come to know a God much more appealing than the one I started with.

I Used to Think God . . .

I used to think God was in charge and had plans. Sovereignty and providence were God's by right and by nature. The king in control was simply who God was, what God did. This image of God depended on a view of space as encompassing territory, and of time as flying forward like an arrow.

The notion of territory requires boundaries—and the late Stephen Hawking tantalizes with a picture of the universe as "finite without boundary."[1] The notion of plans requires sequence and causality—but the tangling of time and light makes clear that all we can talk about is concurrence, and even this is called into question by the dissolution of any specifiable meaning of "simultaneous."

The image of God as a sovereign with schemes depends on views of space and time that resonate with hierarchy and with stories that proceed relentlessly from beginning through middle to end. The Bible often runs counter to these prejudices. It declares the last to be first. Over and over again—as in the parable of the prodigal son— the Bible reflects what Jean-Luc Godard said when told that movies should have a beginning, a middle, and an end: "Certainly, but not necessarily in that order."[2] What if God not only writes the play? What if God is also an actor, the prompter, and the director?

The Bible's a story, not a list of clear-cut principles. My Protestant formation, with its emphasis on the word, and my academic formation, with its high valuation of books that *analyze* stories instead of telling them, gave me a perspective from which I could place everything just where it belonged by thinking clearly that God is in charge, with plans. "Clear-cut" (with a sobering double meaning) I didn't always manage, not even often, but it was the ideal. Clear thinking is nothing to be scoffed at—but it is not to be idolized either. It took Godard's witticism about movies to jolt me free from the obsession with either/or sorting out.

The Bible's subversive current has for centuries been submerged beneath a conception of space and time that serves raw power. Either/or distinctions proliferate: good guys, bad guys; us, them; and, most ominously, the "other" as threat.

But what if the world isn't like this? What if the world isn't hospitable to a sovereign with schemes? What if territory doesn't fit geometry, and time doesn't move relentlessly straight ahead? What if God is more an imaginer than an engineer? Current cosmology renews the lease on the religious imagination, a lease that had lapsed while people continued to refurbish old hierarchical pictures and plots, or simply threw the whole thing over because it made no sense.

And I don't have to depend on scientists. There's the wisdom expressed in 1981 by my then three-year-old daughter, Juliet, in conversation with her six-year-old sister, Miranda, that I overhear while I'm washing the dishes. They are messing with play dough on the floor.

Juliet: "I'm making the foundation of the world." Miranda asks: "Of the whole world?" "Of everything," responds Juliet. Miranda goes deeper: "The foundation from God?" Juliet, immediately: "Yes." "The foundation of you?" "Yes." "And the foundation of space?" "Yes."

Physics and theology converge for me not only when eavesdropping in the kitchen, but also when I read about an exchange between two Nobel laureates. Wolfgang Pauli, at the conclusion of a paper on elementary particles, says to his colleague Niels Bohr, "You probably think these ideas are crazy." Bohr replies, "I do, but unfortunately they are not crazy enough."[3]

The craziness of the universe that underlies all the other craziness was succinctly stated in a note the publicity director of the Metropolitan Opera slipped to Einstein when the great scientist was in the audience: "Relativity: there is no hitching post in the universe—so far as we know." Einstein wrote back, "Read, and found correct."[4]

I suspect that prior to the twentieth century nearly everybody assumed there was a hitching post in the universe, some place that stayed put, a reference point from which and to which we could measure. God need not be that point, need not even be there at that point, but one's image of God is bound to be affected by the confidence that there is a there there somewhere. Einstein raised a fundamental, inescapable doubt about whether there's a there there anywhere.

Cosmology into Story

It is Italian writer Italo Calvino who turns cosmology into story. He makes palpable for me the crazy world that Einstein and his successors opened up.

Calvino offers tales told by characters who live through the unimaginably long stretches of cosmic evolution.[5] He warps time back to "In the beginning."

In "A Sign in Space," the narrator tells of setting up a sign just outside the outer edge of the Milky Way so that he can encounter it again when the galaxy has made its revolution—in two hundred million years. A weird enough notion.

The profound point is the storyteller's inability to recall what the sign was. Since it was the first sign in the history of the cosmos, there wasn't any reference point in terms of which to remember it, nothing to distinguish it from. When he is finally back where the unremembered sign should be, an even more devastating discovery: someone has erased it.

Then comes the profoundest point of all. Once new signs are set up and there are enough to constitute a critical mass for comparison and contrast—the prerequisite for remembering—the narrator is embarrassed because his signs stay put, fixed. "I had left that sign in space, that sign which had seemed so beautiful and original to me and so suited to its function, and which now, in my memory, seemed inappropriate in all its pretension, a sign chiefly of an antiquated way of conceiving signs and of my foolish acceptance of an order of things I ought to have been wise enough to break away from in time."[6]

Whatever my certainties, the signs in which they are coded are themselves subject to the inexorable rule of change. If I try to fix a point, freeze it, the shifting time and space in which it sits will distort it. My sign, my image of God, begins to resemble one of those wilted watches that litter the landscape in Salvador Dalí's paintings.

Here's the moment when my image of God sustained the most direct blow ever, far more devastating than my divorces or my father's suicide.

I propose "a Christian interpretation" of someone else's experience: I quote Romans 8:28 (RSV), "We know that in everything God works for good," to a girlfriend who has just told me of her young brother's death from leukemia several years before. My relationship with her abruptly ends. Whether God works for good in everything I'm not sure. What I am sure of is that in this instant I am using my image of God as a bludgeon, and it has to change.

Calvino deprives me of hitching posts, but I get something wonderful instead: dimensions. I don't really understand dimension talk the way mathematicians do, but when one of them says that a dimension is "a degree of freedom,"[7] I take notice.

The most appealing feature of dimensions is their capacity for coexistence. I don't have to go somewhere else to encounter them; I simply have to understand more comprehensively what is all around me and in me.

"We Were All There"

One of Calvino's stories uses dimensions to drive home a moral argument as fresh as today's newsfeed.

"All at One Point" begins: "Naturally, we were all there—where else could we have been? Nobody knew then that there could be space. Or time either. . . . Every point of each of us coincided with every point of each of the others in a single point, which is where we all were."[8]

He's talking, of course, about the singularity "before" the Big Bang. Calvino is suggesting, in light of modern cosmology, that the answer to the question God asks Job, "Where were you when I laid the foundation of the earth?," is this: "I was there. We all were. In the singularity!"

The philosophical and physical and theological conundrums lurking in origins are touched on lightly and humorously in Calvino's story—as also by Juliet's three-year-old intuition: "The foundation from God?" "Yes." "The foundation of you?" "Yes." "And the foundation of space?" "Yes."—but the implications of our common origin, the common origin of everyone and everything in a single point, is the real burden of the tale.

Calvino's narrator says that certain inhabitants of that point were treated by the others as immigrants, as though they had come "later." "This was mere unfounded prejudice—that seems obvious to me—because neither before nor after existed, nor any place to immigrate from, but there were those who insisted that the concept of 'immigrant' could be understood in the abstract, outside of space and time."[9]

Calvino's story demonstrates that the very notion of "immigrant," a distinction between those who "belong" and those who are allowed in "on sufferance," makes no sense either in the abstract or in space and time. I used to think that we are all sisters and brothers because we are all children of God. I still do, but the history of warfare, of genocide, of abuse, of people lording it over other people, suggests that the image of the family of God isn't particularly effective in promoting harmony.

Maybe the problem lies in the notion that God creates and plays favorites in a universe of up and down.

If my image of God is shaped by a primordial awareness that I and everybody else and everything else that has ever been and ever will be were all in one point, or that all life has a truly common origin (not just the now familiar observation that everything that constitutes us was once a star, but that we and the stars were once the same, none of us unlike anything else), then I have a firm foundation for true diversity.

Here is the irony. What is commonly thought to be God's "favoritism" in "choosing" Abraham for special treatment misses the point of the choice: "In you all the families of the earth shall be blessed." Calvino's story is a commentary on Genesis 12:3, explaining what it means for all families of the earth—indeed, of the galaxy, even the universe—to be blessed. Abraham is singled out to show that we're all in it together. If I see Abraham clearly, I'll realize that "we were all there."

There are no immigrants, nobody has a prior claim on space or time, nobody's territory is exclusive and nobody's calendar is privileged, nobody's particular profile is the standard against which the rest of the universe is to be measured.

IN A WORD

I encounter God's disorienting grace when scientists and storytellers jar me loose from a view of space and time that straitjackets God and favors me.

Grace in Surprise

If I get to choose a time warp to fall into, it would be to join the Seven Sleepers of Ephesus.

It's the year 251, in the reign of Roman Emperor Decius. Seven young men in Ephesus refuse his demand to renounce their Christianity. They hide in a cave. The emperor orders the cave sealed. The young men fall asleep.

Two centuries later they wake up, in the reign of Theodosius II. Their appearance in the city is treated as evidence for the resurrection of the dead, but what interests me especially is their surprise at what they find: the cross over the city gate, the name of Christ freely spoken, and the coins they try to buy things with, bearing the image of Decius, rejected as bogus by the merchants.

This story appears in countless versions in many languages (it's in the Qur'an, Surah 18:9–26); it is even treated with carefree abandon ("slight variations," he calls them) by Mark Twain.[1]

For me, the significance of the Seven Sleepers is best captured by historian Peter Brown, who says that his book *The Making of Late Antiquity* "is an attempt to enter into their surprise."[2]

Brown wants—so do I—to understand nothing less than "what it was like to live in that world,"[3] how persons "came to feel so different from each other."[4] He believes one of the main reasons people come to *feel different* is that they come to *feel differently*, and he believes religion has more bearing than anything else on how people feel.

There is a natural tendency in nearly everyone to assume that centuries long ago were somehow shorter than they are currently. We talk of "the early church" as though it can be set over against "now," failing to recognize that in those first three or four hundred years there was at least as much variety and conflict as there has been since the Reformation of the sixteenth century.

It is easy to homogenize the distant past. In a *New Yorker* cartoon an elderly person says to a younger one at a cocktail party, "Of course, that was long ago, but at the time it seemed like the present."[5]

Imagine you're a drama critic and you get a letter from Lin-Manuel Miranda: "Thank you for your review; you understand better than I do what I'm up to!" That's actually Peter Brown's response to me for an assessment of his work that I published in 1980. For students of Late Antiquity, Brown has remade our understanding of the field the way Miranda's *Hamilton* has remade critics' understanding of musical theater. I count Brown's letter, saying I got him right, among my most precious treasures.

Negative Capability

Brown sustains the historian's version of poet John Keats's "negative capability"[6]—when one "is capable of being in uncertainties, mysteries, doubts, without any irritable reaching after fact and reason"—which has been for me, since I first read it my junior year in college, the surest ground of faith, hope, and love.

Keats does not say that fact and reason are of no value, but that they are not to be rushed at, forced, premature. Uncertainties, mysteries, doubts abound, but for me they are room to move around in, not a pit to try to scramble out of. Some of the greatest havoc ever known has been wreaked—and is still being wreaked—by people who too quickly and too irritably claim to have put an end to uncertainties, mysteries, doubts, whether in the name of God or racial purity or the dialectic.

Keats credits Shakespeare with possessing negative capability "so enormously." That feature of Keats's 1817 letter to his brothers triggered 170 years later the vividest dream I've ever had.

I'm on my way to an exam in Shakespeare; I've just learned about it, so there's no time to prepare. The exam is scheduled for 10:30, and it's now 10:25. I even have a sense I have never studied Shakespeare at all.

I don't know what room the exam is in, but I notice that I'm having a conversation with someone. It's not an ordinary someone, but a sort of wooden statue. The first thing that occurs to me after I wake up from the dream is that it was Shakespeare who was talking to me; the statue figure was enough like various busts of him, or pictures of such busts, to make this plausible.

This statue/person tells me about his early life. It was rather carefree and included rejection of a single imposed order. I think, "He's a kind of existentialist," by which I suppose I mean he operates on the assumption that there's no order, that we have to improvise every moment as we go along.

But then I realize this isn't quite right. I say, "But each of the worlds of Shakespeare's plays"—maybe I said "your plays," though I don't recall recognizing the figure in the dream itself—"has a kind of order, though different from the others." And the person with whom I'm talking agrees.

When the dream began I was very anxious about being late for the exam, but while the conversation is going on I am dimly aware that I'm not worried about that anymore. The key point of the dream seemed to be negative capability—that if my ordered world was coming unglued, the alternative was not chaos, but a differently ordered world. This was the right answer to the exam, and it was a surprise.

The question Brown keeps asking, one that I ask with him, is deceptively simple: What do people actually *do*? How did the people of Late Antiquity spend their days, twenty-four hours long just like ours?

Attention to this question keeps Brown from serving up whole eras on a single dish, makes him sensitive to subtle flavors in the sources. From him I learn that my job as a scholar is more to go out adventuring than to come forth proclaiming.

He takes the measure of Saint Augustine's preaching, an activity the priest and later bishop engaged in every week for thirty-nine years (almost as long as my father did). "In the unselfconscious routine of these sermons we can come as close as is possible to the foundations of Augustine's qualities as a thinker."[7] Brown inoculates me against the temptation to proof-text a theological point with a reference out of context to some particular thing or other that Augustine said. It is Augustine's *qualities as a thinker* that matter.

Brown has come to see that "debates of ordinary [people] as to who they were, to whom they would be loyal, where they felt they belonged, whom they were prepared to accept, and whom they would persist in rejecting" molded the fate of the Roman Empire. Historians of religion must keep their eyes "firmly on the ground."[8] Where to direct my gaze—this is Peter Brown's most important lesson to me.

And his second most important lesson: acknowledge the fact that I'm "dealing with phenomena which I do not readily understand in the world around me, and in myself, any more than I do in the distant past."[9] Being sure about something that happened a minute ago right here is not a lot easier than being sure what happened long ago and far away.

Brown has been instrumental in reorienting theology, for me and for many others—bringing it to ground, thickening its texture, reminding me that practice often—usually—precedes dogma.

In chapter 15, "The Lost Future," of *Augustine of Hippo: A Biography*—as close to a definitive account of the saint as we are ever apt to get—Brown specifies what Augustine's conversion to Christianity meant: Augustine had come to see that we are "bound by the continuities of [our] inner life." What Brown then says about the Augustinian sensibility, I have gone to repeatedly to help make sense of many facets of my own experience. He says that Augustine "has imperceptibly become a 'Romantic.'"

What does this mean, and why does it resonate with my experience? It's the kind of Christian I am: "defined by [the] tension towards something else, by [my] capacity for faith, for hope, for longing, . . . seeking a country that is always distant, but made ever present by the quality of the love that 'groans' for it."[10] This resonates with negative capability—and the inventor of that phrase, my hero John Keats, is among the greatest of the poets who are called "Romantic."

The notion that a *quality of love* can make the unseen present haunts me. I would be hard-pressed to specify further what that "something else" means, but I do know that what it suggests is for me far richer, far more appealing than the dogmatic certainty that is so prominent among many Christians these days.

I would be untrue to my own principles if I doubted the sincerity of those who are so sure. But I would be untrue to my own experience if I said I thought such certainty was the country I am seeking. Like Brown, I am always expecting to be surprised. I, too, wish that I had been one of the Seven Sleepers of Ephesus.

And in a sense, that's what I am up to in this story.

The Seven Sleepers of Ephesus were "surprised" by what they found when they woke up, because it would have never occurred to them that what they discovered could have happened. No way, they would have thought, can the Christian story, having been stamped out by the emperor in their time, become the controlling narrative of the mighty Roman Empire.

The Christian story certainly isn't being stamped out in my own time, but research shows it is eroding. What I see now, at age eighty, is almost as different from what I knew at twenty as what the Sleepers found when they woke up. I wonder whether the waning of the church's influence is like the melting of the glaciers under the influence of climate change—gradual (though at an increasing rate) but probably unstoppable.

In the previous encounter I talked about the way I have jettisoned the notion that God is a sovereign who has plans. I suspect
that "surprise"—both as delight and as trouble—is not just my view
but is also something God knows firsthand.

It's 1989. I have just finished reading *Grand Opening* by my
friend Jon Hassler, whose many novels capture Minnesota both
spot-on and magically. I write to Jon. "I want to thank you for the
gift of a world. Words like 'delicious,' 'exquisite,' 'crafted,' 'etched'
come to mind, and they're all to the point, but they don't get to
the heart of the matter."

And what is that heart of the matter? "Your love for the world
you create. That sounds like God, and I mean it to."

By the time I'm done with *Grand Opening* I'm thinking, "You
must feel a certain terror when you start writing a novel—maybe
not knowing in detail what's to become of characters but knowing
that awful things may, probably will, happen. No matter how much
you love them—precisely because you love them so much—you
must surrender to having bad things happen to good people and
good things to bad people."

And then the theological implication. "This leads me to think
our notion of God as creator simply ringing up worlds for the sheer
overflowing joy of it neglects the divine terror at the prospect of
actually creating one."

IN A WORD

I encounter God's reassuring grace when I wake and
feel at home, even in a rapidly and radically changing
religious landscape.

reassuring

Grace in Politics

The Seven Sleepers of Ephesus woke to a political upending.

In the two centuries they'd been slumbering, the distinction Jesus had made between what belongs to Caesar and what belongs to God had been pretty much obliterated.

It is commonly thought that "Render to Caesar the things that are Caesar's, and to God the things that are God's" (Mark 12:17 RSV) is a clear guideline for Christian action in the public sphere. I find that it settles little, if anything at all.

Whenever I think about the religious and political spheres, I recall a story from many years ago. My parents are on a tour of Ireland, where time warps—known colloquially as "thin places"— are simply part of the landscape.

"Who Belongs to Which Other"

The bus halts for flocks of sheep crossing the road. My mother asks the driver why there are differently colored marks on the animals. "So they can tell who belongs to which other."

Some say Jesus was being sly. Everything belongs to God, so whatever Caesar has is only by delegation. All of Caesar's peremptory claims are spurious.

Some say Jesus is drawing a line in the sand, which must not be crossed. God and Caesar oversee separate turf.

A sardonic paraphrase is included in *The Books of Bokonon* in Kurt Vonnegut's novel *Cat's Cradle*: "Pay no attention to Caesar. Caesar doesn't have the slightest idea what's *really* going on."[1]

I believe "*What* belongs to which other?" is unavoidable—unanswerable, in fact, apart from close attention to surroundings and conditions. Jesus's prescription sharpens the question, doesn't resolve it.

Dispute about what is God's and what is Caesar's has a special character in the United States, concentrated on the relation of religion and politics—and on the company they keep with the rest of the culture.

In 2003 the news organization Reuters banned a United Methodist Church advertisement from its electronic billboard in New York's Times Square. A spokesperson said that in order to preserve Reuters's reputation as an unbiased source of information, the billboard does not carry ads that are "pornographic, political, religious, libelous, misleading, or deceptive."[2] "Political" and "religious" were in pretty embarrassing company.

"Give to politics the things that are politics' and to religion the things that are religion's" is not the same as "Caesar's" and "God's." When the government is, as it is in contemporary America (at least in theory), the people, "Caesar" is not an autocrat but the political process itself. Moreover, when religious pluralism is protected, so that differing identities of God (including "there is none") have equal rights to be heard, the Divine is hard to pin down.

It is here that my quarrel with what passes for "Christian" in media-speak and, more generally, in popular opinion comes into clearest focus. There is a bumper sticker that proclaims "God is not a Republican or a Democrat." I suppose that in technical terms of party affiliation it's true. But not everyone agrees. In recent decades, Republicans have hijacked Christian identity.

I live near Lake Wobegon, the mythical Minnesota town. The reason you don't find Lake Wobegon on maps is like the redistricting of Christianity.

When Minnesota was initially being mapped, "teams of sur-
veyors worked their way in from the four outer corners and, arriving at the center, found they had surveyed more of Minnesota
than there was room for between Wisconsin and the Dakotas"—so
there wasn't any area left to assign to what was actually in the
middle, Lake Wobegon.[3]

Redistricting Religion and Politics

Some Republicans, in drawing the map of politics and religion,
have similarly failed to find space that is occupied by Christians who are Democrats. They pretend to tell you exactly what
counts as Christian and just as exactly what doesn't. Lines drawn
in the sand are quickly fixed in concrete, and walls are built
and reinforced.

In 2004, thinking she has "been invited to a nonpartisan, non-
sectarian" event, a National Day of Prayer breakfast in Plymouth,
Minnesota, Hennepin County Attorney (and, since 2006, US
Senator, and in 2019 candidate for president) Amy Klobuchar, a
Democrat and a Congregationalist, limps in on crutches, having
recently undergone cartilage repair surgery.

Star Tribune columnist Nick Coleman, who was there, recounts
the scene. He sees no other Democrat besides Klobuchar.

"When breakfast ended, a man named Richard Johnson came
over and asked her to call him up and pray with him sometime.
'I didn't know any Democrats are Christian,' Johnson said. He
makes his living selling Noni Juice. . . . 'I assumed that Christians
have been driven out of the Democratic Party,' Johnson told Klobuchar, 'but I pray to the Lord Jesus, and I'd like to pray with you.'"[4]

It isn't just Minnesota, either. In 2003 I hear Dorothy Rupert,
a recently retired Colorado state senator, recount something that
happened to her daughter, Julie Schiola, principal at a bilingual
school. One of the student teachers, a senior at a nearby university,

hears Schiola say she is attending a church, and not just attend-ing—she is in fact a member. The student teacher looks at her, flab-bergasted. Schiola asks if something is wrong. The student teacher blurts out, "I thought you were a Democrat!"

Not everybody, of course, is duped, but the lie, if told often enough, burrows into the popular mind and lodges there, even-tually evicting the truth. I am a Christian, a Democrat, and I pray. I consider the Republican takeover of the Christian tradition to be hostile.

To their credit, some of my Republican friends, with whom I pray, are as embarrassed by Richard Johnson's remark to Amy Klobuchar as I am outraged by it, but the remark must be publicly challenged. The rights of Democrats on Christian turf need to be reclaimed. Richard Johnson appears to think that if Amy Klobu-char is a Christian she must not be a "real" Democrat, and with the help of the Lord Jesus he can bring her around to the place where "real" Christians dwell: the Republican Party.

I don't contest the right of Republicans to the title "Christian," even when I disagree profoundly with them on many points both doctrinal and political. However, I object to their implication that if I don't agree with them on their pet points both doctrinal and political, I've renounced my baptismal identity.

Christian territory is much bigger than Richard Johnson and those who think like him think it is. Republican lawmakers and judges in many states have redistricted Democrats out of legisla-tures and Congress. Republican ideology has redistricted Dem-ocrats out of the church by assuming that "Christians have been driven out of the Democratic Party." We who are Christian and Democrat must redraw the map.

And the map doesn't have clear boundary lines between what is God's and what is Caesar's, what is religious territory and what is political. Moreover, there can be—and are—disagreements over who has the authority to stake out even those blurry frontiers.

IN A WORD

I encounter God's discomfiting grace when I realize that Jesus's saying to give to Caesar and to God what belongs to each is not an answer, but simply the question thrown right back to me.

discomfiting

Part Three

THE BIBLE

Grace in "Whatever"

I've already exposed my hand—I've said that what looks like a straightforward statement by Jesus, about what is Caesar's and what is God's, is subject to qualification. In other words, the Bible doesn't necessarily "settle it."

The Bible is the thread that weaves through the tapestry of Christian identity from the church's beginning to now. I suspect it will continue its course for however long there are Christians.

And the Bible is as time-warped as anything else.

The Bible in Time Warps

In 1900 no one would have predicted that a hundred years later Catholics and Lutherans would be saying the same things about justification by faith; Methodists would have a monastery; Presbyterians would be preaching from a lectionary; Pentecostalists would be the second largest group of Christians (there weren't any Pentecostalists at all until 1906); and theologians (including popes) would be saying that God's covenant with the Jews was not superseded by Christianity, so Christians no longer have a warrant to convert Jews.

Faithful Christians today see, think, feel, and believe things that their ancestors a century earlier would have recoiled from. Nowhere has this revolution registered stronger seismic shocks than in the interpretation of the Bible. I taught Bible courses for many years, so I registered the dynamism of biblical scholarship on my pulse and that of my students.

In the eighteenth and nineteenth centuries the Bible came under unprecedented critical scrutiny. Ironically, it was Protestants, their origin grounded in strident claims for biblical authority, who led the assault that eroded confidence in the Bible's trustworthiness. Likewise ironically, the Catholic Church, which discouraged popular reading of the Bible and insisted on the equal (or even superior) authority of tradition, resisted any critical treatment of the text.

At the beginning of the twentieth century Catholic biblical scholars were forbidden to refer to the works of Protestants. While Protestants were not under similar ecclesiastical strictures, the practical effect was the same. The fundamentalist-modernist controversy was as fierce as any dispute in the history of the church. The story of the "battle for the Bible" could be written by a military historian.

Pope Pius XII inaugurates a revolution. In 1943 he issues an encyclical that turns the world upside down for Catholic scholars.[1] They used to be obligated to justify answers arrived at on dogmatic grounds rather than those of a scholarly discipline. Now they are charged to make good use of all the methods of analysis that had developed over the previous two centuries. They are even to work collaboratively with Protestants.

Early in the twentieth century the Protestant world had arrived at a kind of standoff between conservative and liberal interpreters of the Bible. By the end of the century, however, Protestant voices, in terms of numbers and popular influence, increasingly tilted toward a view not unlike the "originalist" interpretation of the US Constitution.[2] Both constitutional and biblical originalism are grounded in a confidence that we can know exactly what writers from long ago meant, and that what they meant then is directly applicable to our own time.

My own suspicion of originalism is reinforced when I read letters I wrote a half century ago. I'm not at all certain I could say for sure what they "meant" then, much less what they mean now.

No one in 1900 could have predicted the shape of biblical study in 2000. Denominational barriers have dissolved. The terrain has become much more variegated. Few interpreters fit neatly into any one category. From a long and broad view, some roles have been reversed: serious Bible study is a staple of Catholic lay faith formation, while many Protestants are insisting on biblical literalism—as the bumper sticker declares, "The Bible: God said it, I believe it, that settles it."

The lines of connection between Catholic and Protestant biblical interpretation are reminiscent of the Penrose stairs, an optical illusion, popularized by artist M. C. Escher, in which what look like stairways going in opposite directions meet, and parallel lines appear to diverge. On some matters of sexual ethics, traditional Catholics and very conservative Protestants read the Bible the same way, while in matters of social justice, popes and liberal Protestants find the Bible pointing in an identical direction.

During the twentieth century a whole segment of the Christian community hardly participated in these battles at all—the Eastern Orthodox. There were exceptions, of course, but in the main the Orthodox, who had neither a Protestant Reformation nor the Enlightenment to contend with directly, maintained habits of biblical reading that stretched back to the earliest centuries of the church. The term is plural—habits; they were many and varied.

In that part of the Christian world, a truth put succinctly by my teacher, the late Jaroslav Pelikan, is demonstrated: "Tradition is the living faith of the dead; traditionalism is the dead faith of the living."[3] The Orthodox intuition about what tradition really is—including tradition in the Bible—can help spring us free from the either/or boxes we have locked ourselves into.

My friend Anthony Ugolnik, Ukrainian Orthodox priest and professor of English, highlights a feature of Orthodox practice that reinforces this roominess for biblical interpretation. "In Orthodox ritual there is no single bound Bible with that thumping solidity found on a Protestant pulpit," he says. Gospels are placed on the altar; Epistles are a different book; Psalter and Prophets and Wisdom texts are separate volumes on a spinning lectern. The print revolution bound these many books together, "and that one Book has become an icon of its own."

"When the sacred text becomes one thing," Ugolnik continues, "a bound object, even constructed in such a way that it embodies a certain solidity and unarguable solidarity, it can take on the quality of the idol which the Book in its genesis condemned." Nuance, variation, internal tensions—all are obscured.[4]

Christians who used to hit each other over the head with the Bible are now reading it together. Nearly everyone acknowledges that the Bible came from a community and belongs to a community—it is not the private preserve of individuals or even of particular denominations. We *see* the Bible together as well as read it together.

Teeming with Sights and Savors and Sounds

The prophet Ezekiel (3:1–3) was told to *eat* the scroll, and it was sweet as honey. The psalmist (34:8) urges me to *taste* and *see* that the Lord is good. At a moment of revelation to two disciples in the town of Emmaus on the evening of the first Easter day (Luke 24:31), "their *eyes were opened*" (emphasis added). The Bible is teeming with sights and savors and sounds.

For all the fresh, unexpected turns that biblical interpretation took in the twentieth century, it remains primarily *wordy*, locked in literary categories. Imagination has certainly been let loose, but it has not yet been set free. The time is ripe for discovering anew that the Bible is adaptable for life and is not fragile; I cannot "break" it.

The word of God has a strong gravitational pull. It will keep me in orbit even if I circle quite a distance out. The principal aim of interpretation is to stimulate the imagination, not to "get it right."

Earlier ages knew a lot about this. Before scholarship became fixated on words and history, biblical interpreters who expressed what they knew in stained glass and sculpture, in manuscript illuminations, in miracle and mystery plays, in plainchant or polyphony, or on Sistine Chapel ceilings had authority on a par with preachers and professors. Understanding the word of God was not the exclusive province of the learned.

In the wonderful image of Saint Gregory the Great, the Bible is a river in whose shallows a lamb may wade and in whose depths an elephant can swim.[5] The point is this: it is the same river—the shallow water and the deep water are the same water. As the poet Michael Dennis Browne said in a conversation at the Collegeville Institute, in every age the river of the Bible flows in new landscapes, where other streams become tributary to it.

An astute analyst of seismic cultural shifts was Matthew Arnold (1822–88), whom I introduced earlier as one of my favorite conversation partners. Arnold conjures an image that applies directly to the changing role of the Bible in the twentieth century: "We are not beaten from our old opinion by logic, we are not driven off our ground; our ground itself changes with us."[6]

The shifting of the ground is most evident not in the thousands of books and articles published, but in the week-by-week experience of those who participate in Mass and those who go to what are commonly called "mainline" Protestant worship services.

Church unity is still a very distant goal, but it is remarkable that so many Christians these days hear the same biblical passages read on any given Sunday. The "common lectionary," with its readings from various parts of the Bible, including nearly every week the Old Testament, is testimony to the shared conviction that the Bible, as Saint Augustine says, "stoop[s] to all in the great plainness of its language and simplicity of style, yet it require[s] the closest attention of the most serious-minded."[7]

This context of community reading corrects for the theological myopia that often afflicts scholars when they claim to have found *the* key to the meaning of Scripture. The common lectionary reveals the Bible's dimensions and resonances that show the biblical world to be as complicated, ambiguous, and mixed in its promise and peril as my world. It becomes clear that ancient Israel and the early church were not theologically compulsive or obsessive. The texts are interpreted in a thousand different ways, but the hyperlink of the common lectionary keeps everyone spiritually in touch.

There is no one, single, extractable meaning. There was, from the beginning, a variety of messages, not always compatible, as all sorts and conditions of persons tried to make sense of what they had seen and heard.

In 1974 I write a note to the students in my introductory New Testament course. It is the sixth time I have taught it, but "this year I seem to have succeeded even less well than usual in making clear what some of my assumptions are."

The Complexity of Jesus: An Occupational Hazard

It is four pages (writing newspaper columns in recent years has trained me to be briefer). The heart of the matter is this: if "divine revelation occurs in history, that history remains history, and historical documents remain historical documents." Belief in the humanity of Jesus implies a belief that he was to some degree enigmatic to himself—for example, Jesus would one day wake up thinking "I am the Messiah" and the next day wondering "How could I ever have thought so?" Then to the fundamental point: "Belief in the religious significance of history entails belief that religious truth remains essentially elusive, or is at least always subject to reassessment."

I squirm when people talk about their relationship with Jesus Christ as if that is a clear and no-remainder answer to a question that I consider to be very complex and open-ended. I understand and appreciate "What would Jesus do?," but when I ask it of myself, I usually don't have an answer. It's precisely what would disturb other Christians about my relationship with Jesus that makes that relationship very important to me.

The complexity of Jesus—a historical complexity—is an occupational hazard for anyone who teaches the Bible. Almost any time someone tells me what Jesus might do, I can think of another thing he might do, and this in and of itself makes Jesus very significant to me. I am uneasy with people who say it is easy to "put your faith in Jesus." I don't want to short-circuit the blindsiding aspect of Jesus.

One way to keep Jesus in three dimensions is to remember that Jesus had no Gospels to read. It was the scroll of Isaiah he read in the synagogue (Luke 4), and he stood to do so. I may be the only Christian who objects to standing for the reading of the Gospel— or rather, to standing for only it. I find God as much in the rest of the Bible as in the Gospels, and I do not understand why they should be so privileged.

While teaching the Bible to undergraduates, I come to the conclusion that the Bible's upending of expectations is one evidence of its inspiration. I can't believe in a God of total order, but only in a God of the frequently unexpected and sometimes unexplainable.

It's a little like the way Jesus's parable of the good Samaritan (Luke 10:29–37) turns inside out the question posed by the lawyer, "Who is my neighbor?" The lawyer is basically asking, "Whom do I have to love?" Jesus then tells the story of an injured man on the side of the road. Two members of the religious establishment pass by. But a third person, a Samaritan (they and Jews were enemies), stops to help the man, and Jesus's response to the initial question is itself a question: "Which of these three, do you think, was a neighbor to the man who fell into the hands of the robbers?" In other words, the person the lawyer needs to learn to see as his neighbor, and extend love to, is the Samaritan. The parable is a critique of tribalism.

In most churches where the lectionary is used, a reading concludes with "The word of the Lord," and the congregation responds, "Thanks be to God." Usually I am quite happy to give the expected response. But once in a while a reading will seem to me unworthy of the God I worship, and I at best mumble "Thanks be to God."

My moral intuition—even my theological instinct—decisively shaped and deeply informed by the Bible, occasionally tells me that a particular passage in that very Bible is not something to thank God for. From the Bible itself I learn to criticize the Bible.

When the prophet Samuel says to King Saul, "Listen to the words of the Lord. Thus says the Lord of hosts, 'I will punish the Amalekites for what they did in opposing the Israelites when they came up out of Egypt. Now go and attack Amalek, and utterly destroy all that they have; do not spare them, but kill both man and woman, child and infant, ox and sheep, camel and donkey'" (1 Sam. 15:1–3)—no way will I say "Thanks be to God" for this word.

And from the other direction, there are times when the Bible calls me to account, has me squarely in its "Woe to you, hypocrite" crosshairs. I shudder to think how reluctant I am to turn the other cheek and love my enemies. I'm not about to sell all I have and give to the poor. If I'm being honest, I'll gag on saying "Thanks be to God" for these words.

I mention these puzzles to Jayne Thompson, a pastor friend of mine, who says, "I sometimes want to respond to 'The word of the Lord' with 'Whatever.'"

There are occasions on which responding to the Bible with "Whatever" is more faithful than "Thanks be to God."

IN A WORD

I encounter the confounding grace of God when I join lambs wading and elephants swimming in the biblical river, and realize that sometimes "Whatever" is the best response to what I'm finding.

confounding

Grace in Opening Up and Broadening Out

A lifetime of studying the Bible and teaching and writing about it has been for me "not a having and a resting, but a growing and becoming," to adopt a phrase of Matthew Arnold's cited in encounter 2 as a way of characterizing change. The Bible speaks in many different voices on a great variety of topics. Any sentence that begins, without qualification, "The Bible says . . . ," is almost certainly wrong.

In my seventeen years of teaching biblical courses I was constantly reminded that undergraduates who come to the Bible for the first time are caught off guard. They expect it to be a collection of statements about God. They find it is mainly a book of stories. And not only does the Bible tell stories; the compilers of the text were not particularly concerned to reconcile differences or to resolve contradictions.

God visits the sins of your parents on you, and God says that you will suffer only for your own sins. Pharaoh hardens his own heart, and God hardens Pharaoh's heart. Job finally concedes that God makes sense, while Ecclesiastes says that all is vanity. Jeremiah and his opponents agree there is no way they can tell in advance which of their predictions is right—only time will tell.

The Truth of Stories

What is really characteristic of the Bible, however—what gives it coherence in the face of all this diversity—is its insistence that the truth of stories is inextricably bound to their nature as stories.

Joseph says to his brothers—who are startled to discover that he, who they thought was dead, is their benefactor—"Though you intended to do harm to me, God intended it for good" (Gen. 50:20). This is not an abstract theological principle about God's ability to turn evil to good; it is a precipitate from that concrete story. It's true when Joseph says it. It wouldn't be true if the brothers said it, by way of absolving themselves. The truth could not have been arrived at by abstract argument from agreed-upon premises. It doesn't give me warrant for excusing evil I do on the grounds that God can make good of it.

Just as my life fluctuates between order and confusion, so too does the Bible. Sometimes it appears to make coherent sense, while at other times it seems an impossibly diverse collection of partial insights that cannot be brought into any sharp focus—eliciting, at best, a response of "Whatever."

I am a person in history dealing with a book produced in history. Neither the world nor the Bible provides a straightforward key by which to interpret and order the confusion of the other. The Bible is a handbook for pilgrims, not a guidebook for tourists.

What "method" of biblical interpretation do I use? All my experiences enter into my reading. All that I have learned is engaged when I read.

Christian doctrine asserts that God became a human being and dwelt among us. In so doing, God subjected revelation itself to the limitations and rich possibilities of human language and to the ambiguities of history. Jesus is really in history. He is not something plunked down into history that then operates differently.

This drives paradox right into the heart of Christian thought and existence. I have to study the sacred book and the church's origins in all their complex dimensions, with all the tools at the disposal of the human sciences. The Bible is populated with full-bodied and warm-blooded creatures, possessed of five senses.

It is inconsistent to assert, as biblical literalists do, both that God acts in history and that the record of those acts is itself not subject to the uncertainties of history. I must both have and eat my incarnational cake.

When interpreters of the Bible present it as having all the answers, all the schemes worked out, they eliminate a valuable potential: the sort of growth that occurs when a person has to work through—and keep working through—experience and Scripture, both of which are themselves moving back and forth on a line between certainty and uncertainty. This is the situation of the person who is prepared to risk growth, who is not content to stop short either at the assertion that the Bible is all literally true and thus all I have to do is read and believe, or at the assertion that all the variety of the Bible points to one eternal and timeless truth and thus all I have to do is get in touch with my true and timeless self.

I'm as wary of the hyperspiritualization of the text as I am of strict literalism, but there is a middle ground.

A Middle Ground

I came of scholarly age in the heyday of "demythologizing"—the effort to wrest the Bible free of ancient cosmologies (especially the "three-storied universe," with heaven above, earth in the middle, hell below) so it could make sense to "the modern person." In the process, a whole rich way of imagining and speaking got drowned out. I sensed that the "modern person" was in need of as much demythologizing as the Bible.

The demythologizers were imposing their own literalism on people who, more likely, thought and felt and knew poetically. When the psalmist talks about making a bed in Sheol, the place of departed spirits, or dwelling in the uttermost parts of the sea, or ascending into heaven, the psalmist is probably doing what poets always do: being concrete, being suggestive, saying God is too big to get around, too high to get over, too low to get under, and quite impossible to get away from.

For several generations, biblical study had been carried on in effective isolation from the rest of the academy, except for a few schools of philosophical thought.

As I reread the sources of my own story, I realize how fortunate I was to spend the first seventeen years of my career teaching at Swarthmore, an undergraduate college. In such a place, my daily round included interaction with practitioners of other disciplines. I could not escape awareness of revolutionary developments in psychology, sociology, literary criticism, even history of religions.

From psychology, I learned about the irreducible, finally untranslatable function of myth and symbol. From sociology, that consciousness and society are inseparable. Literary criticism clarified the positive uses of ambiguity. History of religions pointed to liturgy and sacrament and community, not doctrine, as chief bearer of religious meaning. The influence of these other disciplines outfitted me with antennae that pick up signals that can be conveyed only through metaphor and myth.

Demythologize the Bible, and people will look to Tolkien's Middle Earth and Lewis's Narnia and Lucas's Star Wars galaxy and Rowling's Hogwarts and the starship *Enterprise* for insight into the true nature of things. Mythology is not a stopgap until we get more knowledge. It is itself a way of knowing. The mythological frame of mind is not a primitive appendix; it is a vital component of the spiritual anatomy.

Equipped with appreciation of the textures and colors and patterns of myth and symbol, I am loosed from the shackles of closing down and narrowing in when I read the Bible. Getting stuck is the ultimate unfaithfulness.

I can of course be challenged by exclusivist claims: "No one comes to the Father except through me," Jesus says in John 14:6; "There is no other name under heaven . . . by which we must be saved," declares Peter in Acts 4:12. But I counter with openings to the outside, such as Paul's Areopagus speech in Acts 17, in which he connects the gospel to the Athenians' "unknown God," and the first chapter of his letter to the Romans. It is not self-evidently clear that the diminishing of Christianity's uniqueness diminishes its worth.

My experience of opening up and broadening out has followed from my long, direct engagement with the Bible but also from my having been catapulted into another part of the religious universe.

Light from Buddhism

I was fortunate to have more than a decade of close association with a Swarthmore College colleague, Donald Swearer, who is in the forefront of interpreters of Buddhism. We even wrote a book together: *For the Sake of the World: The Spirit of Buddhist and Christian Monasticism.*[1]

Early in his career Don was a Presbyterian missionary to Thailand. As demonstrated in his book *Dialogue: The Key to Understanding Other Religions*, he learned that certain basic biblical concepts and images—being in the world but not of it, the new creation, self-emptying, faith and works, liberation, community— are given fresh and specifically Christian cogency as a result of sustained, serious dialogue with committed Buddhists.[2]

Doctrines that on the surface appear contradictory, such as the biblical view of creation and the Buddhist view of the unreality of the world, turn out to cast light on each other instead of annihilating each other when they come into contact in a genuine dialogue between religious persons. Don's book confirms a hunch of C. S. Lewis's, that "those who are at the heart" of their different traditions "are all closer to one another than those who are at the fringes."[3]

In short: I am grateful to have found, through those who have taught me and the teaching I myself have done, a balanced approach to the Bible that takes into account a whole range of techniques and kinds of questions. I do not expect to find *the* answer by any one of them, or by a combination of them. The subject matter itself reflects the elusive complexity of the world.

IN A WORD

I encounter the complex grace of God when I am drawn into the multidimensional world of the Bible and jettison any notion that there is one correct interpretation.

Grace in Verb Tenses

Early in my teaching career I learned the peril of treating the Bible as distinct from everything else. Thanks to one of the most electrifying books I've ever read, I was subsequently alerted to the time warp of "was" and "is."

Here's what prepared the way for my upending.

A Jewish student answers an exam question with details about Moses's life in Egypt that I have never heard before. I challenge him, but he is puzzled by my puzzlement. It turns out my puzzlement is the problem.

My embarrassment motivates me to start filling a huge hole in my training as a scholar of the Bible and early Christianity. In retrospect I am shocked that I know so little about Judaism. Its significance for my study has stopped short at its creation of the Hebrew Bible as I knew it.

It is many years later, in a book by James L. Kugel called *The Bible As It Was*, that I finally see the depth of my problem—the problem that had been revealed in my puzzlement when reading that exam. I'm reading Kugel's book because I have been asked to respond to a lecture of his. In person he is as engaging, and as incisive, as he is in his writing.

For my student, the line of demarcation between the biblical text, which is all I knew, and the multilayered readings built up in Jewish tradition over centuries, simply didn't exist. On that exam

I was judging The Bible As It Was against the norm of The Bible As Modern Historical Criticism Has Remade It.

"Cryptic, Relevant, Harmonious, Inspired"

I knew that ancient interpreters read texts differently from the way I do. I could not have come up quickly and neatly with Kugel's catalog, both succinct and comprehensive, of common ancient assumptions about the nature and character of texts—"cryptic, relevant, harmonious, and inspired"—but when I see his list I feel in familiar territory.[1]

Well, little did I know.

My training in biblical studies, as well as in history more generally, had directed attention to things as they were before they became what they are.

Kugel captures what is so pervasive, so much a part of our mental landscape, that I hardly noticed how odd it is. He says studies are directed exclusively to "the 'pre-Bible.' Students are led backward through the stages of individual books' composition, breaking things down to their putative original components, which can then be studied and explained in terms of the political and social history of the ancient Near East."[2]

The Bible itself talks of breaking things down, whether the walls of Jericho or the mighty from their thrones. The ancient interpreters, from about 300 BCE to 200 CE, whose work Kugel so lovingly and carefully chronicles, can take things apart almost to the atomic level—but always in the interests of building up and planting. I was trained, oddly, to run the film in reverse, to get from the oak tree back to the acorn. Kugel gently, relentlessly, and persuasively asks me: Why do you think the acorn is the only truth of the oak tree?

Kugel intentionally does not organize his material in terms of influences. We automatically think we have "understood" what "B" means if we can demonstrate that "B" is quoting "A." Because we value originality above all else, we are bedeviled by what Harold Bloom has diagnosed as "the anxiety of influence."[3]

Ancient people on the whole did not worry about such things. My understanding of those ancient people is impeded if I impose my anxiety upon them.

Kugel, like Sir Henry Chadwick, submits himself to the discipline of the evidence—he "rereads all the sources." He patiently listens without obsessively interrupting. He comes to understand that the ancient authors thought of the mosaic of readings they had inherited not as interpretation but as a duplication of the biblical text.

What my student wrote about Moses on his exam originated not in some storyteller's imagination but in some commentator's trying to make sense of an obscure verse in Exodus.

Common Flavor

The single thing I most "knew" that Kugel has most shown me I did not know is the degree to which the New Testament and other early Christian literature, even up into the fifth century of the Common Era, has the same flavor as all the other interpretive material from that time. The texts simply cannot be parceled into the traditional boxes I was familiar with, labeled "Jewish" and "Hellenistic" and "Roman" and "Christian."

Tasting this common flavor on page after page of Kugel's book, I realize in my biblical scholarship, as in so many other dimensions of my life, the truth in a distinction classically put by Saint Teresa of Ávila: "It is extraordinary what a difference there is between understanding a thing and knowing it by experience."[4]

By the time I reach the end of Kugel's book, which is about the Bible as it was two millennia ago, I am wondering what a similar project a couple of millennia hence would look like: *The Bible As It Was in 2000 CE*. There is no reason to suspect that we will appear any less odd to faraway-future generations than our ancestors appear to us.

The Future Looks at Us

First, enormous scholarly energy in the twentieth century was devoted to the effort to get to the Jesus behind the Gospels, to the "pre-Jesus" (to draw a parallel with Kugel's category of the "pre-Bible"). The endeavor illustrates both the assets and liabilities of historical criticism.

We have learned a lot about Jesus. But: the century began with the widespread scholarly conviction that Jesus was for sure the preacher of a fiery apocalyptic message, and concluded with the widespread scholarly conviction, based on the same methods of investigation, that Jesus was not like that at all.

What strikes me as worth pondering is not the difference in the portraits but the persistence of the confidence that our method can give assured, no-loose-ends results.

The Jesus we have is the complicated, multifaceted Jesus bequeathed to us by the church of the first century—Jesus as he was to them. My task is to come to terms with that Jesus, not to ferret out the Jesus who lurks behind the text. The doctrine of the Incarnation means God really became historical, didn't just put in an appearance.

What we know about Christ is irreducibly historical: ironic, incomplete, tantalizing, challenging, not packageable in a type or ideal, not decidable by votes of scholars as to the probability of this or that statement's being "authentic." The complexity of Jesus often resists and restrains claims that we know for sure what Christ approves and disapproves. "What would Jesus do?" is a real question, not the answer to one.

Second, feminist criticism provides a powerful modern analogue to the ancient interpretive assumption that texts are cryptic. From a feminist perspective, the strictly historical interpretation of the Bible simply reinforces the patriarchalism that was endemic in the world from which the Bible comes. I must read the text between the lines, through the looking-glass, around the edges, listening for its silences, in order to detect voices and realities that were filtered out by the culture. When I do this, I find myself in a world where God is improviser, storyteller, weaver, imaginer, dramatist. Relationships have priority over order. Lecture formats give way to roundtable conversations.

And this is part of a much larger issue, extending from biblical studies into the whole of theology. I used to think there's "theology," and then there's "feminist theology" and "liberation theology" and so on.

But what justification is there for saying that theology done by white males in North Atlantic seminaries and universities requires any less a designation as "white male North Atlantic theology" than feminist theology and liberation theology need their adjectives? Diversity is not something that "theology" doesn't have that "feminist theology" brings to it.

Third, the whole postmodern tilt of our intellects raises profound questions about whether our monumental attempt to get back to what the text "originally" meant or what "the author" really "intended" has been doomed to frustration from the very beginning.

As I write this, many decades after the student turned in that exam, I can't recall whether I learned enough quickly enough to give him credit for teaching me instead of marking him down for getting it "wrong." If I did the latter, I apologize.

IN A WORD

I encounter the upending grace of God when I am taught that the various tenses of the verb "to be" are a lot slipperier than I once assumed.

upending

Grace in Being *Left Behind*
with *The Da Vinci Code*

There is one time warp that many Christians are eager to slip through that I want to steer entirely clear of. They think it's assured, because it's in the Bible as they read it.

One day I have a vision. I imagine people around me suddenly disappearing, raptured to heaven, while I am *Left Behind*, gazing upward and holding my copy of *The Da Vinci Code*.

In the annals of publishing, the *Left Behind* series by Tim LaHaye and Jerry B. Jenkins, and Dan Brown's *The Da Vinci Code*, are legendary. The former has sold more than sixty-five million copies, the latter over eighty million.

If LaHaye and Jenkins and their millions of followers are right, the day isn't far off when the rapture predicted (according to them) in the Bible will occur. I suspect they do not expect the likes of me to be lifted up. The late Jerry Falwell said, "In terms of its impact on Christianity, [*Left Behind*] is probably greater than that of any other book in modern times, outside the Bible."[1]

Those who expect to be raptured pity me, but I have no need for their pity, because the last thing in the world—or out of the world—that I want is time without end spent glorifying the God who operates the way they believe he (and they most definitely mean *he*) does. I cannot believe God is so masochistic as to prefer an eternity fending off the adoration of Jerry Falwell to an eternity engaging the questions of the Dalai Lama.

Rapture theology is by no means fringe. In 2015 Mike Pompeo, who subsequently became director of the CIA and then secretary of state, said at a "God and Country" rally in Kansas, "We will defend our Christian values and American exceptionalism with all our heart." The battle for those values, he said, is "a never-ending struggle"—never ending, that is, "until the rapture."[2]

When interviewed on the *Understanding the Times* radio program in April 2015, Michele Bachmann, who served four terms in the US House of Representatives from Minnesota's Sixth Congressional District, where I live, and who also ran for president, reiterated her familiar declaration that the end of the world, including the rapture of the church, is imminent. She rehashed some old arguments, but the new wrinkle this time was her linking President Barack Obama's effort to negotiate a nuclear weapons deal with Iran to biblical prophecy as she interprets it.

"Prophets said we look to the future," Bachmann declared. "We long to see those days, live in those days. Why? Because it is the return of a soon-incoming king. Jesus Christ is coming back. We in our lifetimes, potentially, could see Jesus Christ returning to earth, the rapture of the church. These are wonderful times, but we see the destruction. But, this is a destruction that was foretold."[3] Rapture theology purports to fit into place all the pieces of the historical and theological puzzle. This fills its adherents with certainty and passionate intensity.

By inexorable rapture logic, Christians must pray that the nuclear arms deal with Iran not work, because if it did—if Obama turned out to be a peacemaker (Jesus called such people "blessed")—God's apocalyptic timetable would be thwarted. President Donald Trump's rejection of the Iran deal plays right into the rapture story.

My problem with all this is specifically theological. The last thing I want is an eternity spent glorifying the God who operates the way Bachmann believes he (and she, too, most definitely means *he*) does. If Christian identity requires me to sign on to rapture theology, then in the name of God and for the love of Christ I cannot be Christian.

Hell Better Than Heaven

I don't claim that God's ways are my ways, but I cannot believe that God's ways are so inferior to mine as to justify the arbitrariness and cruelty portrayed by LaHaye and Jenkins. If what they say of God is true, my conscience tells me that hell is better than heaven.

Now, this doesn't mean I think the whole Christian story is a sinister fabrication designed to reinforce a power structure, as Dan Brown comes close to implying, but *The Da Vinci Code* is more appealing to me *as a Christian* than the *Left Behind* series. God is more grievously mocked by scenes of divinely ordained carnage in the battles, meteor showers—in one of which a quarter of the world's population perishes—and plagues that saturate the story of the Tribulation Force and the Antichrist than by the suggestion that Jesus and Mary Magdalene had a child.

For Christ's sake, I would rather the Gospels be a hoax than that the book of Revelation, as read by LaHaye and Jenkins and Pompeo and Bachmann, be the script for what's to come.

My dispute with *Left Behind* theology has many dimensions, including how the Bible is read. Biblical literalism, which might be thought traditional, has actually appeared on the scene rather late in the day.

My middle path is in fact a traditional way of being Christian. It not only doesn't require but does not even want the certainty of the rapture crowd. At the same time, it is attracted to but not entirely won over by the skepticism portrayed by Dan Brown.

If I had to choose, though, I would, *as a Christian*, pick hell with Brown over heaven with LaHaye and Jenkins.

A hundred fifty years ago many cultural observers were predicting that religion would gradually wither away. They would have been astonished at the force religion displays in the early twenty-first century.

Much of the Christianity that has risen to prominence recently, and has come to stand for "Christian" in the popular mind, presents a view of God and the world, of human nature and society, that I don't want to be associated with in any way. To people who think like that, I hardly count as Christian at all. To those whose image of the church is molded by what the media pays attention to, I am on the outer edge of Christianity.

I proudly, resolutely, and honestly claim my baptismal identity as a Christian in the center of the tradition. I who will be *Left Behind* with *The Da Vinci Code* am glad of it. I'm not a weak-willed, timid dupe of a godless culture. My God would be more familiar to Jesus than the one who choreographs the rapture.

A doomsday prophet might be expected to behave as one does in a *New Yorker* cartoon—carrying a sign that says, "Yesterday in this space I predicted that the world would come to an end. It did not, however. I regret any inconvenience this may have caused."[4] But such prophets hardly ever "regret the inconvenience." They simply recalibrate, then redouble their efforts.

"We Lose the Mystery When We Have to Be Right"

The dispute between Christians like me and those Christians who would doubt that I am one is pretty fundamental—we interpret what we find in the Bible very differently—and goes to the heart of human identity.

I and Christians like me are not bewildered, befuddled, or bedeviled. At the rapture, as we stand there holding our copies of *The Da Vinci Code*, gazing at the "true believers" grabbed up to heaven, we won't suddenly repent and see the light.

"After the Rapture," LaHaye has said, "I hope our books will become even more popular than they are right now, as people begin to say, 'Hey, I heard about those books. I didn't pay any attention before, but now the Rapture's taken place, I'd better read them, and find out how to get ready."[5] By way of rejoinder, I declare that we already have all the light we need.

I once heard someone tell this horrific story. When he was a child and at the grocery store with his mother, he got separated from her. He looked down an aisle and saw her cart, but she was not with it. "The rapture has happened, and she has been taken and I'm still here!"

I simply cannot believe that God would fashion the world in a way to warrant that child's sheer terror.

And such theological bludgeoning is not at all restricted to rapture theology. There are all sorts of "certainties" that over the centuries and today oppress people in the name of God's will: suicide is unforgiveable (witness the virulent social media comments following the death of comedian Robin Williams); homosexual persons are disordered; unbaptized babies are lost; Black people bear "the mark of Cain," and therefore slavery is justified; the list goes on.

My quarrel is with the conviction that to be Christian is to have the answers. It's not simply that I don't claim to have the answers. It's that I claim *not to have* the answers.

My friend Kathy Langer distills this into an unforgettable axiom: "We lose the mystery when we have to be right." In the popular mind, this puts Kathy and me on the edge of the church (or even over the edge, in outer darkness). But we are attentive to the Bible, respectful of tradition, and alert to what is being thought and felt in the world today. The "edge" we're perceived to be on is actually at, or near, the center.

IN A WORD

I encounter the sly grace of God when I, *as a Christian*, find *The Da Vinci Code* more congenial than *Left Behind*.

sly

Part Four

HISTORY

Grace in Uncertainty

In the previous encounter I said I don't believe there will be a rapture. Do I know that for certain? No. I think the probability is vanishingly small, but I wouldn't be true to my wariness of no-loose-ends answers if I said I'm absolutely sure.

The study of history—what I've been trained to do and which is a kind of daily immersion in time warps—reinforces my skepticism about certainty.

This wasn't always so.

I don't remember whether I learned it in elementary school or in junior high, but I recall with precision the definition of history: "the written record of the progress of man." There are at least three problems with this: "written"—what about archaeology, art, oral tradition?; "progress"—by whose definition?; "man"—what about women? But if this is history, it's pretty clear-cut.

"You Never Know What Is Coming Next"

My work as a historian begins from a very different point, one offered by one of the greatest students of Victorian England, G. M. Young: "The first lesson of history, and it may well be the last, is that you never know what is coming next."[1] Things crystal-clear in retrospect are usually hazy, at best, in the crystal ball.

The grounds for confidence that one knows what is coming

next have been at various times scientific—every effect has a cause,
I just have to trace the series back and then extrapolate forward—
and theological—prophecy, predestination in various forms, even
"God has a plan for my life."

My friend Rachel Gruenwald tells me that someone said to her,
"Your son's death was the plan of God, and now he is with God."
I respond that I don't think the remark itself, or its corollary, "The
loss will all be made up," solves the theological problem. "I believe," I continue, "you have to simply stare the situation down,
and maybe spit in God's face. There is more comfort *and more
faithfulness* in this than in the other attitude."

Quantum theory in physics, with its fundamental indeter-
minacy, and the long series of thwarted theological predictions,
whether cosmic or personal, have cooled such confidence about
"what is coming next" (though in the theological case, not the
predictions).

The unlikelihood of certainty about a particular outcome is
enhanced, for me at least, by a mesmerizing feature of mathematics: factorials.

I'm at a family gathering, taking pictures. I line ten people up,
snap the photo, and then think, "I should arrange them differently.
I wonder how long it would take to get all the options. An hour
or two?"

But then I calculate. There are 3,628,800 possible lineups. Were
I to take a photo every ten seconds, with no breaks for food or
bathroom or sleep, it would take 420 days—a year and almost two
months—to complete the series.

This gets me to thinking about other configurations.

Let's say I'm responsible for seating representatives of twenty
nations around a circular table for a conference. I want to try every
combination. If I were to change alignments every ten seconds
(again, no breaks for anything), it would take *thirty-nine billion
years*—three times the age of the universe—to finish the task.
(I don't believe it either, but it's true.)

Or, if I want to line up the fifty-two cards in a standard deck every possible way, the options are as numerous as the *atoms in six hundred quadrillion Earths.* The options are, for all practical purposes, limitless.

In light of these mind-boggling possibilities, the fact that the world is the way it is—things are the way they are and not some other way—seems absurdly fortuitous. So, even, is the way I think about the way things have already been.

A Finger Slip on the Typewriter Sends Me Reeling

On March 26, 1975, before the age of word processor autotext, I am typing a letter, my finger slips, the year gets an extra digit. I sit transfixed as 19756 catapults me into the 198th century, from which our two thousand years of church history would be no greater a proportion than the first two hundred years are to us. We are part of the "early church" and have as much authority for the tradition, as well as responsibility to it, as those first six or seven generations had.

As I think about the doing of history, I have moments of vertigo, imagining a tumble through time, very much further into the future than even the 198th century, and what it would be like to do history then.

The late Cardinal Anthony J. Bevilacqua, archbishop of Philadelphia from 1988 to 2003, said, "Not in a hundred, not in a thousand, not in a million years" will women be priests.[2] Given the record of change in church policy over the past two thousand years, I find this prediction not especially persuasive. It does, however, set me to wondering about the very distant prospect.

I do some more calculating.

Pope Francis, who has set winds of change stirring in ways reminiscent of Pope Saint John XXIII, is the 266th pope according to Vatican records, and the first of that name. The average length of the first 265 papacies is 7.5 years.

Cosmologists say that five billion years from now the sun will engulf the earth. Rounding up the average papacy length to ten years, this means it will be the five hundred millionth pope who will have the task of issuing an encyclical in the face of the planet's incineration. If that pope happens to choose the name Francis, and the proportion of Francises remains the same (1/266), it will be Francis $\overline{\text{MDCCCLXXIX}}\text{DCXCIX}$ (the 1,879,699th—in Roman numerals, a line over a series of letters multiplies its value by one thousand).

Now of course this is fanciful, literally far-fetched (though Cardinal Bevilacqua might not have thought so). By then, maybe, our descendants will have figured out how to flee Earth for some other habitable world.

But this admittedly whimsical thought experiment serves a serious purpose for me as someone who not only practices history but also wonders about it—and suspects that the best historians are conjurers as well as sleuths.

I admire scholars who, like some of my teachers, master a couple of thousand years' worth of sources to account for how we have come to be where we are. There are even bold adventurers like Will and Ariel Durant, who over a span of forty years in the middle of the last century penned four million words in the eleven volumes of *The Story of Civilization* (they died after reaching Napoleon).

When I picture that five hundred millionth pope trying to make theological sense of a scientifically inescapable "end of the world," I conjecture what authorities (other than his own) he might appeal to. There are biblical passages about a fiery finale. There would be a backlog of several hundred million papal encyclicals and council decrees to cite. There would even be the volumes of the *Left Behind* series, though as sources they would not carry much weight.

But here's the challenge he (or she? Pope Frances?) would be up against: We have enough trouble telling the story of twenty centuries of church history; Pope Francis $\overline{\text{MDCCCLXXIX}}\text{DCXCIX}$

and his contemporaries would have 2.5 million times that many years to make sense of.

When my mind starts spinning off in speculations like these, I wish I were a Hindu. Time for some of them is dizzyingly vast— the universe's age extends to 311 trillion years (making rather laughable the fierce fights between Christians about whether the Bible says the world was created in seven twenty-four-hour days six thousand years ago). Imagining a five hundred millionth pope would be a snap, like little more than the blink of an eye.

Granted, Hindu time is cyclical—those 311 trillion years are followed by the universe's nonexistence for an equivalent period, and then it starts up again. But still, the Hindus are on to something. Maybe my doing of history needs their leavening.

As Open to the Future as to the Past

"You never know what is coming next." "Christ has died; Christ is risen; Christ will come again." Jesus's contemporaries didn't expect him to die. They were surprised when he rose. In both instances, they didn't know what was coming next. Yes, the Gospels say that Jesus alerted them in advance, but their behavior makes clear that the announcement didn't initially register with them.

The third clause in the liturgical affirmation—"Christ will come again"—is just as likely subject to the G. M. Young rule: we really don't know what is coming next. *Left Behind* certainly knows, but in the play-by-play probability sweepstakes, my money is on the astrophysicists' prediction.

In encounter 9 I told about a scholar's analysis of "was" and "is," and how this upended my understanding of the Bible and how to read it. There is a place I sometimes visit that similarly teases my mind with the interplay of "was," "is," and "will": a monastic cemetery.

Its ordered ranks—the order simply by date of death, so no

monk or nun can say with precision, "Here's where I'll be buried"—
seem as open to the unknown future as to the past. What's been,
what's now, what's to come all gets summed up. Those who have
been and who are to come are as much a part of the community
as those who are here now. And all of them—the dead, the living,
the yet to be—are formed by the Rule of Benedict, which claims
to be "written for beginners."[3]

My vote for the most intriguing riff on the second coming goes
to Ernest Digweed.

At his death in 1976, Mr. Digweed, a retired teacher from
Portsmouth, England, bequeathed £30,000 to Jesus Christ. Calculating from the book of Revelation, Digweed expected Christ
to return within twenty-one years, during which time he would
receive both principal and interest. The will further specified that
if the return were delayed beyond 1997, anytime up to 2056 Christ
would receive only the principal, with the interest going to the
state. If Christ were to show up after 2056, he would get nothing;
Digweed declared that his closest living relatives would then get
the money.

The Public Trustee's Office arranged for cousins to receive
the principal immediately, but only on condition that an insur-
ance policy arranged through Lloyd's of London would pay over
£300,000 to Christ as soon as he proves his identity.[4]

My own advice to the British government in the matter of Ernest Digweed's will would be to assign responsibility for identi-
fying Christ to the Salvation Army, that branch of the Christian
community that has specialized in looking for Christ where he
said he would be found.

In a paradoxical way, my uncertainty about history and my appreciation of its myriad possibilities—remember those ways to line
up a deck of cards—underlies my willingness to say "Christ will
come again" without a disclaiming "Whatever." It won't be what or
when or even whom (probably a female, maybe even transgender)
I or anyone else expects. You *never* know what is coming next.

IN A WORD

I encounter the flabbergasting grace of God when I truly acknowledge that I never know what is coming next.

flabbergasting

Grace in the Digging

You never know what is coming next. If you're an archaeologist, you never know what was coming before, until you dig and find it.

There is no way Christian identity can be cut off from the past. The central act of faith for most Christians, the Eucharist, is done "in remembrance." But there are devices for evading the past's vastness, whether by collapsing then and now, as in the cornerstone of a church in Abilene, Texas, that reads, "Church of Christ / Established in Jerusalem / A.D. 33 / This Building Erected / A.D. 1951," or in the conservative Catholic contention that through two millennia nothing essential has really changed.

The Levels of San Clemente

The place that most teases my mind with the depth and elusiveness of the past is the Basilica of San Clemente in Rome, a couple of blocks from the Colosseum.[1]

The church I enter today was constructed at the beginning of the twelfth century, so people have been worshiping in that building for nine hundred years. In the middle of those nine hundred years, in the seventeenth century, San Clemente was affected by the turmoil being experienced elsewhere in Christendom: in 1667 the basilica was granted in perpetuity to the Dominican Order, and just a decade later, when England outlawed the Irish Catholic Church, the displaced Irish Dominicans were put in charge of San Clemente.

Until the nineteenth century it was widely assumed that the church I see today was the one mentioned by Saint Jerome, writing in the year 392. But in 1857 the Dominican prior of San Clemente began excavating under the building. He found a complex and riveting history told by the stones he uncovered.

Peeling back layers, Father Mullooly discovered remains of a previous late fourth-century basilica, which is what Saint Jerome was referring to. At the level below it there are what has been variously interpreted as a Roman nobleman's home (perhaps even connected to Pope Clement's family) or a part of the imperial mint, and a Mithraeum, a place of worship for devotees of Mithras, a religion that competed with Christianity in the first four centuries. Even deeper there appear to be remains of a building burnt in Nero's fire of 64 CE.

It is one thing to read an account of this archaeological detective work. It is something else entirely to visit San Clemente, to go down into its depths, and while standing there to reflect on the narrative of the generations that lived, worked, bought, sold, despaired, hoped, prayed, and died there: (perhaps) house-church Christians, fearing betrayal to the imperial police; the followers of Mithras, sacrificing a bull in hopes of immortality; the Christians of Jerome's time, beneficiaries (if you want to call it that) of Emperor Constantine's flipping the church from outcast to favorite and his successors' exalting membership in it to a requirement for citizenship (remember the surprise of the Seven Sleepers of Ephesus); the medieval faithful, often caught between rival church factions, even a multiplicity of popes.

And there is more.

In the ninth century Saints Cyril and Methodius, brothers who were the apostles to the Slavs (they invented the alphabet still in use today), came to Rome bearing what they said were the remains of the late-first-century Saint Clement, the third pope, who was said to have been drowned in the Black Sea. Doubt about the authenticity of those relics that were "recovered" from the water after more than seven hundred years doesn't apply to the tomb of Saint Cyril, who is buried in San Clemente. Cyril and Methodius are among the most highly venerated of saints in Eastern Orthodoxy, so San Clemente is testimony to a time when the Greek and Latin heritages of the church, with a salute to the Slavic, were on speaking terms.

I once heard my mentor and friend, the late Albert Outler, say that prior to the twentieth century, church history's chief business was to "bolster each church's ingrained triumphalism." This is a specific instance of a much more general tendency of cultural commentators. As Adam Gopnik observes, "Of all the prejudices of pundits, presentism is the strongest. It is the assumption that what is happening now is going to keep on happening, without anything happening to stop it."[2]

The story you told of your denomination was written backward. Where you are now is where the whole story of the church was supposed to end up, so you constructed the narrative to justify you and your tradition as the inevitable, divinely ordained outcome that would "keep on happening, without anything happening to stop it." Other denominations weren't just different. They were wrong.

The ecumenical movement of the twentieth century, in which I have spent much of my career and which will get its due in part 5, was a dramatic reversal of triumphalist history. But the absurdity of claiming historical warrant for absolute, exclusivist prerogatives is apparent to anyone standing in the Basilica of San Clemente—or better, descending through its layers.

There is of course the option of claiming a theological warrant for special entitlement: God arranged things so that no matter how many controversies, even schisms, have roiled Christians over the centuries, "our" way of being Christian is the authentic one.

This can be accounted for by various means, whether apostolic succession or a fresh outpouring of the Spirit or a "return to the Bible." But each of these theological maneuvers straitjackets history, squeezes the narrative into a mold that cannot accommodate all the evidence. As Gopnik further remarks, "Whatever is happening usually does stop happening, and something else happens in its place."

I think about all the ideas, influences, doctrines, disputes, reconciliations followed by renewed divisions—what was understood by one generation and forgotten by the next—and competitions for authority that have coursed through the many levels of San Clemente, decade after decade, century after century. The history of this particular church—indeed, the history of the church and history in general—is like a three-dimensional chess game; or, in a brilliant image of Gopnik's, the story is "not a directional arrow but more like a surfboard, rising and falling on the quick-change waves of history."

And the story is further stirred by that Mithraeum.

I've studied about Mithraism. I know something of its mythology (with striking parallels to parts of the Christian story) and of its vitality during the first four centuries after Christ. But standing in the Mithraeum (it is estimated that there were seven hundred of them in the city of Rome alone), imagining real people, as alive then as I am now, finding and shaping the meaning of their lives by those rituals and ideals and community interaction, I become suspicious of exclusivist claims in the name of Christ—even though scholars have demonstrated that the ground plan of San Clemente was designed to show that Christ keeps Mithras "under."

I think of a question I often asked on exams: "Imagine yourself a faithful Israelite in the early sixth century BCE. Jeremiah, claiming to be a true prophet and with good credentials, says God wants you to capitulate to the Babylonians. Hananiah, claiming to be a true prophet and with good credentials, says God wants you to fight. What do you do, and why?"

I'm not at all sure that had I been a Roman soldier in the second century CE I'd have opted for Christ over Mithras. As a Christian today, I don't fault the Mithraist for remaining faithful to that tradition.

The Danger of Certainties That Exclude Others

Does my respect for "You never know what is coming next"—that is, for the many dimensions of history—make me a thoroughgoing relativist: anything goes, to each their own? It probably looks that way, but I don't think so—though if the alternative is believing that in that Mithraeum I was at the gateway to hell, I'll happily wear the relativist mantle.

I fear rigid, exclusivistic triumphalism far more than I do relativism. It is certainties *that exclude others* that I'm particularly wary of. A favorite hymn by Frederick Faber says it well: "There's a wideness in God's mercy like the wideness of the sea," and "We make God's love too narrow with false limits of our own, and we magnify God's strictness with a zeal love will not own." When those false limits are undone, "There is grace enough for thousands of new worlds as great as this."

IN A WORD

I encounter the recalibrating grace of God when I emerge from the layers of San Clemente knowing that what came before can be as mysterious as what is coming next.

recalibrating

Grace in a Future That Ain't What It Used to Be

Emerging from the layers of the Basilica of San Clemente, I'm thinking again about the improbable pairing of John Stuart Mill and Yogi Berra that I recounted in encounter 3.

Just as Mill and Berra seldom if ever appear together on the same page, historian Peter Brown, who figures prominently in encounter 5, and the baseball great are an unlikely couple. However, Berra's observation that "the future ain't what it used to be" is a commentary on the surprise that Brown and I both savor in our historical sleuthing.

"The future ain't what it used to be" underscores several ways in which my Christian identity works.

Agnostic about History's Direction

First, I am more agnostic than many theologians about history's direction. For me, the jury is out on whether history is a decline from a golden age, a story of progress, a circle, a spiral, or just one damn thing after another. Yogi Berra's insight is seconded by Yoda, the Jedi master, who instructs his apprentice, Luke Skywalker: "Difficult to see. Always in motion is the future."[1]

The tension between the "already" and the "not yet" (which

goes by the fancy technical name of "eschatology") doesn't illuminate anything, because there is much dispute about what that's
going on right now is "already" and what that's going on right now
is "not yet." I believe the recognition of gay marriage is part of the
"already," but many Christians consider it a sacrilege, definitive
evidence of an eschatological "not yet."

Even apart from the fact that Jesus says more about my obli-
gations to the poor than about my sex life, the conviction that the
faith will crumble if gays and lesbians can marry or be ordained
is myopic. While some Christians believe that a "godless culture"
is imposing a "homosexual agenda" on a "beleaguered church,"
Christians like me, who expect God (Creator of all things) to be
as active outside the church as within it, believe that the culture is
coaxing the church into a deeper understanding of what it means
that we are all made in God's image.

It's time for an upending of the title of an epoch-making book
from 1799, Friedrich Schleiermacher's *On Religion: Speeches
to Its Cultured Despisers*. We need *On Culture: Speeches to Its
Religious Despisers*.

And here, incidentally, is the most striking instance of "the future ain't what it used to be" that I have witnessed in my lifetime.

"I believe that a hundred years from now," I wrote in 1999, "the
declaration that homosexuality is 'intrinsically disordered,' and
even odious in the sight of God, will be regarded by most Christians as a curiosity of a bygone age." I posed a challenge: "I ask
those who are absolutely certain of God's disapproval of homosexuality to imagine a future in which their descendants wonder
how they could have been so sure."[2]

Just sixteen (not a hundred) years later, the US Supreme Court
declared that freedom to marry is guaranteed by the Constitution. To be sure, the most vocal opposition to this decision is from
Christians, but polls suggest they are a minority *of Christians*. Even
a majority of US Roman Catholics, whose church officially opposes
marriage for gay people, are in favor of it.[3]

It might be thought that in what I have just said I undercut my claim to be "agnostic" about history's direction. Yes, I predicted what has happened—and much quicker than I expected—but I don't assume that this advance is permanent. There is still vocal Christian resistance. Sustaining the progress requires, at the very least, constant vigilance.

Agnostic about History's Goal

If I'm agnostic first about history's direction, I am also agnostic about its goal.

I certainly find the messianic banquet more appealing than the battle of Armageddon. The sumptuous meal prepared by the housekeeper Babette for the upright and uptight citizens of a remote, windswept Danish village in the movie *Babette's Feast* is explicitly linked to the meal's recapitulation in paradise, but this movie, even with its Oscar, has a lot less cultural clout than the *Left Behind* novels.

And even if there is a fixed goal, I have the same problem as with the "already" and the "not yet." I'm suspicious of claims, my own or anyone else's, to know for sure what it is. Maybe both sides are right. Perhaps the last scene of the historical show will be some people sitting on a hilltop enjoying the messianic banquet while others engage in the battle of Armageddon on the field below, like the picnickers who on July 21, 1861, went out to Bull Run to watch the Union and the Confederacy tear into each other.[4]

Agnostic about the Church's Indefectibility

Third, I am agnostic about the indefectibility of the church. That's a word you don't hear every day. To believe in the indefectibility of the church is to believe that God won't let the church finally go entirely off the rails. It is to take literally Jesus's promise that the gates of hell will not prevail against the church (Matt. 16:18).

I suspect the church could really lose it. Much scholarship about religious traditions uses the past tense. But even if I were to believe in the church's indefectibility (which maybe I do; I said agnostic, which means simply that I don't know), it doesn't follow that I know for sure where the church God is protecting is.

There are some places where two or three or two or three hundred or two or three thousand are gathered together in Jesus's name and I seriously doubt whether Jesus is there in the midst of them. There are other places where Jesus's name isn't spoken at all and I suspect he is there. Jesus warned that my saying "Lord, Lord" doesn't mean he'll come running (Matt. 25:11–12), and chances are good that I won't recognize him when he shows up.

"The future ain't what it used to be" captures both my agnosticism about the future and my hopes for it. I have no guarantees, but I'm not stuck.

"Churchy" and "Christiany"

My hope for the future of the church is grounded in its resistance to the temptation to be "churchy" and "Christiany."

These terms leap off the page from a news story[5] in 2003 about a New Testament published in fashion-magazine format,[6] aimed at girls ages twelve to seventeen. A fifteen-year-old from Nashville voices a marketer's dream: "My friends, they don't like to read the Bible, but once they saw it they were like, 'I'm going to have to get me one of those.'"

I doubt there are many theologians who get past the first paragraph of this news story, but if so, they miss a fresh and compelling insight. The publication's managing editor praises the firm that designed the layout: "They're great because they don't make things look churchy or Christiany."

I am sure there are Christians who are offended by the way some in our culture treat the tradition. Over his years on *The Daily Show*, Jon Stewart poked fun at religion. I, as a Christian, frequently cheered him on. He was satirizing not the church and the Christian, but the churchy and the Christiany. I would rather spend time in his company than in that of those he was needling.

Two biblical stories—Saul and the woman of Endor (1 Sam. 28), and Jesus and the Syrophoenician woman (Mark 7:24–30)—remind me that the future ain't what it used to be. They provide a compelling alternative to a life that is either churchy or Christiany—or both.

King Saul is desperate. The standard ways of consulting God are giving an "unexpected error" message. There seems to be no way to reboot. Saul asks his aides to find a soothsayer.

Imagine the bind this puts them in. Previously the king had ordered them to eliminate all such practitioners from the realm, so if they find one, they are admitting they did not do their job. Saul persists, so they take him to a woman who calls up the shade of Samuel—and then she is terrified, for the masks are off. She realizes it is the king who is consulting her. She has to think it's a trap, a sting operation. But Saul grants her immunity.

Then comes a reversal, an upending, an episode of "last shall be first and first, last" that is resonant with the heart of the gospel. Saul hasn't eaten all day. The woman says to him, "I've risked my life in speaking to you, now you listen to me"—remember, she's an outlaw addressing the king—"I'm going to give you some food and you need to eat it." He refuses, but the woman and Saul's servants prevail "and," the text tells us, "they ate. Then they rose and went away that night."

The church is about this sort of welcome, where rank and status blur, where motives mix and don't all have to be noble, where happy faces aren't required, where the tragic is not denied and the comic is appreciated (the scene is in fact pretty funny). Christ makes a place for us at the table, for all of us, and says "Eat, that you may have strength when you go on your way."

The woman of Endor is a type of Christ—and she is neither churchy nor Christiany.

And Saul's future ain't what it used to be. In outline, to be sure, it is. Samuel told him that God had withdrawn favor. Saul died as the prophet said he would. But in those last few hours of his life Saul knew the warmth of welcome and the liberation of giving up control—"Now you listen to me," the woman said, and he listened and followed her instructions. In a way, the woman was holding on to God for Saul when he couldn't hold on himself.

In the story from Mark's Gospel of Jesus and the Syrophoenician woman I see features similar to those of Saul's encounter with the woman of Endor.

There's something clandestine. Just as Saul's cover is blown when he asks the woman to summon up the shade of the prophet Samuel, Jesus enters a house, doesn't want anyone to know he is there, and "yet," as Mark tells us, "he could not escape notice." The Syrophoenician woman hears where he is, comes immediately, and begs Jesus to heal her daughter. Jesus says no, as Saul had initially said to the woman of Endor when she urged him to eat something.

Jesus's response is quite harsh, certainly neither churchy nor Christiany: "Let the children be fed first, for it is not fair to take the children's food and throw it to the dogs." The woman beats Jesus at his own game, turning an image of exclusion into one of inclusion: "Even the dogs under the table eat the children's crumbs."

I wish people who ask "What would Jesus do?" would pay more attention to this sort of interaction between Jesus and others. He acknowledges the challenge and praises the woman for it: "For saying that, you may go—the demon has left your daughter."

There is no better evidence of the Jewishness of Jesus than this kind of repartee, which is neither churchy nor Christiany. The Jesus we think keeps others out is teasing us to invite them to the table. This gentile woman's riposte to Jesus is a hinge on which history turns, and the future certainly ain't what it used to be.

IN A WORD

I encounter the humorous grace of God when I see that neither "churchy" nor "Christiany" is a mark of faithfulness.

humorous

Part Five

COMING TOGETHER AFTER COMING APART

Grace in Ecumenism

I have been fortunate to spend half my career in the ecumenical movement, where the future certainly hasn't been what it used to be.

The century we recently left behind is among the most revolutionary in Christian history. Understanding the depth and range of that transformation—how Christian energy was redirected from fission to fusion—is crucial for explaining how I have become the sort of Christian I am.

Until 1910, churches had been splitting apart—indulging in caricature and stereotypes, jumping to conclusions, judging before listening, deploring the joys of other Christians and savoring their miseries. Dismemberment of the body of Christ, most often by self-mutilation, had proceeded almost unabated.

Even a tradition such as the one I grew up in, the Christian Church (Disciples of Christ), which started in the early nineteenth century as an effort to achieve unity by restoring the patterns of the New Testament church, had divided by the beginning of the twentieth century. The denomination's founder, Thomas Campbell, writing in 1809, bemoaned "the bitter jarrings and janglings of a party spirit," the biting and devouring of one another[1]—which reappeared a hundred years later in the tradition he started to end them.

The dispute? Over the installation of organs in sanctuaries. One group said they were acceptable because instrumental music in worship is not forbidden in the New Testament. The other group said no, because the New Testament does not explicitly sanction instrumental music. "Where the Bible speaks, we speak; where the Bible is silent, we are silent" doesn't forestall conflict.

During centuries of division, anathemas, and bloodshed, few observers would have predicted that the ecumenical movement was "coming next."

The modern ecumenical movement is generally said to have begun at the World Missionary Conference in Edinburgh in 1910. In Africa and Asia, when Christian missionaries of various denominations attempted to perpetuate the distinctions and antagonisms of their churches back home in Europe and North America, potential converts were both mystified and scandalized.

The missionaries came to realize that in their new context, so like that of the earliest Christians in the Roman Empire, the differences paled. They were forced by their circumstances to recognize each other as sisters and brothers in the faith—*the faith*, deeper than any of their particular expressions of it.

Ecumenism was born in the missions, not in libraries and seminar rooms. It began when people who were preaching the gospel grasped that they could no longer talk about other people who were preaching the gospel the way they had been taught to talk about them.

The mission field was the arena in which doctrinal differences began to move to the periphery of concern.

Simultaneously, the traditional center of Christendom, the North Atlantic, saw a burgeoning of common social effort by Christians, initially in the devastation following World War I, then in the vaster catastrophe of World War II. To the issues labeled "Faith and Order" were added those called "Life and Work"—these latter in so many ways expressions of the mandate from Jesus in Matthew 25 to feed the hungry, give drink to the thirsty, welcome the stranger, clothe the naked, care for the sick, and visit the imprisoned.

"We Intend to Stay Together"

What began in Edinburgh developed through the rest of the twentieth century into the most powerful engine of reform and revitalization in the church's history. "Faith and Order" and "Life and Work" coalesced in the founding of the World Council of Churches in 1948, with its declaration, "We intend to stay together."

The Catholic Church joined the movement when the Second Vatican Council (1962–65) opened the windows to other Christians and beyond. Both the World Council and the Vatican Council punctuated a movement that had already in 1942 been called, by Archbishop of Canterbury William Temple, "the great new fact of our era"[2]—a bold thing to say, with bombs falling on London.

The registering of that fact in histories, news stories, and encyclopedias gives the impression that ecumenism is a matter of organizations and large gatherings, of scholars meeting for years to find points of convergence, of agreed communiqués, and church unions. That story is grand, it is momentous—and it is not the whole story. The twentieth century has a whole other dimension.

It was my privilege to spend twenty years as executive director of a place where that other dimension has come vividly to life: the Collegeville Institute for Ecumenical and Cultural Research. It's the reconciliation not just of churches but of the identities of people who claim to be Christian. Polarizations get resolved—mind and spirit, civilization and nature, worship and work, art and science, academy and church, the urgent and the truly important. In our setting, people let others say, at length and without immediate rejoinder, things they think outrageous, weird, heretical, nuts, benighted, politically correct (or incorrect), passé.

The institute's character was realized in 1994, when a conference initially called "Transmitting the Ecumenical Tradition" transformed into "Ecumenism Among Us."[3] I can still recall the electricity in the air when that seismic shift occurred in the program committee. We were acknowledging that ecumenism is not a project; it's a new way of knowing. That moment solidified what I believe is my contribution to management lore: when an idea comes out of a meeting that no one came into it with, pay very close attention.

The new name, gently but inexorably, extricated the conference from the control of any particular ecumenical genealogy. Ecumenism would be found among us all and by us all, not imposed on any of us. Everybody would be equally responsible for success or failure. "We are not providing a conference with a predetermined content and agenda," we said in the invitation. "Rather, we are providing an arena in which the engagement of persons with each other, which is the conference, can happen."

And we expected everyone to practice what the institute had pioneered as first-person discourse. The institute's style is like the corrective lens that was added to the Hubble Space Telescope: ecumenical discussion becomes clearer, sharper, and probes deeper when the blur of "others think" gives way to the precision of "I believe." Jargon is jettisoned in the interests of direct communication: not "one might conjecture," but "I say." When asked, "What should I bring?," we responded, "Only your life." If that's all that's brought, no one is more "expert" than anyone else. It's a level playing field. There are no religious strangers in the room.

The 208 participants in "Ecumenism Among Us," ranging in age from seventeen to eighty-seven, from forty-one different Christian denominations, made clear that ecumenism was not the preserve of professionals.

This democratization was itself a recovery of tradition. Much early ecumenical leadership was provided by laypersons and by young people. The Student Christian Movement, the World YMCA, and the Interseminary Movement galvanized energies and shaped careers.

John R. Mott (1865–1955), awarded the Nobel Peace Prize in 1946 and credited by many as the chief architect of the World Council of Churches, was a Methodist layperson. He formulated what most practical-minded ordinary Christians would immediately recognize as an appropriate plan of action, free of theological gobbledygook and pious posturing: "Organize as if there is no prayer; pray as if there is no organization."[4]

It is hardly surprising that a movement that began among laypersons was soon being managed by clerics and denominational officials. Ordinary Christians could be heard bemoaning bureaucracy, disparaging "out-of-touch professionals." They complained either about overconcern with theological quibbles in the face of the world's crying need or about excessive social action without attention to theological fundamentals. Ecumenism, like so many vital human motivations and actions, came to seem like something "they" do, which meant it could be left to "them." "They" could be blamed for whatever you did not like.

"Ecumenical" without Knowing It

The part of the ecumenical story that I have seen most intimately, and about which I am most encouraged, is the discovery by many people that they are part of "the great new fact of our era" without knowing it, because the term "ecumenism" is over the horizon of common vocabulary. One of the greatest ecumenists, the late Father Thomas Stransky, CSP, when asked in one of the Collegeville Institute's board meetings, "What is ecumenism?," replied, "Ecumenism is something which, if we had a better name for, we would have more of."

I am riveted by the very word. "Ecumenism" is linguistically noble and colossal—it comes from Greek and means "the whole inhabited world." In a Christian framework, ecumenism resonates with "God so loved *the world*" and Christ's prayer that all his followers be one. It names the effort by members of specific denominations to overcome the splintering of the church of Jesus Christ by acknowledging and claiming the gift of unity.

And the expansiveness of ecumenism allays the uneasy fear of many Christians that Christian identity itself isn't good for people—that it requires building walls when what the world needs is bridges for people to cross. The Collegeville Institute's mission statement puts the alternative succinctly: "the mission of the church *and* the renewal of human community."

While the theological motive for ecumenism is the unity Christ prayed for, much of the energy of popular ecumenism comes from experience in the human community—with neighbors, friends, family. As noted in encounter 7, faithful Christians today say, think, feel, and believe positive things about other Christians that would have made their ancestors a century earlier cringe. Ecumenism has changed the world in which ecumenism happens.

Almost universally these faithful Christians, whether they call themselves ecumenists or not, report that the more they appreciate the faithfulness of others, the more they grasp the faithfulness of their own traditions. Unity does not require uniformity; it is actually allergic to it. The gospel is about liberation, not claustrophobia.

"Bent into Shape"

The consequence of ecumenism is what my friend Kathleen Cahalan calls getting "bent into shape." "If I get too much enmeshed in my own tradition," she says, "I get bent out of shape. To get bent into shape, I need to visit other rooms in God's house that has many of them."

And the shape I get bent into? The image of God I was created in to begin with, or at least closer to that image than when I was too cramped. When writing an essay in 1998 about themes of World Council of Churches assemblies, I muse on the upending since the initial assembly in 1948 in Amsterdam, where the theme was "Man's Disorder and God's Design." It seems to me that the ecumenical message now is "Our Designs and God's Disorder." I can rejoice in hope because God disrupts our designs, our schemes, our little systems that have their day, whether academic or political or ecclesiastical.

Early on, I wondered whether it's possible—theologically, psychologically, culturally, intellectually—to be both rooted somewhere and open to the other. There are lots more "others" now than there were in my grandparents', and even my parents', generation.

Thanks to the ecumenical movement—and in gratitude for my opportunity to be part of it—I know, as my friend the late James P. Shannon translated an aphorism of Saint Thomas Aquinas, "If it has been done, it must be possible."

Though there's still a long way to go, nobody would have imagined how far we've come.

It's 1995. I'm in Albuquerque at the Thirty-First National Workshop on Christian Unity. We are guests of an intercultural ecumenical agency that is pioneering fresh ways of getting church and world into phase with one another. At the concluding worship service, however, the barrier of the Eucharist proves impregnable. While sitting there I remember Saint Thomas's aphorism, and think, "The reason frequently given why we don't commune together is that 'we don't because we can't.' But, in practical terms, it might be that we can't because we don't, and if we did, we could. Let's no longer say we can't, then don't, but rather let's do it, and then we can."

In 1998 I attend the National Workshop, in Saint Paul this time. Near the end I talk with a reporter for the *Pioneer Press*. She asks me what I think people should do who want to further the aims of the ecumenical movement. I surprise myself with the answer: not set up a commission or study it, but "Pray for it."

To get to where I could say that—to make my own John R. Mott's "pray as if there is no organization"—I had had to go through a spiritual maturing. Since I grew up so close to the church, it was hard for me to acknowledge that it's possible honestly not to know God, and to dishonestly know God. I had to realize that a relationship with God is not a "given," and that prayer is not "natural."

Prayer originally came to me too easily. Maybe the much-bemoaned lack of church involvement on the part of young people today is an ecumenical blessing. Maybe people will come to prayer with more difficulty and won't have to unlearn as much as I did. Even now, when I'm praying publicly, as one in the business of word-mongering I'm concerned to impress people with the quality of my prayer prose (and occasionally even poetry).

It's 1990. I am invited to deliver the homily at Saint John's Abbey Church in the Week of Prayer for Christian Unity. I conclude, "God grant us all a double portion of the spirit of adventure, a delight in risks, boldness and brashness and freshness in imagining what we could do and be together." A prayer, a dream, yes, but with a century's transition from fission to fusion to back it up.

IN A WORD

I encounter the reconciling grace of God in the current state of relations between churches—not perfect, to be sure, but unimaginable to my ancestors a century ago.

reconciling

Grace in the "Cannot"

In my years at the Collegeville Institute for Ecumenical and Cultural Research I got to know hundreds of people whose stories of discovery, of U-turns, of wanderings and surprise, of heartache and grace constitute the definition of ecumenism for me. Among them, Joan Chittister, Herbert Chilstrom, Richard Mouw, and Margaret O'Gara told tales that stake out the territory. Conversations with them, over many years, weave throughout the tapestry of my story.

Benedictine Sister Joan Chittister is set on an ecumenical course when she is in second grade. Her mother was Catholic, her stepfather Presbyterian. Joan rushes home. "What did you learn in school today that has you so wound up?" her mother asks. "Sister said that only Catholics go to heaven." "Oh, really? And what do you think about that, Joan?" "I think Sister's wrong." "And why do you think Sister would say a thing that's wrong?" "Because Sister doesn't know Daddy." "Sister," says Sister Joan, recalling this moment, "was missing some of the evidence."[1]

"Missing Some of the Evidence"

As I have come to know, throughout my life, an ever-widening range of people, I have wondered where our cramped notion of God, like that of Joan's teacher, came from. Mine was never terribly narrow, certainly not like that of people I knew who thought it was bad enough to be a Buddhist or an atheist but worse still to be a Catholic. However, I "knew" God had standards. A blind spot I'm especially chagrined by is what I used to think when hearing a Pentecostal sermon on the car radio: "God certainly prefers me to them!" My subsequent acquaintance with many Pentecostals has taught me that I "was missing some of the evidence."

I condense into a single word the consequence of uncovering the missing evidence. Ecumenism is grounded in a "cannot"—not "I will not believe" or "I choose not to believe," but "I cannot believe." The ripple effect of this "cannot" extends far. Today it would be difficult to find a Catholic nun who thinks the gate of heaven is barred against Presbyterians (or even Buddhists, for that matter). To round out the irony, I know a Presbyterian nun.

Herbert Chilstrom told me that when he was growing up Lutheran in Litchfield, Minnesota, he would quickly move to the other side of the street if he saw a Catholic priest or nun walking toward him. (Back then, social distancing was mandated by theology, not by public health.) When, at the end of the twentieth century, Chilstrom retired as the first bishop of the newly united Evangelical Lutheran Church in America, Archbishop John Roach of the archdiocese of Saint Paul and Minneapolis was an honored guest at the retirement party. Think about it: within a single lifetime to go from crossing the street to avoid a nun to welcoming your good friend, the Catholic archbishop, to your retirement festivities.

What happened in the intervening half century is a seismic shift in Christian identity. In a way, it's no less dramatic than the fall of the Berlin Wall. It is a measure of the power of the "cannot" that most Christians would find it as unthinkable today that Archbishop Roach would not be at that party as they would have understood in an earlier era why Catholics and Protestants didn't want to encounter one another on the sidewalk.

The history of ecumenism is an account of how something that

many would not have dreamed of—except in their nightmares—
has come to seem the most natural thing in the world. It's not just
thinking outside the box. It's rethinking the shape and the size
of the box itself. Herb Chilstrom and John Roach discovered it's
a lot bigger than they thought, has more dimensions than they
suspected. The box is still shape-shifting in ways we can't foretell
or forestall.

I believe that in all the joint services following 9/11, when
priests, pastors, rabbis, and imams prayed for our nation, most
American Christians assumed that the prayers were being sent to
the same address, or would at least be forwarded and not dropped
into a dead mailbox. If this is what we think, what's to stop our
welcoming adherents of many other faiths to our own retirement
parties? Following Jesus has for me, as it did for Peter, Andrew,
James, and John, led to places I never dreamed of.

Richard Mouw, for twenty years president of Fuller Theological
Seminary, and a major voice in evangelical Christianity, learned
through sustained contact and conversation that people in other
churches are not as scary as he once thought. Things that had
sounded strange began to sound normal, and vice versa. "Now
when I speak about other groups of Christians, I remember that
I have friends in those groups," he said. In fact, "there are also
times, now, when I take part in groups with members of my own
denomination and wish my Orthodox and Roman Catholic friends
were there, because they would understand what I was saying.
I have built up new loyalties to Christians from those other traditions. I have very much needed them to help me explain who I am
as a Christian."[2]

Mouw discovers spiritual kinfolk among those he used to think
of as aliens. People he thought might as well be from another galaxy turn out to be soul mates. He learns one of the fundamental
ecumenical truths: people can use very different language to mean
much the same thing, and the same language to mean something
very different.

Chittister's and Chilstrom's and Mouw's are twentieth-century ecumenical stories. There are also tales that reach back directly into earlier eras.

"The Ecumenical Gift Exchange"

The late Margaret O'Gara, a leading Roman Catholic ecumenist, coined a phrase, "the ecumenical gift exchange," that is illustrated by a moment in a theology class she was teaching in the 1990s.[3]

The final day's discussion turns to personal reminiscences. A woman mentions the name of her great-grandmother. A man says his great-grandmother had the same name. A rapid genealogical excavation unearths the connection.

Two sisters had grown up in an Anglican family in Nova Scotia. One had become Catholic and married a Catholic. Her Anglican family cut off all contact with her. The two sisters never saw each other again. All the knowledge their descendants retained was that a branch of the family was missing.

Those two sisters were the grandmothers of the two students who were seeking priesthood, he as a Catholic, she as an Anglican. That summer there were two ordinations, and both families attended each. The ceremonies included a prayer that their ministries would be an instrument for the reconciliation not only of their families, but also for their whole church families, so that they could live again as sister churches.

Robert S. Bilheimer, my predecessor as executive director of the Collegeville Institute for Ecumenical and Cultural Research, often said that the job of the ecumenical movement in general, and of the institute in particular, is to help people who are already ecumenical but don't know it to recognize their true identity—in short, to wake them up. These are people who have more in common with their counterparts in other denominations than with many in their own traditions.

In some instances, ecumenical identity is a recovery of something they knew as children, as Chittister did, but may have forgotten as they grew older. In others, it is a confirmation of what has become clear only with mature experience, as in Chilstrom's case. In yet others, such as Mouw's, acquaintance with different traditions expands horizons.

Here is what is discovered in all such stories: one's own church is too small. There is not just one family room in God's house; there are many. And each family room, if not sealed off from the others, is a good place to be.

It may appear that I have just undercut one of my own claims: that ecumenism is for everyone, not the preserve of an elite. A nationally prominent nun (who has been a write-in candidate for president of the United States), a former bishop, a seminary president, and a theology professor—these are hardly your average church folk. But my point stands—is in fact undergirded by these examples.

When ecumenical stories are told, everyone is on a level playing field. The "experts" are no more alert than anyone else—and no less, either—to the surprises that lie in wait. Ecumenicists defy what the great Cambridge classicist F. M. Cornford formulated a century ago, with tongue in cheek, as The Principle of the Dangerous Precedent: "Every public action which is not customary, either is wrong, or, if it is right, is a dangerous precedent. It follows that nothing should ever be done for the first time."[4] Ecumenism is a compendium of "dangerous precedents."

Chittister, Chilstrom, Mouw, and O'Gara know (and, in O'Gara's case, alas, knew) instinctively what another theologian friend of mine, Mary Bednarowski, says is our calling as human beings: "to become caretakers of one another's stories."[5] This can't happen until I have heard the stories, really listened to them. I have been privileged to be in settings where genuine conversation takes place, where stereotypes and caricatures simply dissolve. The "cannot"—"I cannot any longer believe about those others what I once did"—is transposed into the key of "must"—"I must now incorporate their stories into my own."

IN A WORD

I encounter the sneaky grace of God when discovery of "more of the evidence" turns what I do into "I cannot," and then into "I must."

Grace in Reconciling Memories

I can boil down my task as an ecumenical engineer to reconciling memories.

This is a big challenge, because churches like to live in their own pasts, which were shaped by their opposition—sometimes even lethal—to other churches. The resolution of all those memories—those pasts that were not even past—requires feats of imagination.

Deweaponizing Memory

The ecumenical tool kit has several methods for achieving memory ceasefire; here are seven that I have found both useful and distinct. To be effective, the implement needs to suit the task.

First is reconciling by addition. If we tell our stories to each other often enough, everybody's story becomes part of everybody's story. I long for the time when I, whose experience is far removed from that of Pentecostals, can say, with conviction and so that it matters, "I was at Azusa Street," the mission in Los Angeles where Pentecostalism began in 1906.

Second is reconciling by subtraction. Sometimes the act of remembering intensifies controversy beyond necessity. Sir Henry Chadwick, whom I saluted in encounter 2, was working on the eleventh century. In 1996 he wrote to me about his discovery that three decades after 1054, the year traditionally designated as the definitive break between the Western and Eastern churches, the pope in Rome was inquiring of the patriarch in Constantinople whether there had been some sort of schism that no one had told him about.[1]

Third is reconciling by overlooking. The great teacher here is Erasmus, writing in the maelstrom of the early sixteenth century. In *The Praise of Folly* is a phrase I nominate as a motto for an ecumenical coat of arms. Folly proposes for the smooth functioning of human communities that we "make mistakes together or individually, . . . [and] wisely overlook things."[2]

This runs counter to what is too common in academic and church life: lying in wait, hoping to catch the other person in a gaffe, an error, even a heresy, on which I can pounce. If we are going to get anywhere, my dialogue partner and I have to give each other permission to take things back, or else we'll both be too afraid to try things out for fear they'll be held against us forever.

Fourth is reconciling by the "to wit" clause. According to English common law, certain crimes could be prosecuted only if committed in England. The reach of law extended as far as Dover, not to Calais and beyond. By a charming fiction, however, this was no problem. After the actual site of a crime was stated (for example, Hamburg), the declaration would continue, "to-wit, in London, in the parish of St.-Mary-le-Bow in the Ward of Cheap."[3]

At the risk of seeming flippant—though I am completely serious—I propose "to wit" as a solution to one of the most intractable of memory conflicts. The Filioque controversy (in the Nicene Creed, does the Spirit proceed from the Father, as the Eastern Orthodox say, or as Christians descended from Latin tradition put it, from the Father and the Son?) is theologically and historically both complex and consequential. I suggest that Western Christians, when reciting the creed, say "We believe in the Holy Spirit, the Lord, the Giver of Life, who proceeds from the Father and the Son—to wit, from the Father—and together with the Father and the Son is worshiped and glorified." Theology aligned via English common law.

Fifth is reconciling by the humor maneuver. When, uncommonly in ecumenical documents, there is a light touch, it leaps off the page, shimmering, as in a recent agreement between the Evangelical Lutheran Church in America and churches in the Reformed tradition.

On the issue of the Eucharist: "Both Lutheran and Reformed churches affirm that Christ himself is the host at this table. Both churches affirm that Christ himself is truly present and received in the Supper. Neither communion professes to explain how this is so."[4]

On the issue of predestination: "To put the situation sharply: rather than being divided over the doctrine, both sides seem to be united in an equally lukewarm endorsement and an equal embarrassment over any form of predestinarian teaching as part of their theological commitment."[5] "Equal embarrassment"—a fair percentage of church-dividing issues could be resolved by such an admission on both sides, followed by a good laugh.

I say "followed by a good laugh" because of an expression used in a scene that is etched indelibly in my memory. This story describes a model for any ecumenical gathering—for just about any meeting of any sort for any purpose.

It's from the autobiography of one of my heroes, Nelson Mandela. He recalls, from his days as a teenager, gatherings of elders at Mqhekezweni, provisional capital of Thembuland. "At the very end of the council, a praise-singer or poet would deliver a panegyric to the ancient kings, and a mixture of compliments to and satire on the present chiefs, and the audience, led by the regent, would roar with laughter."[6]

Sixth is reconciling by the honesty policy. The best example I know is from long ago, at the Seventh Ecumenical Council, held at Nicaea in 787, about which I did my doctoral study at Yale. Its task was to undo the prohibition of icons that had been enacted thirty-three years earlier by a council calling itself the Seventh Ecumenical. The question for the council fathers is this: How to repudiate their parents without losing the inheritance of the apostolic tradition?[7]

Could they really say the church had been mistaken? Can you disavow the immediate past without putting other parts of the past, or even the whole past, under suspicion? Hypatius, bishop of the host city of Nicaea, speaks for several when he says, "We were not intimidated or forced, but we were born in this heresy of ours, and were educated and nurtured in it."[8]

Patriarch Tarasius of Constantinople manages a reconciling of memories with the skill of a Balanchine choreographing a ballet. He makes sure that Bishop Gregory of Neocaesarea, who had participated in the earlier council, is seated at Nicaea, and that it is Gregory who reads out the decisions of that council prior to their refutation. The fathers of Nicaea II admit that "the hierarchs had become heresiarchs,"[9] and pray in repentance: "for the rejection of ecclesiastical tradition, let us ask pardon for our sin."[10]

Note that they do not say, "We have now received back into the church those who were opponents of orthodoxy and truth." The Seventh Ecumenical Council demonstrates that memories can be reconciled by admitting—honestly, boldly, and carefully—"*we were wrong.*"

Seventh is reconciling by the listening mandate. If all are sure of their own command of the truth, there is no incentive to pay attention to what others are saying in order to learn something; you pay attention only as a preparation for ambush. I shudder to think how many times this is precisely what I've done.

The power of listening for the reconciling of memories is dramatically illustrated by the 1999 Joint Declaration on the Doctrine of Justification, issued by the Lutheran World Federation and the Pontifical Council for Promoting Christian Unity.[11]

Lutheran and Roman Catholic theologians concluded, preliminarily, that while their ancestors in the faith "did not simply or altogether miss the point," the mutual condemnations of the sixteenth century do miss the point of the new understandings reached in the recent dialogues. "The diversity between the Lutheran and Catholic understanding of justification is mutually open rather than mutually exclusive."[12]

"Mutually Open Rather Than Mutually Exclusive"

The expression does not cover the whole ecumenical breakthrough of the twentieth century, but as shorthand goes, it is remarkably comprehensive. It reminds me of the balance between Bentham's "What is the meaning of it?" and Coleridge's "Is it true?" detected by John Stuart Mill, as detailed in encounter 3. Diversity is not eliminated, obliterated, denied, or papered over. It is acknowledged and acclaimed. It is not something we tolerate because we cannot agree. Nobody claims to have figured everything out. We celebrate diversity because God revels in it.

Listening is a reconciler of memories not only because traditions have learned to hear each other. They have also learned to hear themselves. Lutherans and Catholics have been listening to each other, but Lutherans have also been listening to Lutherans in the presence of Catholics, Catholics to Catholics in the presence of Lutherans. Neither tradition, it turns out, is a monolith. Each tradition has a huge task in reconciling its own memories.

People with long involvement in these dialogues have told me that time and again someone from one tradition will formulate the case for the other tradition more cogently than any of that other tradition's spokespersons. "Not only have I heard and learned from your way; I'm handing your way back to you so you can see it afresh." Lines don't disappear, but they do blur. The reality of a common Christian tradition—the middle, if you will—older and deeper than the competing versions, simply stares the group in the face—specifically, in the faces of those around the table.

It's 1989. I hear about an ecumenical women's prayer group in

Minneapolis that has met every week for more than half a century. There is no "organization," there are no officers. Their prayer hour is not a discussion group. Then the ecumenical clincher: "Discussion follows over sandwiches at lunch. We do not always agree or understand, but we don't misunderstand."

IN A WORD

I encounter the reshuffling grace of God when memories that seemed mutually exclusive turn out to be mutually open.

reshuffling

Part Six

DIVERSITY

Grace in Variety

Ecumenism still has lots of work to do. Despite much reconciling, there are still deep divisions between churches (and within them). One of the sharpest points of division is what to make of other religions.

At the beginning of the twentieth century William James wrote *The Varieties of Religious Experience.* At the beginning of the twenty-first century, the reality for many is the experience of religious variety.

People in America encounter more people of other races, ethnicities, and religions today than ever before. More US presidents have been Episcopalian than any other tradition, but there are now more Muslims than Episcopalians in the United States,[1] and a greater variety of Buddhists than in any other country (with huge implications for Buddhist ecumenism).[2] By mid-century the racial "majority" in the US will be the minority. The statistics tumble over one another, all of them reinforced by the globalization of commerce and communication. The World Wide Web cares hardly a fig about geography.

But the experience of religious variety starts much closer to home. I experience myself as "diverse"—the Patrick of today, including Patrick the Christian of today, would in many ways be unrecognizable to the Patrick of ten or thirty or fifty years ago, or maybe even yesterday.

If I ponder my own story, I get on the pulse a sense of what is writ large on the entire social map. I have a sense of coherence, despite parts of my story, including my Christian story, that don't fit together neatly at all. My recognizing that I have gone beyond, even rejected, earlier positions I took, without necessarily regretting having taken them, makes me open to views other than the ones I have now.

"Never Burn Your Bridges behind You"

One of the intellectual blessings that came to me when I moved from being a professor to administering a research institute was my regular encounter with nonacademic types, especially businesspeople (who constitute a major "diversity" category for PhDs). From many of them I learned that embracing diversity is not simply a matter of broadening the mind or even opening the heart. It gets to the bottom line.

As Elizabeth Villafana, a board member of the Collegeville Institute, said to me about the recently deceased H. C. (Bob) Piper, CEO of Piper Jaffray and chair of the institute's board, who was notable for not holding grudges, "He knew what every good businessperson knows: you never burn your bridges behind you, because you never know when you might have to cross over them again." Professors, cloistered by tenure, can burn bridges at will.

Some people blame John Calvin and, especially for America, his profound follower Jonathan Edwards for the spirit of intolerance. But Edwards, most notoriously known for his sermon "Sinners in the Hands of an Angry God" (which is more about God's mercy than about God's wrath), wrote some of the most passionate theology you'll find anywhere about beauty and the wild, glorious diversity of creation. Edwards teaches me that while the eco-havoc we are wreaking on our planet is evil, it is also ugly. The God of justice made the world, yes, but also the God of beauty.

Calvin isn't the culprit. It's our culturally conditioned competitiveness, our bedrock assumption of scarcity, our fear that God hasn't really supplied all that we need. We suspect that the world is, at best, a zero-sum game; more likely the bottom line is way in deficit. In the *Left Behind* series, Christ slays millions upon millions, and a few survive.

If this is how I see the world, if this is how the world feels to me, then diversity—indeed, anybody else—is bound to appear threatening. By confronting me with the radically other, God is at best testing me—more likely, punishing me. From this perspective, God created a diverse world not for my delight but to hedge me in.

The opposite perspective is grounded in the ecumenical conversions dependent on the "cannot" recounted in encounter 15— the discovery by many Christians in recent decades that forms of Christian practice and belief that they used to think abominable are pleasing in the sight of God.

Rooted Somewhere and Open to the Other

The dynamic of this transformation cannot be halted at the borders of the explicitly Christian community.

For a week each in 1999 and 2000 the Collegeville Institute for Ecumenical and Cultural Research gathers American Indians, Buddhists, Christians, Hindus, Jews, and Muslims to talk about "Living Faithfully in the United States Today." As we tell the stories of our lives to one another, surprises are around every corner. "The doors of my heart are open for others to enter," says one, and another: "When you go from here you take a part of me, and I'll have part of you."

One of the Muslims says, "I will consider all children as my own children, all men as my brothers, all women as my sisters, and all elders as my own parents." Each day a particular faith group holds a service and invites the others to attend. When the Hindus are going to do their puja (devotional worship), this Muslim, whose story goes back to the violent partition of the subcontinent into Pakistan and India, asks them if he can start their service by chanting one of the Vedas, their holy scripture, in Sanskrit. Animosity between religious communities as bitter as any the world has known—periodic news reports remind me that Hindu-Muslim relations can still be murderous—is overcome in this moment, on both sides: his offer, and their acceptance of it. My response is immediate and unequivocal: If *this* has been done, then *anything* is possible.

The transformation that our time calls for—experiences of religious variety bringing people together instead of tearing them apart—was anticipated by someone who is often credited with being the first "modern person," Michel de Montaigne (1533–92).

To provide historical context: when Montaigne was one year old Martin Luther published the entire Bible in his own German translation; when Montaigne was three, John Calvin published the first edition of his *Institutes of the Christian Religion*; and when Montaigne was twelve, the Council of Trent was called to stem the tide of the Protestant Reformation. In other words, Montaigne's world was shaped by a monumental cultural and religious revolution in which claims to certainty were steadily ratcheted up.

In the midst of all this bickering and bashing, Montaigne was "more enchanted than alarmed by the bewildering variety of human practices."[3]

There is something about Montaigne's particular blend of curiosity and self-awareness that makes him seem much more my contemporary than Luther or Calvin or the cardinals of Trent. It is this "more enchanted than alarmed" that instructs me most.

God Revels in Variety

The enchantment rather than alarm is theologically sound, even mandated. The God who revels in that bewildering variety—who, after all, created it—has been hiding in plain sight in the Bible.

As Jacob discovers in Genesis 28: "Surely the Lord is in this place—*and I did not know it.*" He thought he already knew where

God was—and God gave him a really big surprise. As any therapist could have told Jacob, having your eyes opened, really seeing what is right in front of your face, is one of the most difficult of human accomplishments.

It's April 1989. I'm at a conference I helped plan, called "Religious Education for Dialogue and Peace." This event covers, in the great scheme of things, a very small swath of the overall diversity spectrum, but in American academic history it is pretty radical.

Saint John's University, Luther Seminary, and the University of Minnesota—three institutions not a whole lot like each other—have teamed up to bring representatives of about a dozen religious traditions together to consider this question: "How does my tradition account for the fact that there are other traditions whose adherents are as deeply committed to them as I am to mine?"[4] What we are getting at is not "What do you *think about* tradition X or Y?" but "How do you *account for* the fact of X and Y, and the adherence of people to them?"

Answers are all over the place, not only because divergent viewpoints are simply the nature of such conferences but also because it is not always easy to keep participants focused on the question. But the question, always worth asking, is key to a deep appreciation of diversity. The fundamental challenge of the other is not the distinction between our ideas, but how does my set of ideas account for the fact of that other set of ideas?

I'm not proposing a relativist, "anything goes" abandonment of judgment and standards. There are certainly times when the way I account for another's view that differs from mine is to say, simply, "They're wrong." Sometimes, "dangerously wrong." But often I've learned, after getting to know someone, that the conclusion I'd originally jumped to was a mistake, so I hesitate to claim that my initial way of accounting for some "other" is sustainable.

Life is short. I really don't have time to waste, whether drawing lines and excluding and lording it over others, or dwelling on trivialities. I'll never forget a scene in Anne Lamott's *Traveling*

Mercies. She is fretting over whether a dress she is trying on makes her look big in the hips. Her friend, dying of cancer, says "as clear and kind as a woman can be, 'Annie? You really don't have that kind of time.'"[5]

From Duty to Delight

The profoundest experiences of diversity have the character of conversion, of transforming both mind and heart. The reward is immense. What likely begins as duty—"I ought to appreciate those different from me"—transforms into delight. One mark of true conversion is my astonishment that I could have ever thought and felt the way I used to.

Some years ago I was handed language that clarified something I had suspected for years but never knew what to call it. It's a phrase coined by the late Krister Stendahl, who was dean of Harvard Divinity School and subsequently Lutheran archbishop of Stockholm. He speaks of "holy envy," the sense of longing for what someone in another tradition or from another culture has that I know I can't have because it requires that whole other atmosphere for its own breathing.[6]

A specific instance of this for me is the Jewish tradition of religious life centered around the family, especially the table. When I sit with Jewish friends at a Passover Seder, I can imagine trying to emulate it, but it will never really be like what it is for them, steeped in generations of household worship and prayer.

The brilliance of Stendahl's term is the modification of "envy," one of the seven deadly sins, with "holy." The envy is no longer my wish that you didn't have what you have and I want but can't have. The envy becomes my celebration of your having it, of its being part of the whole human story, of your being my friend.

The experience of religious variety has been for me, repeatedly, the passage from resistance, through bafflement and conversation, to holy envy. Sometimes it's scary to find what others say intriguing, but then I reach the point of saying, "I want to know more—even if it worries me, tell me."

My friend Mary Bednarowski, who in encounter 15 challenged me to become a caretaker of others' stories, sums it up: "Life is so short. How can we bear the thought of missing out on what so many different kinds of people can offer each other?"[7]

And this does not result in homogenization, or descent to the least common denominator.

I'm looking not for sameness, or even agreement, but for solidarity. This implies that I celebrate the ways you are different from me, and you the ways I am different from you. I get hints that friends in other traditions, whom I envy, envy me in turn. The God I know, the God of surprise, looks on this kind of envy and pronounces it very good.

IN A WORD

I encounter the inclusive grace of God when my suspicions turn into holy envy.

inclusive

Grace in a Fugue

My experience of religious diversity is set within the larger framework of the diversities that are a hallmark of twenty-first-century life.

During my first two or three decades I was aware of diversity, of course, but I was not part of the diversity. I and people like me were the norm. Everyone else was more or less "diverse" from that norm—in short, a deviation. God looked at me and said not only, "You are good," but also, "You are the standard."

My current understanding of diversity is radically different from what I thought in the middle of the last century. This way of putting it doesn't get it quite right, however. Back in the 1950s I didn't even *think about it* in any systematic or self-conscious sense. A world whose norm I was was just the way it was.

I am grateful for the liberation I have undergone in being some-times nudged, sometimes jolted out of the complacency that is the lethal side effect of thinking and feeling oneself the norm. I now know that I cheat myself if I stay only where I can breathe easy. It is actually a huge relief. Nothing could persuade me to go back to the way it was.

The civil rights and feminist revolutions, which have moved the ground on which I stand—I've experienced a seismic shift—are part of the whole atmosphere change that is labeled "post-modernism"—the upending of the notion that unity depends on a single authentic narrative, a story against which all other stories are measured. I have learned to listen, not for nuggets I can fit into patterns of thinking I have inherited, but for whole new patterns into which I can fit inherited nuggets.

Ducks Not in a Row, but Flying Around All Over the Place

I used to think that the test of intellect, of understanding, was my ability to get all the ducks in a row. Now I think it's my ability to be amazed that the ducks are flying around all over the place and to try to watch them all.

Diversity is not one thing, any more than life itself is one thing. It has many components, features, nuances, pitfalls, delights, sorrows. I play tricks on myself if I think I'm thinking clearly about it. A single, controlling story about diversity would be self-contradictory.

Understanding diversity requires the discipline of really listening, especially to voices that have been ignored or discounted. I once heard a woman professor say that when a male colleague asked, "What are you working on?" and she replied, "An autobiography," he immediately queried, "An autobiography of whom?"

It is frequently said that we have to come to terms with diversity because of recent changes in our society. But diversity has been a reality a lot longer than many have realized.

Just as I grew up being so much the norm that I didn't even think about it, so also did our culture—or rather, those on top in our culture—go along for decades oblivious to unnoticed, unheard stories—of Blacks, American Indians, women, the poor. Diversity was hidden in plain sight. As soon as I begin to notice what has been hidden in plain sight, I start to wonder whether there is yet more, whether my peripheral vision is in good working order.

So, diversity is a social reality. It is also a theological one.

The Normative Narrative Trap

It is especially easy for a Christian to slip into the normative narrative trap. The Bible appears to be the ultimate privileged story—the plotline worked out from creation to the new heaven and new earth, from alpha to omega with all the other letters falling right into place in the interim. The many passages about people falling away, about golden calves and betrayals, simply reinforce by way of contrast the central conviction that there is a way, one way, the only way to live an authentic life expressing what I am meant to be.

The normative trap is built into the Christian story. It closes especially tight when it is set in the midst of a society where nearly everybody adheres to the story. There is the allure of a single narrative—the mainline track one wants to be on so as to avoid a train wreck. The success of the *Left Behind* series, discussed in encounter 10, is stunning testimony to the appeal of certainty. As Tim LaHaye, one of the coauthors, states, "Well, we know that we're right, so we just present our position."[1]

There is another theological starting point, though, one that's at least as strongly rooted in the Bible as is the "tiny remnant" image. God created the world wildly diverse. "The earth is the LORD's and all that is in it, the world, and those who live in it"—Psalm 24:1 says it best. I once heard a friend say that the best homily he'd ever heard was a single sentence: "What part of *all* don't you understand?" Attention to diversity should not have waited until diversity was just down the street. Diversity is theologically prior to demographics.

What do I think the existence, the insistence, the inescapability of all this diversity tells me about the character of the God who made it all? What part of "all" don't I understand? How could it ever have occurred to me that God made me the norm?

A participant in the "Religious Education for Dialogue and Peace" conference I recalled in the previous encounter conjured an image for this diversity that is imprinted indelibly in my memory. He said that we are in a saltwater marsh, where there is constant motion, teeming life, and an ever-shifting boundary between sea and land. Our task is not to figure out where we are, but to notice what is going on all around us.[2]

I have a choice. I can read the Bible to mean that the diversity is a mistake, a consequence of the fall, and that my vocation is to find my way out of the saltwater marsh and to bring as many with me as I can.

Or I can read the Bible to mean that God delights in the diversity, that the saltwater marsh is where I am supposed to be, and the consequence of the fall is my not understanding all parts of "all." Choosing to read the Bible this way—the other way is equally a choice, not an inevitability—springs me free from the normative Christian trap.

Diversity Makes Us Safer

Demographics and theology are reinforced by the experience of diversity. My friend Grant Grissom said it best: "I have found that, when I have a more-than-superficial encounter with people whose experience is markedly different from my own, I feel a connectedness that makes the world seem a better, safer place. I have also recognized wonderful qualities in others that are possibilities inside myself that were undiscovered, or atrophied."[3] The world seems *safer*.

The experience of diversity is not just one-way. Diversity is not something I don't have that others bring to me. If they're worth my time, there's a presumption that I'm worth theirs. I have to be careful to avoid the trap of normality, where I'm the standard and they're "diverse."

The center of gravity of my own thinking about diversity has shifted over the years from the prayer of Jesus in John 17, "that they all may be one," to the image of God's house with many rooms, in John 14.

I remember a motto on the door of Bernard Saffran, a colleague at Swarthmore College, in the economics department, who was as fascinated by religion as he was skeptical of it: "Do not do unto others as you would have them do unto you—your tastes may be different." The image of God's house with many rooms allows for very diverse styles of decoration. In this day when many Christians join me in recognizing, even celebrating, gay marriage, I'm reminded that in God's house there are many rooms, not closets.

Theology as Choreography

It's 1955. I am in high school. My mother takes me to a performance of the Royal Danish Ballet in Dallas; it is their first US tour. The concluding work is Benjamin Britten's *The Young Person's Guide to the Orchestra: Variations and Fugue on a Theme of Henry Purcell*, op. 34. The ballet company is divided into segments corresponding to the sections of the orchestra. All are dressed in primary-color costumes (the brasses are red).

At each variation, the dancers for that part of the orchestra are on stage and turn into motion the character of the instruments. Then, at the end, when Britten takes the theme through all the double helixes of a fugue, everyone is on stage. Art and discovery and learning and delight all come together. Unity in—not just in, but through—complex diversity is woven in front of my eyes and ears. I come to understand that diversity and unity ratchet each other up—it's not just both/and.

Many years later, in 1993, my memory of the Royal Danish Ballet is triggered in Chicago's Grant Park.

I'm at the Parliament of the World's Religions, commemorating the first such gathering a century earlier. My main responsibility is to moderate a conversation between Christian and Buddhist monastics. One member of that discussion, His Holiness the Dalai Lama, is the featured speaker at the concluding plenary.

The plenary is drawing to its close. Representatives of about thirty religious traditions pronounce blessings on the audience. The mix of languages, dress, and styles presents a face of religion far more diverse than most Americans are used to.

Then a multiethnic dance group encourages everyone to clap

in rhythm. Hundreds, including me, start dancing in the aisles. I think: The Parliament has reached a fitting conclusion. Ritual action together—a kind of fugue—finally puts all the millions of words of the previous week into perspective. Peace is a dance more than it is a document.

From those moments in Dallas and Chicago until now, I have suspected that the answer to how we can have unity without a privileged story lurks not in the charts of a sociologist or the categories of a theologian but in the imagination of a choreographer, who knows that a fugal model of understanding does full justice to the yeses, nos, and maybes—loosens the knots we intellectually tie ourselves into.

IN A WORD

I encounter the choreographing grace of God when diversity becomes a delight.

choreographing

Grace in Finding an Old Sermon

In 2007 I slip through a time warp when I inadvertently come across a sermon I had preached nearly a half century earlier.

It's August 2, 1959, the summer between my junior and senior years of college. As the son of its minister, I have grown up immersed in the life of the Northway Christian Church in Dallas. I am the "obvious" choice for preacher when a student-led service is planned. I am on track to follow the family profession (as I noted earlier, both my grandfathers were also pastors). I suppose this occasion is a kind of initiation rite.

In those days the Christian Church (Disciples of Christ) did not require seminary training prior to ordination—my father was ordained at age seventeen, while still in high school. Less than three months after I preach the sermon, I express reservation in a letter to my parents: "I have thought and thought and thought about the ordination. I hope it does not sound as if I'm equivocating or am not sure of myself when I say that I believe it would be better to wait a while for the official service. Part of the freedom for which I am so very grateful is my freedom to express my desires on this quite frankly."

This is the first step in what becomes a riff on "the priesthood of all believers." A few years later I finally acknowledge a call that goes the other way: God is calling me not to the ministry but to be a layperson. My sermon and its near aftermath very nearly mark the moment at which vocation for me begins to transpose from the key of ordination to that of the lay state.

There is a certain resonance between my call to nonordination and the most authentic and persuasive story of a call to ordination that I have ever heard. My friend, the late John Jankowski, an Episcopal priest, was for a couple of decades a successful computer software engineer. He kept feeling a call to the priesthood. He attended a spiritual retreat some distance from home. On the drive back he said, audibly, "God, do you want me for a priest?" He reports that he heard a voice loud and clear: "I don't care!" God didn't have "a plan" for John's life. The decision was John's.

When I find that old sermon lurking in a file folder, one feature gives me pain, and one causes me to wince.

Language Matters

What really hurts is my unselfconscious use of exclusive language: "Men have often asked," I say. "This has not been apparent to men always." "A man's individual existence." I'm hardly a quarter of the way into the sermon.

Now it's 1976. Old Testament scholar Phyllis Trible and I are leading a convocation at Maryville College in Tennessee. The subject: "Who Speaks for Man?"

In my opening remarks I say that "I hope everyone will understand that when I say 'man' I mean both genders." This is a slight advance over the unqualified use of "man" in the sermon fifteen years earlier, but hardly sufficient.

My opening remarks also plant what proves to be a time bomb. "At the beginning of the semester I always say to my students, 'There's a requirement that's not on the syllabus. To complete this course successfully, you must during the semester say at least one absolutely outrageous thing.'" The point is to unlock the chains of academic caution.

It's now the final day of the convocation. Phyllis has to leave early. I ask if there's anything she wants to say by way of wrapping up.

"Yes, Patrick. You've been absolutely outrageous. Why do you keep using language that hurts millions of us, all the while insisting that you aren't?"

I am to lead the closing worship service. Whatever it is I have planned gets jettisoned. It's repentance time.

I fashion a story about Chaos and God, where I'm playing Chaos. God says to Chaos, "Let there be light." Chaos responds, "That just doesn't speak to my condition"—just as, when women censure me for my use of sexist language, they aren't speaking to my "condition" of "blamelessness," since in my own consciousness I'm not being exclusive when I use terms like "mankind" and it's too bad if others are misled by what I say. It's only when Chaos—up until then entirely comfortable with the formless void and the blanket of darkness for security, like me in my linguistic smugness—relents and gives light a chance, that creation happens.

I say that Phyllis has made clear to me that the important thing is not what connects with my experience, but the impassioned voices of millions of women who are saying that the common terminology is an insult, a put-down. The fact that I mean no harm by the terms I use is no excuse for my not listening to those who tell me they are harmed by my use of those terms.

The challenge is to my conviction that I know what is best for everybody, to my North American white male understanding of how the world is put together. I want to be open. What Phyllis says initially hurts—but in the moment it hurts, I know it is for my good. I learn that truth-telling is finally life-giving even if it initially appears to be death-dealing, and failure is often full of teaching.

From Maryville on, when I periodically read things I wrote before then, such as that sermon in which I was excluding half the congregation, I will find it terribly hard to believe that through all those years I didn't "get it."

I suspect, too, that in my early years I used a metaphor that, thanks to my subsequent experience, I've come to see is hugely prejudicial, as bad in its way as the generic "man," and that's the use of the term "stepchild" as a put-down.

My visceral reaction to a March 2, 2005, editorial in the *Star Tribune* woke me up to the error of that common usage. The editors castigated legislators who, they said, had "treated city and county officials as naughty stepchildren."

My letter was published the next day. "As a stepson who has a stepdaughter, I object to the ease with which the step-relation continues to be used as though it automatically demeans. Eventually there will be enough stepfathers, stepmothers (what an awful press they've had!), stepchildren, and stepsiblings so no one will even dream of the put-down. Newspapers are language arbiters. Please think about the stepchildren and stepparents you know (and perhaps even are), and cease treating them as a cheap metaphor."

I am fortunate to have a stepdaughter, Christina, who shows me repeatedly that the step-relation is in no way inferior to the blood one, as was also demonstrated by my stepfather, whom my mother married several years after my father's death. Whenever I hear some group disgraced as "stepchildren," I bristle. The figure of speech is simply wrong. The ranks of those it humiliates are legion.

Cycles and Straight Lines

If my male chauvinist language causes me, in retrospect, pain and embarrassment, what causes me to wince is a theological insight that I was very proud of—it still has some merit—but if stated without nuance is seriously misleading. One trajectory of my own spiritual and intellectual life can be traced back to the discovery that a fundamental premise of my 1959 sermon is wrong.

"Biblical faith contests this [Greek and Oriental] cyclical view of time. . . . Time is a straight line, with unknown possibilities for the future. The actions of individual men [*sic*] in large measure determine history, so that every man's [*sic*, again] life is of incalculable worth."

The sermon's title comes from *West Side Story*, which I had seen a few months earlier on Broadway. Its retelling of the story of Romeo and Juliet, with the Jets and Sharks gangs in place of the Montagues and Capulets, overpowered me. I wrote to my parents: "One of the most poignant lines I've ever heard is spoken by a lesser member of the Jets when the whole group is being pursued by the police: 'Why can't it be yesterday?'" From that sentence the sermon is born.

This memory ricochets to a tangent that is crucial to my story.

A family friend, Charles Meeker, was in charge of the State Fair Musicals. Each summer he brought half a dozen Broadway shows to Dallas, and I saw nearly all of them. The 1940s and 1950s were the glory days of musical theater.

Carousel, Oklahoma!, Annie Get Your Gun, My Fair Lady, The Music Man, The Most Happy Fella, Candide, The King and I, Damn Yankees, South Pacific, Kiss Me, Kate, West Side Story—these were my *Sesame Street*, my *Mister Rogers' Neighborhood*. Their mix of romance and social commentary and, occasionally, tragedy, staked out much of what I understood about the world.

Then there is my all-time favorite: *Brigadoon*.

As I look back, I realize that it was my first encounter with time warping.

Two New Yorkers visit Scotland and come upon a town called Brigadoon. One of them falls in love with Fiona, who tells him Brigadoon's story. In order to prevent the town's corruption by the outside world, the local pastor, two hundred years ago, prayed that it would disappear, and reappear for only one day every hundred years.

Such a situation is of course ripe for all sorts of complications. The show deals with them deftly, humorously, poignantly. The man smitten with Fiona eventually makes it back to Brigadoon. The rule that the town comes back only once every century is momentarily broken so he and his true love can be together.

"Why can't it be yesterday?" is what sent me off on this tangent.

The question points to the liability in the biblical conception of time as I outline it in the sermon: "Our mistakes, our sins of the past cannot, as in the cyclical view, be redeemed by the passage of more time. . . . It is very important to realize that on the issue of time, biblical faith and Oriental religions are at sharp odds."

By a curious coincidence or special providence, my retrieval of the sermon occurs less than a week after reading an essay by Bruce Grierson in *Time* magazine that resonates with my spiritual state.[1]

Grierson reports that a Chinese student said to University of Michigan psychologist Richard Nisbett, "The difference between you and me is that I think the world is a circle, and you think it's a line." The remark generated a book from Nisbett, *The Geography of Thought.*

"To Western thinking," Grierson continues, "the world is linear; you can chop it up and analyze it, and we can all work on our little part of the project independently until it's solved. The classically Eastern mind, according to Nisbett, sees things differently: the world isn't a length of rope but a vast, closed chain, incomprehensibly complex and ever changing."

At first glance it might seem that what I am reading in 2007 simply confirms what I said in 1959. But no. What happened to me in those intervening decades shifted the whole framework of my thought and feeling.

The contrast between "West" and "East" is still useful, but the conflation of "Western" with "biblical" and, by extension, "Christian," implicit in my sermon, no longer makes sense to me. The Bible is far more "Asian," and Christianity far more "Eastern," than I knew back when Eisenhower was president.

"The East" covers a lot of territory. Grierson, and Nisbett to whom he refers, clearly have in mind mainly Asia, its spirit embodied in Taoism and Confucianism and Hinduism and Buddhism—in all their myriad varieties.

Buddhism is one focus of my attention. I am grateful to Buddhists I have worked with for alerting me to a feature of Christian doctrine that I, as a "Westerner," was almost oblivious to. This discovery comes not in discussions of doctrine or theory, but in reflections on practice.

First, though, back to the sermon. Here's what I say about cyclical time: "If the wheel of fortune does revolve from its high point to its low, it will inevitably return to the top. In some distant tomorrow, then, yesterday will return. A man's [sic] individual existence in this view is not highly worthwhile—he [sic] is merely carried along in the unchangeable movement of the cycles of time."

In theory, perhaps. But when I say this, I have yet to learn that some very wise Christians have thought time cyclical. Origen, the great third-century scholar, believed all things would eventually revert to what they were in the beginning. When I say this, I have yet to learn what T. S. Eliot wrote—that in our exploration we return to where we started. When I say this, I have yet to learn of the Buddhist bodhisattva, the practitioner who gets right up to the verge of nirvana and then, expressing the fundamental virtue of compassion, pulls back in order to help others not yet so far along. In other words, when I say this, I have yet to learn that Christians can be cyclical and that individual Buddhists can consider their own existence worthwhile.

Over the decades, as I have studied more deeply in Christian mysticism, have encountered Buddhism, and have had a sequence of feminist conversion experiences, I have come to see circles where before I noticed only straight lines, webs instead of arrows, and have also discerned the many different patterns within the Bible. I long ago gave up an irritable reaching after the unique and unrepeatable.

Yesterday Keeps Coming Back

Within a year of each other—1992 and 1993, respectively—an episode of *Star Trek: The Next Generation* (a show of which I was a
devotee, and which will get its due in encounter 29), called "Cause
and Effect," and a wildly popular movie, *Groundhog Day*,[2] answer
the question I posed in 1959, "Why can't it be yesterday?," in ways
both harrowing and humorous.

In the movie, a disgruntled TV meteorologist, Phil Connors,
is assigned, as for many years previously, to cover the emergence
from the ground on February 2 of Punxsutawney Phil, the Pennsylvania groundhog whose sighting or nonsighting of his shadow
predicts whether there will be six more weeks of winter.

On the way home, the TV crew is caught in a snowstorm that
Connors had forecast would miss the area. They are forced to return to Punxsutawney. The next morning Connors wakes up to
find it is February 2 again. Of course this keeps happening over
and over again (the time lapse is left ambiguous but is speculated
to have been at least ten years).

Connors is aware of what is happening—he has memories of
the previous day—but no one else in Punxsutawney is. For all of
them, each day is just like it was the last time around, except when
Connors changes his own behavior and affects theirs. Before long
he learns that he can do whatever he wants, with no consequences
for himself.

Doing "whatever he wants" soon becomes tiresome. Eventually
he captures Punxsutawney Phil and drives both the groundhog
and himself to a fiery death in a crash. But the next day February
2 starts all over again, and it keeps doing so even after subsequent
repeated deaths from marmotcide and suicide.

The repeating Groundhog Day stops when Connors, coached
by his colleague Rita (whom he has unsuccessfully tried to seduce),
learns that he can help other people. He wakes up on February 3
to a Punxsutawney where he is respected and loved. Yesterday

happens often enough for Phil Connors, finally, to return to where he started and see it—and himself—afresh.

On March 23, 2368, the starship *Enterprise* gets caught in a time loop, which the crew is first alerted to in a situation where repetition is about as remote a possibility as can be imagined—a poker game. (As I noted in encounter 11, the number of ways the cards in a deck can be arranged is beyond astronomical.) They have a vague but dogged sense that they've been here "before." As I peer in at their game, I see that the same cards are dealt every time.[3]

It's not just poker that repeats. The *Enterprise* is destroyed in a collision with another spaceship. Everyone dies. Then the cards are dealt again. The collision happens again. Through a hunch that a hint could be sent from one rendition of the time loop to the next (a hint that gets encoded in the poker game itself), the android, Lieutenant Commander Data, manages to avoid the action that triggers the collision, breaking the ring after seventeen days; for the other spaceship, it has been eighty years.

Cdr. Data functions as a bodhisattva, who manages to intervene to halt a destructive cycle. Or like the prophet Jeremiah, who, when the Babylonians are about to conquer Judah, buys a field from a relative and gives instruction that the deed is to be buried in an earthenware jar to "last for a long time." In other words, when this time capsule is unearthed, God's promise—"houses and fields and vineyards shall again be bought in this land"—will be confirmed (Jer. 32:15).

My Fundamental Nature Is Not Darkness but Light

I mentioned earlier that Buddhists alerted me to a submerged feature of Christian doctrine.

The occasion is a project I edit under the title *Benedict's Dharma: Buddhists Reflect on the Rule of Saint Benedict.*[4] Four Buddhists, each from a different tradition (Zen, Theravada, Ma-

hayana, Tantric), ponder the intersections and divergences between their own spiritual practice and experience and the pattern
of monastic life outlined in the sixth-century Rule, which establishes a community structure and organizes its daily life.

In my 1959 sermon I emphasize the role of sin and repentance
in Christianity. The good news is forgiveness. I still think it is. But
the Buddhists perceive in Benedict the balancing truth I didn't
emphasize back then: my fundamental nature is not darkness but
light. It's not just repentance that's called for. "Sinner" doesn't exhaust my identity.

The Buddhists—and Phil Connors and Cdr. Data—help me
learn that the answer to "Why can't it be yesterday?" is Yogi Berra's
insight, discussed in encounter 13: even if it's yesterday, "the future
ain't what it used to be." Eliot says not only that we return to where
we started—but that we "know the place for the first time."[5]

IN A WORD

I encounter the challenging grace of God when I'm
called to repentance and can hardly believe I didn't
"get it" before.

challenging

Grace in Christian Autobiography

Religious variety, and diversity more generally, can be portrayed in broad swatches. However, the general needs to be complemented by the particular. Christian autobiographies are a good source. The writers invite me into their own time warps.

In 1947 W. H. Auden called his time an age of anxiety.[1] Ours is an age of suspicion. We instinctively suppose people mean something other than what they say. Literary analysis known as deconstruction purports to expose the illusion that there is an actor and a speaker in the first place.

On the other hand, I've been in academic cocktail conversations that go something like this: "Isn't *everybody* writing autobiography? Isn't the self-conscious, admitted autobiographer the only honest, non-self-indulgent person around? Isn't Walt Whitman's unapologetic 'I sing myself' the true epigraph to every literary work?"

Still, whether I as a reader am drawn in or on guard, trusting transparency or wary of being hoodwinked by the author's clandestine motives, autobiographies are a primary source for the category "human"—with the caution that when an author is both informant and anthropologist, as an autobiographer necessarily is, there is bound to be some distortion.

I taught a course called "Religious Autobiography" several times, never with exactly the same reading list, always with a unique group of students, each instance at a different stage of my own spiritual development.

In May 1983 my father died. A few months later I taught the course for the last time. A parent's death would by itself have given an edge to my rereadings of the texts; the fact that his death was from suicide made the edge especially sharp. His fascination with the poetry of John Berryman, who also died from suicide, became in retrospect a haunting motif in my father's biography.

Memory Wiped Out

Some years later I was brought face to face with the depth of the shock and how it was registered in memory—or rather in the eradication of memory.

I have composed hundreds of recommendation letters, maybe at least a thousand. Here is one I wrote on December 8, 1991.

When I got a letter from Leigh Kyle recently asking if I would write a graduate school recommendation, I had no recollection. The name was familiar, but I couldn't even remember whether it was Leigh (masculine) or Leigh (feminine).

You have never received a letter of recommendation that starts in this inauspicious way. Please read on.

I called the number in the letter, and got an answering machine. At least I now knew it was Leigh/she.

She called me back. The sound and inflection of the voice made a crack in the memory barrier. And then the lightning flash: "You directed my senior paper in the year 1982–83, but just before the oral exam you had to leave because of a death in the family or something like that." In mid-May 1983 my father, with virtually no warning (to me, at least), committed suicide [what I wrote in 1991; I have since learned the importance of saying "died from suicide"; we don't say someone "committed cancer"]. Leigh's reconstruction of that spring told me what

I had never realized: the trauma obliterated the whole previous year from my active consciousness.

I tell you this because Leigh's request, of a sort that can be a professor's nightmare ("What can I say if a student asks for a recommendation a decade later?"), has helped me identify and resolve an unfinished consequence of a personal nightmare. My recommendation is an act of profound gratitude to her.

The letter continues with a circumstantial account of Leigh's excellence as a student, especially in that senior paper, "Religion in the Art of Ingmar Bergman: Some Things Which Are Better Left Unsaid." She helped me understand that the moviemaker's "self-contradictory remarks are not willfully obscure, but are the only way he could talk about what cannot really be talked about directly without serious distortion." Leigh understood that Bergman's film-making is an instance of religious autobiography.

Her impression on me went beyond the academic.

I recall appreciating the way she reminded me, when so many students were succumbing to caution and calculation, of the boldness, brashness, irony, seriousness, and humor of the students of the late '60s and early '70s. (I was not nostalgic for some of their tactics, but I longed for a revival of their spirit, and Leigh had a good portion of it.)

My letter concludes:

Writing this letter has been for me an experience unlike any other I have ever had. If you had called me a month ago and asked for my opinion of Leigh Kyle, I would have drawn a virtual blank (not a total blank; a professor, even a former professor, with a deleted memory, can always find something to say). But voice, letters, transcript, a picture (she suspected a "visual aid" would help, and it did), and papers have brought

her vividly to life for me, and I can say with conviction: Admit
her: she's a treasure.

My own growth, with its clear sailings and rough patches and
U-turns and byways and roads both less and more traveled, chronicled along the way by markers like my letter for Leigh, certainly affects
how I read what others write, especially their life stories. However,
whether I consider my own development, or that of an author, to be of
the spirit or the mind or the soul doesn't matter a great deal. As Saint
Teresa of Ávila winsomely says, "They all seem the same to me."[2]

Motives for Writing about Oneself

A Christian's writing an autobiography is sacrilegious as well as
sacramental. Self-centeredness is not a virtue, but the autobiographer can't avoid it—though Augustine's *Confessions* is a three-
hundred-page prayer directed entirely to God. His book does not
address me at all. I simply eavesdrop on Augustine's long colloquy
with God.

C. S. Lewis, with a purpose more common among autobiographers, says that *Surprised by Joy* "is written partly in answer to
requests that I would tell how I passed from Atheism to Christianity and partly to correct one or two false notions that seem to have
got about."[3] In other words, he wants so satisfy his friends and
confound his enemies.

The most disarming motive I've ever seen for writing about
one's spiritual expedition is the beginning of Anne Sexton's opening poem in *The Awful Rowing Toward God*: "A story, a story! (Let
it go. Let it come.)"[4]

Exploring the self can be inward, as in Dag Hammarskjöld's
Markings. It can be outward, downward, and upward all at the
same time, as in Thomas Merton's *The Seven Storey Mountain*
(where Dante's imagery of the Mountain of Purgatory disorients
me geographically to show me the topography of spiritual life).

Sexton's "you're climbing out of yourself"[5] is neither inward nor outward, but both. It can even be "through the looking-glass," as with Augustine, who says to God, "Lord, you turned my attention back to myself. You took me up from behind my own back where I had placed myself because I did not wish to observe myself, and you set me before my face."[6]

A particularly poignant moment in my spiritual autobiography resonates with Augustine's. It's 1999. I'm in Boston for a convention. While there, I visit the New England Holocaust Memorial.

It's in the open, a series of six glass towers, each fifty-four feet high, on which are engraved millions of numbers to indicate both the scale of the murders and the Nazi scheme of tattooing numbers on prisoners to dehumanize them. A memory of a survivor from the camps is etched on the walls of each tower.

Shortly after my return home, I write to Stanley Saitowitz, the architect who designed the memorial.

I expected to spend a few minutes. But the Memorial won't let go. I lingered, meditated, lingered some more, went back at night to see it in the dark.

What most moved me was your use of the double qualities of glass, both window and mirror. I focused on the words of a survivor, then refocused through those words to the numbers on the next pane of glass, and focused again beyond that plane and found myself staring back at me.

The memorial, like Leigh Kyle's letter eight years earlier, set me before my face.

Standing on Holy Ground

When reading an autobiography, I'm standing on holy ground, like Moses before the burning bush. I have to "take off my sandals," as Moses did, because an autobiography is, to one degree or another, a revelation—at least a Christian, who believes we are made in God's image, thinks so.

I get a glimpse of what someone else has come to know about God, the God who became incarnate and thus has come to know about us. In one way or another, a religious autobiography occupies a mysterious space between two of Saint Teresa of Ávila's phrases: "Praised be the Lord, who has delivered me from myself,"[7] and "the only service I have rendered the Lord is to be what I am."[8] A bit like Ingmar Bergman's "only way he could talk about what cannot really be talked about."

I am incurably curious. Autobiography intrigues me because it lets me in on other people's lives. But more, the autobiographer, despite superficial appearances of self-indulgence and self-regard, is engaged in an essentially communal activity. Like the bodhisattva in Buddhism, who, as I noted in encounter 19, gets right up to the gateway to nirvana and then turns back to aid those still on the way, the autobiographer offers a gift to others, "a bait to [our] soul,"[9] as Saint Teresa puts it, allowing readers "to learn to understand themselves."[10]

The most dramatic and winsome demonstration I have ever seen of autobiographies being "a bait to the soul" happens during a meeting at the Collegeville Institute for Ecumenical and Cultural Research. It is the Feast of the Assumption. Some of the Catholics lead the group in prayer. Paul Bassett, a learned church historian from the Wesleyan Holiness tradition, is acutely uncomfortable. Instead of pouting, he goes on a quest to discover why his dear friends think those crazy things. "These are people I know and love," he says. "I owe it to them and to myself to learn why this day means so much to them." He goes to the library and checks out several autobiographies of Catholics, to understand better how their hearts and minds work.

When Paul does this, it activates a memory of mine. In the summer of 1969 I visit Mount Athos, the Greek peninsula, dedicated to Mary—on which, ironically, women are not allowed. It is home to more than twenty monasteries. For the Orthodox, it is the most sacred and revered spot on earth.

The terrain is unbelievably rocky, steep, forbidding. I am ill prepared, lacking water, wearing shoes designed for carpeted floors, and the maps are all but indecipherable. I am close to delirious with thirst.

I see, far down the hillside, a boat. My shouts and hand waving get the skipper's attention. On the boat I find myself uncontrollably praying, repeatedly, "Thank you, Mother of God, for protecting me on this, your holy mountain." Being a good Protestant, I am not supposed to believe or say things like this. I'm neither Orthodox nor Catholic, but in this moment I understand, viscerally, how their hearts and minds work, because mine work that way too.

Few if any Christian autobiographers reflect what critics of religion often taunt as "Come weal or come woe, our status is quo." On giving an account of their life from the perspective of their faith, they do not maintain that they have stayed put. Autobiographers whom I trust display, either directly or indirectly, a lingering affection for their own self prior to the transformation which is often the point toward which the whole story moves. I consider an author's not being totally alienated from her or his own past one mark of authenticity in Christian autobiography.

"The Roughness and Density of Life"

A second criterion for authenticity is suggested by a phrase of Lewis's, characterizing the difference he senses between religious imagination and secular imagination.

While still a committed atheist, Lewis began to notice that the authors who most appealed to him—G. K. Chesterton, John Milton, Edmund Spenser, Samuel Johnson, and, among the ancients, Plato, Aeschylus, Virgil—all had the annoying quality of being profoundly religious. "Writers who did not suffer from religion and with whom in theory my sympathy ought to have been complete—[George Bernard] Shaw and [H. G.] Wells and [John Stuart] Mill and [Edward] Gibbon and Voltaire—all seemed a little thin; what as boys we called 'tinny.'" He found them "entertaining, but hardly more. There seemed to be no depth in them. They were too simple. The roughness and density of life didn't appear in their books."[11]

As what I said in encounter 3 makes clear, I sharply disagree with Lewis's appraisal of Mill, whom I find both deep and complex, but Lewis's general point is sound.

The roughness and density of life. When Christianity is touted, often by very vocal critics of "secular humanism," as a panacea for all ills both public and private—when, as I noted in encounter 1, they "dump isolated Bible verses or happy faces" as though these constitute the gospel—the tradition is made to sound "tinny."

The Bible is rough and dense—"My God, my God, why have you forsaken me?" says Jesus—and so is Christian self-understanding. It torments me, it brings me joy, it brings me both and convinces me they are in essence the same thing—and sometimes it deprives me of both.

Saint Teresa remembers a time when "I had neither any joy in God nor any pleasure in the world. When I was in the midst of worldly pleasures, I was distressed by the remembrance of what I owed to God; when I was with God, I grew restless because of worldly affections."[12]

When I'm in the presence of someone who can say that—even if in my own story I'm skeptical of the sharp distinction between "worldly affections" and what is "owed to God"—I'm on holy ground.

IN A WORD

I encounter the therapeutic grace of God in the stories others tell of their own journeys—inward, outward, up, down, in circles—in many cases, all of the above.

therapeutic

Part Seven

IMAGINATIONS:
RELIGIOUS AND SCIENTIFIC

Grace in Science

From grace in autobiography to grace in science might seem a stretch. In my experience they're just a step apart, because both are holy ground where God's grace catches me off guard.

In 1999 I was intrigued—startled, even—by the Arts and Entertainment Network catalog of "the hundred most influential people of the [second] millennium." It sandwiched Martin Luther in third place between Charles Darwin at fourth and Isaac Newton at second. (Heading the list is Johannes Gutenberg.)[1] Such rankings are quirky, soon forgettable, but the concentration of science and religion so near the top suggests an interface that bears repeated visits.

In recent decades scientists and people of faith (the same person more often than is popularly supposed) have been engaged in sustained conversation. This significant reconnection has had negligible impact on churches, however. What is being talked about has seemed too esoteric or too technical—or too dangerous—for both clergy and laypersons, whose energies and attention are already taxed to the limit. There is neither time nor room for one more thing.

"Life, Too, Is Probably Round"

What is happening at the science-religion interface is not "just one more thing." It has potential for reversing the flattening of spiritual and cultural life that is so widely perceived these days. Vincent van Gogh identified the problem more than a century ago: "People used to think that the earth was flat. . . . Science demonstrates that the world as a whole is round. . . . For all that, people still persist in thinking that *life is flat* and runs from birth to death. But life, too, is probably round."[2]

Science and religion have developed different—often competing—*worldviews*. Each has a *language* not readily intelligible to the other. Distinct *professional communities*, with little overlap, have created folkways, practices, habits that form their inhabitants in radically dissimilar ways.

Both realms are aided and hindered by the organizational and institutional cultures they have created. While neither science nor religion is a monolith, both have well-developed schemes for marginalizing outliers (who are themselves subject to what C. S. Lewis called the temptation of "the inner ring"[3]).

However, if I focus on *imaginations*, which of course are shaped by worldview, language, community, marginalization, and many other factors, I probe a deep level where experience binds people together—whether they are self-conscious about the play of science and religion in their lives or are not aware of it but might find such reflection enlightening and enlivening. Scientists and people of faith—the humans who *do*, who *practice* science and religion— are put at the center. The abstractions "science" and "religion" lack equipment to have a conversation.

I'm not a scientist, but I have an appreciation for what scientists do that was shaped by a decision I made in college.

The Challenge of Physics 1

In my first year I spent a single day in Physics 1. I then opted to satisfy the "general education" requirement by taking a natural science course that was popularly known as "Biology for Poets." It wasn't disgraceful, but it wasn't particularly difficult or rigorous either.

During my last two years, two of my roommates were among the brightest physics majors in our class (one, Paul D'Andrea, later wrote his doctoral dissertation on Shakespeare and has become a noted playwright—go figure). I decided I needed to know more about the world they inhabited. In my senior year I enrolled in that introductory physics course—the one for majors and potential physicians—that I had run from three years earlier.

It was the toughest intellectual challenge I ever faced. It pushed mathematics beyond what I had mastered. The lab work tested my patience and my persistence. I realized that I was still only at the border of what my roommates knew and did, but at least I had a notion where their horizon was. I got a taste of how science is informed by imagination.

There are people in churches who fear that the scientific imagination will rob them of what sustains their spirit. Others feel cramped by a too-small God and universe, a too-narrow conception of themselves, theology painted on a tiny canvas. For many of these latter, the scientific imagination has made the grandeur of God accessible. There are people who go to the laboratory every day who say good riddance to God. There are others whose sense of mystery and wonder deepens and widens the more they explore—mystery that is not "what we haven't yet figured out," but that intensifies "the more we figure out."

When Einstein spoke of "holy curiosity" and "imagination [that] encircles the world,"[4] he was describing a real and practical and fundamentally human experience, generally available to people, not only to saints and Nobel laureates. The interface of science and religion is not an easy place, not always even a safe place—it is often turbulent—but there is movement and adventure there. I find room for the play of intellect, for exploration, for trying things out, for making mistakes, for beginning over, for returning to the starting point and seeing it, anew, for the first time.

In 2008 I am at that interface. I am a respondent to an address by Natalie Angier, Pulitzer Prize–winning science journalist for the *New York Times.*

I write to her afterward:

> It may surprise you to know that I'm a Christian who finds your atheism far more attractive than the dogmatic load that is often treated by the media as the norm for theology and religion. Your insistence that scientists are adventurers, that uncertainty is what they love, seems totally familiar to me. When Dave Stevenson [whom she had quoted] says, "People need to understand that science is dynamic and that we do change our minds. We have to. That's how science functions," he's describing the way my religious imagination works. Avoiding the "temptations of dogmatism and certitude" is something that Christians like me are trying to do all the time.
>
> I don't expect these texts [some things I'd written that I enclosed with the letter] will alter your fundamental convictions, but I hope they will be a window into a religious and theological world that is less cramped than what you find forbidding, distasteful, dangerous. I don't like that stuff any more than you do. Indeed, I suspect I like it even less.

The Jazz Ensemble

The institute where I worked spent time at that interface. We brought together two dozen people—some who occupy most of their time in laboratories, others who preach, study the Bible, or do theology, some early in their careers and others in retirement—for a week in each of three successive summers under the theme of "Visiting Religious and Scientific Imaginations Afresh." Three Russians participated, and many of us had a fourth occasion to gather, at an international conference on science and faith at the Saint Petersburg School of Religion and Philosophy.

Our image for the project was the jazz ensemble. Participants had practiced a lot. Jazz improvisation works because all the players know the chord progressions. They create in real time. Everybody is an authority. There isn't a conductor for the orchestra. There aren't even principal chairs in each section.

Jazz draws on and draws out competencies from various sources. We expected to be surprised by what turned up as people told narratives about the interplay of science and religion in their imaginations.

And we suspected we would come to know what C. S. Lewis knew, as put in the mouth of one of the characters in the first volume of his Space Trilogy: "When you and I met, the meeting was over very shortly, it was nothing. Now it is growing something as we remember it. But still we know very little about it. What it will be when I remember it as I lie down to die, what it makes in me all my days till then—that is the real meeting. The other is only the beginning of it."[5]

While I am not yet "lying down to die," I believe the institute project on science and faith has helped make in me something valuable in how and what I see.[6]

Views Long, Deep, and Wide

We learned to take a long view.

The science-religion tension seems new, but it isn't. The hammering out of Christian doctrine in the first few centuries was, in many ways, an effort to square Incarnation and Trinity with the science of the day (or rather, sciences; there were many competing theories of how the world actually works).

And it is always worth remembering that the newly rediscovered science of Aristotle, with which Saint Thomas Aquinas reconciled the whole of Christian dogma, was greeted with as much theological suspicion in the thirteenth century as Darwin was in the nineteenth. In 1277 the bishop of Paris, seconded the next year by the archbishop of Canterbury, declared some of Aristotle's propositions heretical—teaching them would get you excommunicated (though Thomas was exempt; he had died three years earlier).[7]

In addition to the long view, there is the deep view.

Religion could be dismissed by the scientific. The Russians tell of seventy years in which there was no dialogue. A Soviet journal, *Science and Religion*, had the sole purpose of showing science beating religion at every turn. Consultation participant Natalia Pecherskaya, rector of the Saint Petersburg School of Religion and Philosophy, relates that the university mathematics department even had a hymn that began, "Mathematicians are the salt of this world; physicists, our younger brothers, sing glory for us." Orthodox theology was deprived of dialogue with contemporary thought.

Or, science could be dismissed by the religious. "I went home at Christmas to my parents," says Gregory Maslowe. "We were talking about what I was studying, and I said cosmology and religion. My mother told me to stop: 'Creation isn't a story, it's biblical truth.' I haven't been able to integrate my own ideas of science and religion with the people I'm closest to."

Dawn Adams, a Choctaw scientist, says how alien to her are the dualisms that bedevil the debate. "I would say to people in church that I wanted to be a paleontologist; they said, 'What about religion?' This was like responding, when I said 'I want to drive a truck,' 'But what about cars?'"

And besides the long view and the deep view there is the wide view.

What is needed is not just a science-religion interface, but safe space. Reid Locklin made an especially winsome suggestion. "I started thinking about religion and science as roommates. They aren't consistent, they change all the time. They probably don't live up to each other's expectations. They are short on common activities but they have to share common space. They need a duty roster, some common activities, and separate spaces."

Roommates is only one image. Anne Foerst called to mind a picture that is both a vase and two faces, "but you cannot see the two simultaneously. Someone says it's much more a vase than two faces, another says the opposite, and a fight breaks out. Take the vase as religion, and the two faces as science. The two are completely interactive; they can't be without each other."

Science and Religion as Practices

What I begin to see through all the lenses—long, deep, wide—is some resonance between what science and religion are as practices, as what people do: in the words of David O'Fallon, both "combine urgency with playfulness, letting go with passion to carry through."

Science and religion in practice have the both/and characteristic that I learned early on from John Stuart Mill's essays on Bentham and Coleridge—but both science and religion can be corrupted, stopped dead in their tracks, by dogmatism. Catherine Nelson nails it: "You take a position and then start defending it, build up armor around you. It becomes not a conversation, but a war."

It needn't be this way.

Nelson continues. "Science is a matter of presenting yourself without armor, of stripping away the garbage that you bring in your mind and going at it one more time." She sees this as parallel to a relationship with God. "You show up in the lab the same way you show up in prayer. You have to get rid of the crap that gets in the way before you can have a conversation." And most of the time you get disabused of your prior assumptions, "simply because you are limited by the questions that you're able to ask. We are not very good at asking the right questions."

The right questions. Yes. That's my challenge—and my opportunity. I have as much privilege and responsibility to link religion to the thought of my time, including its science, as the Christians of previous ages, including the earliest ones, had in theirs.

IN A WORD

I encounter the adventurous grace of God when I realize that both religion and science combine urgency and playfulness.

Grace in a Hazelnut

The long view, the wide view, the deep view. Yes, science and religion need all three. Once upon a time they all came together in a hazelnut. But first, the context.

Science and religion are not abstractions, ideal types isolated from the flux of time. Fashioned by humans, both science and religion are as historically conditioned as anything else we do, even though proponents of religion and proponents of science often insist that their knowledge is timeless.

Dogmatism, whether religious or scientific, is driven by the passion to get everything settled. It has the allure of repose. I get to a place where I no longer have to worry, puzzle, lie awake at night wondering about things that don't fit or fretting about people who don't agree with me.

The so-called warfare between science and religion is really a chapter in the much larger story of the warfare between dogmatisms. If the dogmatists in both camps hijack the discussion, warfare is what we get. Drawing battle lines is what dogmatists do.

The story of the relationship between science and religion has been plotted on a variety of grids: conflict, strict separation, dialogue, among others. These all fall prey to abstraction, to treating science and religion as "things-in-themselves," pipers that play the tune to which their adherents dance. But I choreograph my life by imagination and improvisation, not by direct access to the divine will or to the blueprint of the universe.

I have three guides: Dame Julian of Norwich (ca. 1342–1413) from the fourteenth century; John Keats (1795–1821) from the nineteenth; and T. S. Eliot (1888–1965) from the twentieth.

First Guide: Julian—Analogy

Dame Julian holds a hazelnut in her hand and sees that it contains the whole universe.[1] She is not anticipating the Big Bang of current cosmology, which says that in the beginning the whole universe was a singularity much smaller than a hazelnut. She gets beneath and beyond particulars to what is universal. No, that isn't right. She is so clear-eyed about the particulars that she sees right into the heart of the universal.

Julian is illuminating the power of analogy to make meaning and intelligibility. There is nothing new in my highlighting analogy as a feature of human thinking, whether in science or religion or anything else. What is fresh about Julian is the way she wrests the analogical imagination free from hierarchy. In the classical "analogy of being," the lower I go "down" the series from the perfect original, the fainter the analogy becomes.

Julian means something else entirely. The analogy is in her perception, not in the object perceived. She is not probing to some underlying "essence." It's an optometric deepening of observation. She is seeing things rounded, because they are related to other things and finally to all things. I am in the realm of enlightenment, awakening, not in that of logic, whether deductive or inductive.

Analogy, in both religion and science, is an intuition, an experience. It's as if the imagination is supercooled so that interference disappears and unhindered superconductivity takes over.

If Dame Julian of Norwich instructs me about analogy, John Keats teaches me about discovery.

Second Guide: Keats—Discovery

Keats's first volume of poetry, published at age twenty-one, includes "On First Looking into Chapman's Homer."[2] It was not a scientific experiment that precipitated his amazement, though it might have been—Keats studied to be a doctor and passed his medical exams—but his reading of the *Iliad* and the *Odyssey*.

Nonetheless, I am sure that many scientists and many persons of faith know exactly what Keats means when he says that he felt "like some watcher of the skies / When a new planet swims into his ken," or like an explorer climbing a hill and seeing the Pacific Ocean spread out before him. This latter image includes two phrases especially significant for the character of discovery in both science and religion: "wild surmise" and "silent."

Both the person of faith and the scientist have moments when surmise pushes beyond established boundaries, surmise that appears wild. As I noted in encounter 4, physicist Wolfgang Pauli turned to his colleague Niels Bohr and said, "You probably think these ideas are crazy." Bohr replied, "I do, but unfortunately they are not crazy enough." When the earliest followers of Jesus, gathered on the day of Pentecost, started speaking in tongues, onlookers thought they were drunk. Peter had to quell suspicion by noting that it was only nine o'clock in the morning (Acts 2:1–15).

Surmises can seem wild. Sometimes, as Keats knew, words cannot express the truth of breakthrough. He would have understood the Zen admonition "Speak only if you can improve on the silence."

From Julian, analogy; from Keats, discovery. What from T. S. Eliot?

Third Guide: Eliot—Recognition

Eliot's great poem cycle, *Four Quartets*, published between 1936 and 1942, was written after his conversion to Christianity. The

poems are powerful for many reasons, not least because Eliot remembered what it was like to be without faith.

The Waste Land, published in 1922, is still cited as the clearest evidence of an early twentieth-century culture on the edge of
meaninglessness and despair. Eliot knew that hope could not paper
over hopelessness. He had to win his way through by taking the
way down, by unflinchingly facing his worst fears—by deciding
what to keep and what to throw away.

Because he will not fool himself, because he refuses cheap
grace, because he goes, as a scientist would, where the evidence
takes him, Eliot's report of what happens to him—and could happen to me—rings true.

Four lines near the end of "Little Gidding" (already referenced
in encounter 19), the last of the *Quartets*, have served me, for the
past sixty years, as the clearest chart of my experience:

> We shall not cease from exploration
> And the end of all our exploring
> Will be to arrive where we started
> And know the place for the first time.[3]

From Eliot I learn about recognition. The world is full of surprises, but often they have a quality of the familiar, like Mary Oliver's heron that appears above, in encounter 2.

"Something More Generous, Frightening and Authentic"

Scientists in recent decades have recorded many instances of such
comings full circle in their explorations. Fritjof Capra's *The Tao of
Physics* and Murray Gell-Mann's "eightfold way" theory that brought
order to the chaos created by the discovery of some one hundred
particles in the atom's nucleus are examples of correspondence between science and the ancient religious traditions of the East.

Anglican priest Angela Tilby grew up in a conservative evangelical family in England, went to Cambridge University, threw

religion away, studied physics, and found science reviving a sense of wonder in her. She then discovered that the Greek church fathers have a theology that resonates with current cosmology.

It was a second-century bishop, Irenaeus, Tilby says, who broke the chains of determinism, moralism, and rigidity that bound her, so she could enter "into something more generous, frightening and authentic." Tilby, remembering her own early years, remarks that "in all fundamentalism there is a refusal to acknowledge the beauty of complexity." She credits Eastern Christian theology with the virtue of not presuming "to know too much."[4]

Analogy, discovery, and recognition converge for me in an epigram that Jaroslav Pelikan called the motto of the scholarly life. It is Goethe's Faust who speaks the words:

> What you have as heritage,
> Take now as task;
> For thus you will make it your own![5]

I do not mimic, I do not echo, but I do not have to invent everything for myself. What I do is join the chorus.

IN A WORD

I encounter the compelling grace of God in the recovery, by both science and religion, of life's roundness, making the heritage of analogy, discovery, and recognition my own so that those who come after me will not cease from exploration, wild surmise, silence, and further exploration.

compelling

Grace on Darwin's Grave

In Westminster Abbey I have a really surprising encounter with God's grace, confirmed years later when I see the Bible and *On the Origin of Species* slapped together.

The crowd is pressing around so tight I cannot move. I glance down. I am standing on the grave of Charles Darwin.

I know Isaac Newton is buried here, so precedent favors the honoring of a great scientist. (Later, in 2018, Stephen Hawking's ashes would join the bones of Newton and Darwin.) But Newton thought of himself as a theologian—his writings on Scripture are more voluminous than his scientific works—while Darwin has for a century and a half, especially in the United States, symbolized the alleged incompatibility of science and religion.

Standing on Darwin's remains in church, I wonder: What does it mean for me, a Christian, to believe God is better served, even glorified, by Darwin, who eventually doubted God, than by those who, claiming to be God's defenders, consign Darwin and his followers to outer darkness?

On the Origin of Species, published in 1859, generates immediate resistance. When Bishop Samuel Wilberforce and Thomas Henry Huxley debate at Oxford in 1860, Wilberforce snidely asks Huxley whether he is descended from an ape on his grandmother's side or his grandfather's. Huxley's brilliant defense of Darwin's theory concludes with the rejoinder, "I would rather be the offspring of two apes than be a man and afraid to face the truth."[1]

The focal point of the argument is 1925, when John T. Scopes, a twenty-four-year-old high school mathematics teacher and coach—and substitute biology teacher—is charged with breaking a law that prohibits teaching, in any state-funded school in Tennessee, "any theory that denies the story of the Divine Creation of man as taught in the Bible, and to teach instead that man has descended from a lower order of animals."[2]

William Jennings Bryan, three times Democratic candidate for president, and secretary of state under President Woodrow Wilson, is the lead prosecuting attorney. The American Civil Liberties Union, founded only five years earlier, secures the services of prominent lawyer Clarence Darrow to lead the defense.

The trial ends with Scopes's conviction and a $100 fine (almost $1,400 today). A year later the verdict is overturned on a technicality by the Tennessee Supreme Court. In 1968 the United States Supreme Court declares that such laws are primarily religious in nature and therefore ruled out by the Establishment Clause of the Constitution.

The Scopes Trial in the American Imagination

The Scopes Trial plays a peculiar role in the American imagination, because historical recollection is interwoven so intricately with creative imagination. The 1955 play *Inherit the Wind*, made widely known by the 1960 movie, takes a clearly pro-Darrow slant, but this is as much a response to the cultural chill of Senator Joseph McCarthy's witch hunts of the mid-1950s as it is a commentary on the trial itself.

The play is full of words—eloquent, funny, biting—but the moment etched in my memory is the final scene, with no words at all. Alone now in the courtroom, Henry Drummond, the character modeled on Darrow, notices a copy of *On the Origin of Species* on a table, and picks it up.

> He rotates the volume in his hand, this one book has been the center of the whirlwind. He is about to put it into his briefcase when he notices the Bible at the end of the Judge's bench. He picks up the Bible in the other hand, looks from one volume to the other, balancing them thoughtfully as if his hands were scales. He half smiles, half shrugs. Then Drummond resoundingly slaps the two books together, side by side, jams them into his briefcase, neither one on top. Slowly, he climbs to the level of the empty town square. . . . Curtain.[3]

The significance of this scene is not historical in the strict sense. If I were in that courtroom in Dayton, Tennessee, in July 1925, I'd probably see nothing of the sort. But in a more profound historical sense, the image tells much about the decades since the Scopes Trial. The "half smile" and "half shrug" of the stage directions illuminate the slightly comic character of the dogmatisms on both sides.

There are, to be sure, scientific dogmatisms. Evolution can do without God; to say, further, that it rules God out is not itself a scientific statement. There is much debate in scientific circles about the details of evolution, but it is entirely wrong-headed for defenders of the biblical account of creation to claim that disagreement between scientists undermines the theory.

Churches these days send mixed messages. The Roman Catholic Church, which could be said to have learned a lesson from its disastrous treatment of Galileo, officially endorses evolution as compatible with Christian teaching.[4] Many conservative Protestants stoutly resist any story of how things came to be that doesn't adhere literally to the account in Genesis. The Creation Museum in Petersburg, Kentucky, operated by the organization Answers in Genesis, in its first decade of operation had over two and a half million visitors, who, according to the website, have learned "why God's infallible Word, rather than man's faulty assumptions, is the place to begin if we want to make sense of our world," and have been "shown" that humans and dinosaurs were contemporaries.[5]

What Counts as Human?

The theological puzzle, however, is not centered on the challenge to the biblical portrayal of the special creation of human beings. Rather, it's in the question of what counts as being made in the image of God—where to draw the line? What about Neanderthals? Or, in the other direction, what about our further "evolution" toward artificial intelligence? As theologian and AI expert Anne Foerst asks, "Can [*Star Trek*'s Commander] Data, as flawless machine, be treated and perceived as a person, not a human but nonetheless worthy of personhood and dignity?"[6] Her answer, both learned and subtle, seems to be yes—in part, at least, because the category of "person" is itself so fluid. (And the conclusion to the first season, in 2020, of the new series *Star Trek: Picard* transposes the question into yet another key: Picard dies—or "dies"—and a scan of his brain, perhaps to be called "himself," is implanted in a "body" identical to his.[7] Season 2 will invite further theological reflection!)

The discovery that I share 99 percent of my genome with chimpanzees and bonobos further complicates the picture. Does that 1 percent difference constitute the image of God? It used to be thought that self-consciousness and a moral sense set us apart, but recent research in the behavior of various other species, both what can be observed directly and what is detected by brain scans, is eroding confidence that these traits belong to us alone.

Paul Bassett, the Wesleyan Holiness theologian who in encounter 20 assembled Catholic autobiographies to learn what the dogma of the Assumption means to Catholics, is grateful to his mother for lowering the theological thermostat when he, as a child, came home and asked about evolution. She replied: "It's not something you really have to worry about. I wonder if the apes will ever forgive us?" Another theologian friend, Nancy Howell, says, "I'd like to go into the field to work with animals who are crossing lines in the sand that we draw." When he preached to the birds, Saint Francis may already have intuited what Darwin demonstrated.

I don't have a clear answer to the question about the image of God and Neanderthals and bonobos and androids. I do not know what we will eventually come to accept. A clear answer would require putting the brakes on breathtaking research discoveries that are happening at warp speed every day. The history of theology is littered with discredited "definitive" resolutions.

Evolution, Creationism, and Medicine

This encounter began with the question of evolution in the classroom in Tennessee almost a century ago. It ends with a more recent question of evolution in a hospital room in Florida—that in fact spills over into classrooms today.

I'm visiting my daughter Juliet at the Mayo Clinic's Saint Luke's Hospital in Jacksonville. She has had a pancreas transplant—major surgery by any standard—and a series of infections has prolonged her hospital stay.

Sitting by her bed, my thoughts are focused on what is right here: Juliet, the nurses and doctors and orderlies and housekeepers, the tubes and machines, the pills and IVs and blood draws. A hospital provides constant incentive to live in the moment.

After I leave to return home, however, something I saw repeatedly while at Saint Luke's moves front and center in my consciousness, jolts me out of the moment into cosmic speculation.

Every room in Saint Luke's is equipped with a computer on which the patient's information is recorded (medical charts used to be measured in pages, now in gigabytes). When a doctor or nurse is not entering data, the screen saver scrolls through Mayo's mission statement, its vision statement, and its motto. The motto, words of Charles H. Mayo, reads, "Heal the Sick, Advance the Science."

These six words, etched indelibly in my memory, are the rejoinder to those who insist that creationism, and particularly what is called "creation science," is on a par with evolution as an explanation for the way the world is.

What worries me, as a Christian, is the rallying of so many Christians to creationism and their malign influence on school boards. They think they are defending God by insisting that Genesis is an account of how the world came to be as it is, and that its account is on a level playing field with evolution. Those who champion creationism as saving God from Darwin remind me of Job's so-called comforters (who appeared in encounter 1). They said all the "theologically correct" things about God and were subsequently scolded by God for getting it all wrong.

In order to heal the sick, you have to advance the science. Every instance of healing in Juliet's room is a testimony to the powerful, comprehensive, expansive, and rigorous truth of the theory of evolution. Eminent geneticist Theodosius Dobzhansky—of whom a colleague said, "He would work as a scientist all week and then on Sunday get down on his knees and pray to God"—declared in the March 1973 issue of *The American Biology Teacher*, "Nothing in biology makes sense except in the light of evolution."[8] When your daughter is in a hospital bed, believe me, you want biology to make sense.

God is dishonored by those who snipe at evolution and distract schools from teaching sound biological science. Those professionals at Saint Luke's Hospital—a place named after the patron saint of physicians—demonstrate that God is glorified when science is advanced, even when some of the scientists who do the advancing don't talk about God at all.

In Westminster Abbey I was standing on the grave of one whose insatiable holy curiosity revealed, in a fundamental way, how the world actually works. Any deity dislodged by such knowledge isn't worthy of worship, or even of defense.

IN A WORD

I encounter the resilient grace of God when I recognize that Darwin's doubts about God are more faithful than the dogmatic certainties of his opponents.

Grace in *Scientific American*

An aphorism with an uncertain pedigree—as is true with so many—was recently cited by Rowan Williams shortly before his retirement as archbishop of Canterbury: "You have to preach with a Bible in one hand and a newspaper in the other."[1] I seldom preach, but I think and write a lot, and I find *Scientific American* as useful and necessary as the newspaper.

At one level, the magazine draws me in because it provides challenge and resources simply in terms of information.

For example, the cover story in the February 2015 issue is headlined "Inside the Neandertal Mind."[2] As I noted in the previous encounter, I am intrigued and puzzled by the place of other species of the genus *Homo* in the scheme of things. Are Neanderthals, who were dominant for hundreds of thousands of years, made "in the image of God" as much as I, a *Homo sapiens*, am (note how we salute ourselves by the name we give ourselves)?

The question is made even subtler by the recently uncovered evidence that Neanderthals and my direct ancestors interbred. I carry Neanderthal DNA. Moreover, current study is demonstrating a Neanderthal cultural sophistication that far exceeds what had been surmised before. In a 2014 article called "Our Neanderthal Complex: What if our ancient relatives did 'human' better?" Lydia Pyne, a researcher at the Institute for Historical Studies at the University of Texas at Austin, puts the issue succinctly: "We have moved from one narrative, about human superiority, to another, about familial belonging."[3]

The *Scientific American* article doesn't solve my puzzle, but it cautions me against making any definitive theological judgment that depends on there being a sharp demarcation between what I consider human and what not.

At the other end of the spectrum of what counts as human is an article in that same issue about a breakthrough in computing technology. Electronic components that act like neurons can both calculate and store information, increasing exponentially computer speed and efficiency. At what point does "artificial" in "artificial intelligence" become moot? I can't peremptorily rule out the possibility that a robot might count as a person.

And there is nearly always in an issue of *Scientific American* some new mind-blowing discovery in cosmology, such as the likelihood of planets even better suited than Earth for life, or the theoretical possibility (probability?) that there are multiple universes. On this latter point, it is worth noting that some early church theologians thought it very well might be so.[4]

But it isn't just information that *Scientific American* gives me. There are three dimensions of it that correspond to fundamental theological motifs that I've spent my career studying.

First is *tradition*.

Tradition—"50, 100 & 150 Years Ago"

Scientific American is of course concerned to report the latest thing. Many articles upend what has been believed before. Jesus's "You have heard it said . . . , but I tell you" is not unlike a common refrain in the articles. But the magazine, which began publication in 1845, in its monthly feature called "50, 100 & 150 Years Ago: Innovation and discovery as chronicled in *Scientific American*," testifies to the dependence of "the latest thing" on what has gone before.

The February 2015 issue recalls a warning in 1965 against "widespread use of pesticides and detergents without preliminary tests of their effects on environmental pollution," and an alert to the dangers of a high-altitude nuclear explosion over the Pacific. In 1915, when World War I is in full swing, the importance of new portable X-ray machines for use in military hospitals is highlighted. In 1865, people in Paris are becoming anxious about smallpox, and vaccination directly from cows is proving effective.

These specific instances are simply "for example"—though concerns for the environment, the use of technology for healing (medical X-rays) and not mass destruction (nuclear explosion), and vaccinations for public health all have clear and ongoing theological ramifications.

The chief significance for me of the regular appearance of "50, 100 & 150 Years Ago" is the reminder that science is properly understood as a human activity exercised through time. Even when a conclusion is superseded, it is seldom suppressed or buried. I quoted Jaroslav Pelikan in encounter 7, relating to religion: "Tradition is the living faith of the dead; traditionalism is the dead faith of the living." *Scientific American* says something like this about science.

Exploration

Exploration—the corollary to tradition as "living tradition"—is the second dimension of *Scientific American* that corresponds to fundamental theological motifs.

Regularly in reading *Scientific American* articles I get caught up in the excitement of discovery. There are "strange new worlds" to explore right here and now. That's what I'm doing every month when I read *Scientific American.*

Many of the writers have already published their findings in more technical journals. I'm sure that in most cases it would take skill way beyond what I have, especially in mathematics, to detect in those publications the adventure that led to the conclusion. But when they are writing for the lay public, they are really good at making intelligible without dumbing down (or the magazine's editors are really good at helping them be clear). They tell stories of adventure.

Sometimes they go full speed ahead and reach the goal. More often, there are fits and starts, dead ends, and, my favorite, a conclusion that says we have a long way yet to go. Acknowledgments of help along the way far exceed gloatings over rivals vanquished.

While not all the writers (maybe very few of them) would put it the way cosmologist Brian Greene does, I believe they generally trust the universe to be enticing them, if not guiding them.

"The universe in a sense guides us toward truths," Greene writes, "because those truths are the things that govern what we see." In consequence, "we're all being steered in the same direction. Therefore, the difference between making a breakthrough and not often can be just a small element of perception . . . that puts things together in a different way." Greene's desire for breakthrough shows me an end run around certainty of either a dogmatic or a skeptical sort.

Greene evokes what I detect over and over again in *Scientific American* articles as the scheme of scientific advance. "I like to say things more than one way," he writes. The reason for this is a paradox of scientific method. "Everybody's looking at a problem one way, and you come at it from the back. That different way of getting there somehow reveals things that the other approach didn't."[5]

This "coming at it from the back" resonates with so much of what I believe to be essential in religion: Erasmus's admonition that we "make mistakes together or individually, . . . [and] wisely overlook things,"[6] which I proposed for an ecumenical coat of arms; Augustine's declaration to God that "You took me up from behind my own back where I had placed myself because I did not wish to observe myself, and you set me before my face";[7] the illumination brought to Scripture by feminist attention to its silences; and Sir Henry Chadwick's disarming "I'm rereading all the sources."[8]

Community

The third dimension of *Scientific American* that corresponds to theological motifs, after tradition and exploration, is *community*.

Community is essential to religion, but sometimes scientists do it better than religious folk. Geographical boundaries are regularly brushed away in the sciences. In the course of an article, reference may be made to teams of scientists whose individual bases of operation are as disparate as the United States and Japan and Brazil, or Taiwan and Italy and Ukraine.

And while scientists are no less (but, I suspect, no more) subject to rivalries and envy and the temptation of "the inner circle" (to use C. S. Lewis's phrase) than denizens of any other field, they are increasingly embedding themselves in large research projects, especially in particle physics, in which a resultant article will have scores, even hundreds of names attached.

Tradition, exploration, and community—these are the thematic resonances between science and religion that I detect in *Scientific American*. There is an article in the March 2007 issue that relates directly to my ponderings on memory.

MyLifeBits

It poses directly the question: What if I could remember *everything*?

The article reports that Gordon Bell, of Microsoft Research, is working on MyLifeBits, a project "to record all of his communications with other people and machines, as well as the images he sees, the sounds he hears and the Web sites he visits."[9]

Everything I read, look at, every breath I take and beat of my heart and precise spot on earth I'm at at any moment—for sixty years or more—can be stored on a flash drive. Bell celebrates this. My reaction as I read: it's creepy.

And I think: What technology is making possible has long teased imaginations into great works of literature. First in rank is Marcel Proust's *Remembrance of Things Past*, where the taste of a madeleine dipped in tea sparks seven volumes of recollection, often of tiny details.

At first glance Bell doesn't seem so different. "Digital memories allow one to vividly relive an event with sounds and images, enhancing personal reflection in much the same way that the Internet has aided scientific investigations." But this sounds to me a lot like what I too often say when taking a photo on a vacation trip: "I'll really look at this when we get back."

If I retrieve a web page I visited five years ago, have I really "enhanced personal reflection"? Retrieving is not the same as remembering. Proust didn't need MyLifeBits. It was sufficient for him that "the mind feels overtaken by itself." The remembering that happened when his mind was thus overtaken he fashioned into something that enhances the personal reflection of anyone who bothers to read his book.

There is a moral problem, as well as an intellectual one, in Bell's project. "The cost was high: it took a personal assistant working for several years to complete the task." In other words, while Bell was recording everything, even "logos on coffee mugs and T-shirts," his assistant's life was consumed by Bell's life. Granted, the digitizing of so much these days means capture can increasingly be automatic, but it is still likely that some lives will be measured out in others' lives.

Bell says that thanks to MyLifeBits, "future historians will be able to examine the past in unprecedented detail." I'm not sure those future historians will be grateful for information about every website I visited. I suspect that at the end of a day drowning in terabytes they will say, "Let's get a cup of tea and a madeleine."

Skepticism without Cynicism

For 214 issues, from April 2001 to January 2019, there is one regular feature of *Scientific American* that I haven't yet mentioned. Anyone familiar with the magazine might assume I have intentionally left it out: "Skeptic: Viewing the world with a rational eye." This monthly column was by Michael Shermer, publisher of *Skeptic* magazine and—no surprise—not a fan of religion.

Shermer can be biting and caustic, but usually with good reason. I often find his critique more appealing than the view he is opposing. Moreover, he isn't just negative; in fact, that's not his usual angle. Rather, as the title of the column says, he "views the world with a rational eye." He wants to make clear that a rational eye is neither myopic nor bloodless.

He is even-handed in his judgments. In the February 2014 issue he outlines several technologically grounded stratagems for utopian futures and then says of them, "I am skeptical of these schemes but not cynical about them. New ideas have to come from somewhere."[10]

"Skepticism without cynicism"—that's an attitude that should undergird tradition, exploration, and community, in religion as well as in science. Tradition has to guard against traditionalism; exploration can become an ego trip; community is susceptible to sabotage by "the inner circle." Being alert to these subversions— being skeptical but not cynical—is the best antidote.

IN A WORD

I encounter the tentative grace of God when I find that coming at religion or science from the back reveals new truths, justifying an attitude of skepticism without cynicism.

Part Eight

DISTURBANCES OF DOGMA

Grace in Coventry Cathedral
and on the Hudson River

In the 1929 interview in which he observes that "imagination encircles the world," noted in encounter 21, Albert Einstein also muses on his own identity. "If I were not a physicist, I would probably be a musician. I often think in music. I live my daydreams in music. I see my life in terms of music."[1]

A musician has most compellingly shown me how imagination encircles *the world*—doesn't escape it or leave it behind.

Composer Benjamin Britten appeared earlier, in encounter 18, where the Royal Danish Ballet's rendition of *The Young Person's Guide to the Orchestra* became a visual and visceral image of diversity in unity. He appears again, here, because in a single sentence he captures an essential feature of Christian identity.

First, though, the context.

In 1940 the medieval Coventry Cathedral was bombed by the Nazis. The ruins, on which the then provost had inscribed the words "Father, forgive," remain alongside the newly constructed cathedral, which was dedicated in 1962. Britten's *War Requiem*, composed for the occasion, weaves together the traditional Mass for the Dead and nine poems of Wilfred Owen, among the greatest of war poets, who was killed in France just a week before the armistice that ended World War I.

In 1964 Britten was chosen, from among more than a hundred nominees, as the first recipient of the Robert O. Anderson Aspen Award in the Humanities. The award, given by the Aspen Institute, honors "the individual anywhere in the world judged to have made the greatest contribution to the advancement of the humanities."

In his speech accepting the award, Britten says that when given a commission, "I want to know in some detail the conditions of the place where it will be performed, the size and acoustics, what instruments or singers will be available and suitable, the kind of people who will hear it, and what language they will understand— and even sometimes the age of the listeners and performers." He realizes that "the text of my *War Requiem* was perfectly in place in Coventry Cathedral—the Owen poems in the vernacular, and the words of the Requiem Mass familiar to everyone—but it would have been pointless in Cairo or Peking."[2]

"Performance Imposes Conditions"

Then, generalizing from this specific instance to what I consider a profound theological principle, Britten says, "Music does not exist in a vacuum, it does not exist until it is performed, and performance imposes conditions." This he does not regret. On the contrary, the conditions "are not only a restriction, but a challenge, an inspiration."

"Performance imposes conditions." Three words that encapsulate the irony of an incarnational religion.

Becoming human entails dying. When Jesus predicts his own death, Peter, who has just identified Jesus as the Messiah, objects: "This must never happen to you!" Then Jesus calls Peter Satan, and accuses him of "setting your mind not on divine things but on human things" (Matt. 16:21–23). In other words, Peter has failed to realize that God's performance as human imposes conditions.

Britten said, "It is the easiest thing in the world to write a piece virtually or totally impossible to perform—but oddly enough that is not what I prefer to do; I prefer to study the conditions of performance and shape my music to them."

In 2009 the world was riveted by another instance of performance imposing conditions, with similar theological implications.

Flight 1549

"I needed to touch down with the wings exactly level . . . the nose slightly up . . . at a descent rate that was survivable . . . just above our minimum flying speed but not below it. And I needed to make all these things happen simultaneously."

Three and a half minutes, and all in a day's work for Chesley "Sully" Sullenberger as he recounted it to Katie Couric on the television news magazine *60 Minutes*.[3]

Sullenberger's remarks, about the January 15, 2009, landing of US Airways Flight 1549 in the Hudson River and the survival of all 155 people on board, riveted me because they were so understated, so matter-of-fact. As I listened, mesmerized, I realized that Flight 1549 is not only inspirational but also instructive.

First, I should always honor expertise, which is not necessarily the same as confidence. Sully could honestly, without bragging, say, "I was sure I could do it," because "my entire life up to that moment had been a preparation to handle that particular moment."

I'm in favor of prayer, but had I been on that plane I'd have hoped the pilot wasn't praying. Sully said he wasn't: "I would imagine somebody in back was taking care of that for me while I was flying the airplane. My focus at that point was so intensely on the landing. I thought of nothing else."

Because he was thinking of nothing else, Sully managed "to make all these things happen simultaneously."

Second, leadership and teamwork are two sides of the same coin. Once the captain made the "brace for impact" statement, he heard the flight attendants shouting their response: "Heads down. Stay down." "I felt very comforted by that. I knew immediately that they were on the same page. That if I could land the airplane, they could get them out safely." You don't want a slash-and-burn "leader" in the pilot's seat.

Third, hospitality comes naturally in crisis, so why can't it be normal operating procedure in less trying circumstances? One reason everybody survived the crash is that no one tried to be the only survivor. Nobody was "voted off the island."

According to a passenger, Gerry McNamara, "There was some panic—people jumping over seats and running toward the doors, but we soon got everyone straightened out and calmed down. . . . Everyone worked together—teamed up and in groups to figure out how to help each other. . . . I witnessed the best of humanity that day."[4]

And hospitality wasn't just on the plane. Boats, including Hudson River ferries that are not designed for rescue, showed up almost instantaneously.

Fourth, everybody is finally connected to everybody else; no story is isolated. One of the survivors had lost a brother, a firefighter, in the collapse of the World Trade Center on September 11, 2001.

In a particularly poignant *60 Minutes* moment, Sully and his wife read their favorite letter, from someone whose eighty-four-year-old father had called from his apartment house in Manhattan to say that the plane could have hit a building like his and killed thousands. "As a Holocaust survivor my father taught me that to save a life is to save a world, as you never know what the person you've saved or his or her progeny will go on to contribute to the peace and healing of the world."

This resonates with an insight from David O'Fallon, spoken in the consultation on religious and scientific imaginations I talked about in encounter 21. "We need to protect ideas and images, especially those of young people, and hold them for the time when they might be useful again. You never know when a piece of our cultural DNA that seems useless, even 'junk,' right now might be just what we need in ten years or a hundred or a thousand."

Flight 1549 is about the renewal of human community. Expertise developed through practice is to be valued, not distrusted. Leaders are servants, not bullies. We all do better when we all do better.[5] We're all part of the same story. That's certainly not the whole of Christian theology, but it's a piece of it.

Sully's contribution to theology is very different from that of Rayford Steele, pilot of the transatlantic Pan-Continental flight that begins the first volume of the *Left Behind* series.[6] More than a hundred passengers suddenly disappear. "First one, then another cried out when they realized their seatmates were missing but their clothes were still there. They cried, they screamed, they leaped from their seats." Steele realizes that he and the remaining passengers have been "left behind."

The God I know is revealed in US Airways 1549, not Pan-Continental 3597.

Crosses were made from nails that had held together the ancient roof of Coventry Cathedral. One of the crosses is above the altar in the new cathedral. Another of those crosses was given to Kaiser Wilhelm Memorial Church in Berlin, which was destroyed by Allied bomb attacks and is also kept as a ruin alongside a newer building.

Flight 1549 linked those passengers and 9/11 and the Holocaust and generations yet to come. Imagination does truly encircle the world.

IN A WORD

I encounter the demanding grace of God when performance imposes conditions.

demanding

Grace in Art

If performance imposes conditions, in the life of artists those conditions can be perilous.

Murder, grand larceny, arson, kidnapping, libel—art could bring all these charges against religion. In the name of religion paintings and sculptures and mosaics and windows have been smashed, toppled, burned, ridiculed, satirized.

Yet when I walk through virtually any museum I realize that without religion many walls would be bare and display cases empty. Divine beings gaze out at me. I suspect that viewers unfamiliar with religious traditions find art museums peculiarly unknown territory.

I recommend to museum curators that when they hear reports of some sort of religious revival, they increase two budget allocations: acquisitions . . . and security.

Constantia's Consternation

It's the fourth century. I have an appointment with Constantia, sister of Emperor Constantine—he who has publicly endorsed Christianity, though he'll wait until his deathbed to be baptized, since he's pretty sure he'll have to do some skulduggery in his role as emperor.

"I've asked Bishop Eusebius of Caesarea to send me a picture of Christ," Constantia tells me. "I thought my request innocent enough, even pious, in good religious taste. But Eusebius was not pleased. What he sent in reply was not a picture but a stinging rebuke: 'The true Christian does not need material props for faith.' The bishop was disappointed in me; he thought I had advanced beyond what he calls the weakness of 'spiritual infancy.'"[1]

I respond to Constantia that Eusebius's is not the last word.

"Four centuries from now," I tell her, "one of your brother's successors—a woman, Empress Irene—declares that objecting to pictures of Christ is heretical because it implies that Christ didn't become fully human. After all, being human means a picture can be made of you. The arguments are fierce. In the course of decades, people on both sides get put in prison, even killed."

Moving ahead another eight hundred years, "Bishops of Rome in the period we call the Renaissance commission artists to portray Christ," I inform Constantia, "and even God the Father, not to mention the cherubim and seraphim, the glorious company of the apostles, the goodly fellowship of the prophets, and the noble army of martyrs, on the walls and ceilings and altars of churches. Make your request twelve hundred years from now and you receive an enthusiastic response—especially if you offer to pay handsomely for the picture."

On to the twentieth century. I tell Constantia about theologian Paul Tillich. "He argues that the art with the greatest religious depth is usually concerned with apparently 'secular' subjects. When he gets your request he responds that your instincts are right but you are mistaken in what you ask for. What you really want is not a portrait of Christ but a still life by Cézanne."

If I take Constantia as a model for Christians who are serious about their faith but untrained in the fine points of theology, I see how confusing the relation of Christianity and art is.

In the fourth century her request is denied; in the eighth it provokes bitter, even lethal dispute; in the sixteenth it is superabundantly granted; in the twentieth she is told to look elsewhere.

As if this were not puzzle enough, her confusion quickly becomes worse confounded.

"Even a century ago," I tell Constantia, "when the church was in the shadows, pictures of Christ that are reminiscent of the traditional figures of Roman emperors and philosophers started appearing on sarcophagi and in Christian places of worship. In other words, Eusebius's opinion is not unchallenged even now."

I carry her consternation forward to the sixteenth century. "If you happen to pose your question to John Calvin instead of to the pope, you are subjected to a withering denunciation of all images of God in any of the three persons: 'All those who seek for God in a visible figure, not only decline, but actually revolt, from the true study of piety.'[2] Eusebius tells you your faith is weak. Calvin declares your desire wicked."

And in the twentieth century, "Tillich's acknowledgment of the religious dimension of 'secular' art is counterpoised by the theology of Karl Barth, who insists on a radical distinction between the word of God and cultural life," I tell her. "Barth's love of the music of Mozart is famous, but someone I know once asked Barth how he reconciled his passion for Mozart with his theological asceticism. Barth quickly changed the subject."

Does Constantia get the point? I can't be sure. An emperor's sister learns to be circumspect. But my visit to her time and to subsequent eras makes one thing evident: the search for a simple, clear-cut, no-loose-ends answer to the question of the relation of artistic imagination to the Christian tradition is futile. What one Christian calls heresy another calls a bedrock of orthodoxy, and what is kitsch to one Christian is another's connection to God.

Whatever the connection is, though, art moves me at levels far deeper than the rational. Artists are like a spy I meet in one of John le Carré's novels, who "walked the wide streets, analyzing nothing, alert to everything."[3]

I don't expect to find the definitive answer to the relation of art and religion. I am always on the lookout, though, for fresh and unexpected clues. I find one among people who repeatedly show me an ancient and ever new way to be Christian: Benedictine monastics.

Saint John's: Entanglement of Bible and Abbey Church

To provide context, I go far afield and invoke a concept from quantum physics, which allows me to correlate two very different works of art: the Saint John's Abbey Church[4] in Collegeville, Minnesota, built in the 1950s, and the Saint John's Bible,[5] created in the first decade of the twenty-first century, the first illuminated manuscript of the Bible commissioned by a monastery in five hundred years.

During the celebration of the Solemnity of the Holy Trinity in the Abbey Church on June 18, 2011, I see Donald Jackson, one of the world's foremost calligraphers, walk up the central aisle to present to Abbot John Klassen the final page of the Saint John's Bible. In a conversation with a Saint John's monk many years earlier, Jackson said his dream was to handwrite the Bible ("the calligrapher's Sistine Chapel," as he put it).

This stunning vellum page, blue and red and gold, placed on the altar of the church built a half century earlier, prompts in me a cascade of connections across time and space.

High on the world's weirdness list according to modern physics is the phenomenon of "entanglement"—a particle at the quantum level "knowing" what another particle, perhaps even on the other side of the universe, is doing, and reacting to it. Einstein called it "spooky action-at-a-distance."[6] Many physicists recently speculate that entanglement operates also on larger scales.[7]

The folio on the altar suggests to me an entanglement between the architectural imagination of Marcel Breuer and the artistic imagination of Donald Jackson. Each "knew" what the other was up to and reacted accordingly. The passage of time doesn't matter.

In the early 1950s the monks of Saint John's decide to build a new church. "Who says it needs to look like 'a church'?" they wonder.

The monks understand that tradition is not doing *what* predecessors did (traditionalism) but *as* they did. So they ask a pathbreaking architect, a Jew, to reimagine what might count as a church. As Marcel Breuer said, "In architecture you buy something that doesn't yet exist."[8] This was as true of Gothic arches in twelfth-century Paris as it is of pleated concrete in twentieth-century Collegeville. Abbot Suger of Saint-Denis and Abbot Baldwin of Saint John's both had to break with traditionalism in order to keep tradition alive.

Benedictines are true keepers of tradition, because they know that what seems traditional to us was the result of boldness and innovation—and they know that things take time. If something doesn't get settled this quarter or this year or this decade or even this century, there is no warrant for giving up. They know, too, that things must be done together, and they will have to overcome resistance and discouragement (not all the monks initially think Breuer's plan is God's will). Like monks in every age, those of Saint John's don't get stuck in the past, nor do they suppose the story culminates in them.

Saint John's, at the very end of the twentieth century, remembered forward for the twenty-first century.

One might suppose that contracting for a handwritten, illuminated Bible would be an instance of doing *what* their forerunners did, not *as* they did.

Sometimes, though—after a hiatus of five hundred years, for instance—what is very old becomes very new once more. A Bible written and illuminated by hand, with persistence and patience over a period of thirteen years, is these days so startlingly countercultural that people all over the world take notice. Words, their flavor diluted in oceans of printer's ink, can suddenly be tasted again.

In the past two or three centuries advances in science and encounters with other religious traditions undermined confidence in the Bible as a trustworthy guide. The genius of the Saint John's Bible is to turn the problem into an asset.

Imagery of what has been seen as a threat—double helixes of DNA and planets in orbit and menorahs and Buddhist prayer wheels and the voice print of an American Indian chant and so much more—is incorporated joyfully, winsomely into the illuminations. They don't just "illustrate." Each of them is like a plucked sitar string, which then sets up resonances both in the words of the Bible and, especially, in the white spaces where the mystery that's behind it all dwells. The text sounds different because you're getting the chords, not just the single note.

I wish Constantia had slipped through a time warp to sit beside me on Trinity Sunday in 2011. She'd not have found the answer to what she asked Eusebius, but I suspect that gazing at that folio on the altar in that church, she'd have come up with a more interesting request.

IN A WORD

I encounter the enduring grace of God when in art, repeatedly, what is very old becomes very new once more.

enduring

Grace on a Baseball Diamond

The grace of God can be encountered anywhere—on a baseball diamond as well as in an abbey church.

I reach into the cupboard and take out one of those souvenir cups where hot liquid on the inside changes the picture on the outside. As I pour the coffee, baseball players slowly emerge from a field of corn. I am tossed back to April 28, 2007.

My younger son, Brendan, and I are in Dyersville, Iowa. He has brought me here as a sixty-eighth birthday present, to a town that has been a pilgrimage destination since 1989 (almost a million visitors).

We're here to see the baseball diamond in a cornfield that figures as both reality and symbol in the movie *Field of Dreams*.[1] The film, nominated for an Academy Award, is based on the 1982 novel *Shoeless Joe* by W. P. Kinsella. I saw the movie with my older son, Stephan, shortly after it came out.

The film's protagonist, former 1960s hippie and current Iowa farmer Ray Kinsella, hears a voice: "If you build it, he will come." Ray knows that "he" is Joe Jackson, accused, probably falsely, in the "Black Sox" World Series scandal of 1919. "It" is a baseball field.

Ray's wife, Annie, after a brief initial skepticism, encourages him to take the voice seriously. Despite all the reasons not to do it, Ray does it.

When the field is finished Ray says, "I have just created something totally illogical," to which Annie responds, "That's what I like about it." The neighbors, staunch and skeptical farmers, and especially Annie's banker brother, think Ray is crazy. They call him to "reality."

The Fluid Boundary between Perception and Reality

God and Jesus hardly figure in what all these people say—the former is named sixteen times, half of them in "Oh my God!"; the latter only once, and not in a worshipful way—but the story is theologically profound. It draws me into the fluid boundary between perception and reality. It doesn't claim that the world is only what we think it is but rather demonstrates that when we think only in terms of scarcity, of "me first," of fear, we get reality wrong.

The question "Is this heaven?," when first asked, provokes the response, "No. It's Iowa." By the time it's asked again, the question starts a conversation that begins with Iowa but concludes with Ray smiling and nodding, "Then maybe this is heaven."

Still Iowa, but not at all the same. Or rather, as T. S. Eliot would say, Ray has arrived where he started and knows the place for the first time. As with Mary Oliver's heron that "rises into the air and is gone" back in encounter 2, "it isn't a miracle, but the common thing."

Hospitality That Goes Beyond Even the Living

The Field of Dreams, incongruous out here in the corn, feels like sacred ground because what happens here is hospitality. It's hospitality that goes beyond even the living. Ray Kinsella provides a place for baseball players dead for decades.

He also offers two homecomings. One is to a disaffected and disillusioned writer, based on the notoriously reclusive J. D. Salinger. The other is to an unsung (but thanks to the movie, now widely sung) physician, Archibald "Moonlight" Graham of Chisholm, Minnesota. In 1905 Graham has the shortest major league career on record—he plays right field for the New York Giants for two innings but has no at-bat.

The tale is driven by a series of enigmatic directives, not unlike instructions delivered to Old Testament prophets, such as "Prophesy to these bones" heard by Ezekiel (37:4), or, to Jeremiah (13:1), "Go and buy yourself a linen loincloth."

"If you build it, he will come" is followed by "Ease his pain." Annie asks the obvious question: "Ease whose pain?" When Ray admits he doesn't know, she blurts out, "This is a very nonspecific voice you've got out there, Ray, and he's really starting to piss me off." Jeremiah did not use exactly this terminology, but he did bewail his becoming a laughingstock. As with Ray, "all my close friends are watching for me to stumble" (Jer. 20:10).

Ray connects "Ease his pain" to a memory of a baseball story written many decades earlier by Terence Mann, an author who has effectively disappeared. Ray drives to Boston and finds Mann, who initially thinks him as crazy as his Iowa neighbors do.

When Ray says to Mann, "You once wrote: 'There comes a time when all the cosmic tumblers have clicked into place, and the universe opens itself up for a few seconds, to show you what is possible,'" Mann shouts, "Out! Out!"

But then the tumblers click. Both Ray and Mann, at a game in Boston's Fenway Park, hear the voice: "Go the distance." It's Mann who knows what it means.

The two men drive to Minnesota, where they learn that Archibald Graham, MD, died fifteen years earlier, but the memory of his good deeds is deep in the town of Chisholm. As the town's motel manager says, "It's like all these memories we have of Doc had gone to sleep and sunk way down inside us. But once you started asking about him, and started us talking about him, why, they swum back up to the surface again."

On the way back to Iowa, Ray and Mann pick up a young hitchhiker who is looking for a chance to play baseball. Of course it's Graham as he was nearly a century earlier. When they get to the diamond in the corn he joins in the game with Shoeless Joe and many other greats from baseball's past. He knocks a long fly ball and it's caught, so there's no hit—but the runner on third base scores and Graham gets a "run batted in," more of a baseball record than he got in "real" life.

Later, as the ghostly players are readying for another game, Ray and Annie's daughter Karin suddenly chokes on a hot dog. She will likely die before they can get her to a hospital. Young Archie Graham walks toward the stands, past a time-warp barrier that he won't be able to go back across. He becomes the elderly Doc Graham, who skillfully dislodges the obstruction from Karin's throat.

With exquisite precision, the moment demonstrates what Terence Mann had earlier said when in Chisholm: one inning could change the world, for if Graham had gotten a hit in 1905 he might well have stayed in the major leagues. The people of Chisholm (and Karin) wouldn't have had Doc Graham.

There is still one twist the story has yet to take. As he leaves the field, Shoeless Joe calls Ray's attention to the catcher: "He will come." It's Ray's father, John, when a young man.

Ray, prompted by Annie, introduces his father to Karin, though he is careful not to disclose the fact that either of them is related to John. After mother and daughter return to the house, John and Ray have the conversation that concludes with "Then maybe this is heaven." That question having been settled, the two men engage in the timeless father-son ritual of playing catch.

Part of the magic of Dyersville is that the conclusion of the story isn't my memory of the movie. Brendan and I come with baseball, gloves, and bat, and engage in the timeless father-son ritual of pitches, hits, catches, and running the bases. The Field of Dreams becomes the field not just of dreams dreamed, but of dreams lived.

"Ease His Pain" and "Go the Distance"

What's real? What's imagined? Seeing the movie in the company of one son, and visiting the field in Iowa with the other, blurs that distinction for me.

My father played baseball as a young man. He loved the game throughout his life. I don't fully understand the despair that led to his suicide, nor do his grandsons. But Ray and Annie and Karin Kinsella, urging us to ease his pain and go the distance, give him back to us with astonishing force.

Some years later I come across a photo of my dad as a teenager with fielder's mitt held high on a sandlot in Texas. I send copies to my sons. The circle is complete. All the cosmic tumblers click into place.

The Field of Dreams, on the screen and on the ground, makes real for me a goal I once heard stated by a Catholic priest friend, Timothy Power, alluding to the title of a 1972 song by country music singer David Rogers: "to see if I can be as aware of when 'all heaven breaks loose' as I am of when 'all hell breaks loose.'"

As I drink my coffee, the baseball players fade back into the corn. When I'm finished, they are gone. The memory is indelible.

IN A WORD

I encounter the bewildering grace of God when "Is this heaven or is this Iowa?" (an uncommon question to be asked by a Minnesotan like me—the states' rivalry is legendary) transposes from query to clue.

bewildering

Grace Where I Don't Expect It

A church, an illuminated Bible, even a Field of Dreams—these are places I might expect imagination and anticipation to prepare the ground for an encounter with the grace of God. But TV's *Ally McBeal* and the big screen's *The Hunger Games*?

The National Public Radio feature *Composers Datebook* concludes each day with "Reminding you that all music was once new." This obviously true statement startles me every time I hear it. Isaiah's vision in the temple was once new. Paul's Damascus road conversion was once new. So was Jesus's "Do this in remembrance of me."

One religious impulse is to take what was once new and repeat it over and over. There is another equally religious impulse that is alert to occasions when something that is now new illuminates a traditional truth better than a repetition does.

I find little theological nourishment in Mel Gibson's *The Passion of the Christ*,[1] a movie that portrays in relentlessly graphic fashion the suffering of Jesus on Good Friday.

The most powerful commentary on Golgotha I've ever seen makes a very different point. Near the end of the movie *Spartacus*,[2] thousands of slaves are strung up on crosses lining the Appian Way. The moment I see this scene my image of the Crucifixion is forever altered. Thanks to the history of art, we see those three crosses all alone against the sky. The whole thing seems totally singular. Seeing *Spartacus*, I realize that the citizens of Jerusalem on Good Friday would probably have paid no more attention than to a familiar billboard.

As Paul Tillich might have predicted, I have found more sustenance—more of the substance of the gospel—in *The Hunger Games*[3] and *Ally McBeal* than in Gibson's movie. It is not beside the point that in both instances the protagonists are women. All music—all art—was once new.

Katniss Everdeen and the Hunger Games

Katniss Everdeen, age sixteen, lives a century from now in the nation of Panem, a twelve-district police state where the United States used to be. She is caught in the seventy-fourth edition of the Hunger Games, Panem's fiendish transformation of "reality TV" into a gruesome yet entertaining punishment for a revolt many decades earlier.

Every year each of the dozen districts must supply one boy and one girl between the ages of twelve and eighteen to compete in a survival scenario that can be controlled by producers and editors. Everyone in the nation is required to watch. The Games conclude when only one of the twenty-four "tributes" (as they are called) is left alive.

At the end of the film, Katniss returns home (along with Peeta, the other District 12 tribute, thanks to a last-minute rule change). She is mutedly triumphant, traumatized but not really guilty of murder, and poised for the next installment in the narrative.

The Hunger Games is multilayered, with echoes of Greek myth and the Bible and Shakespeare. The story resonates with two questions a recent writer says are unavoidably posed by the Titanic, another classic mythical event: "Who will survive?" and "What would I have done?"[4]

"Who will survive?" is the engine that drives the Hunger Games. Part of the appeal to the people of Panem is that there is a definite answer, no loose ends or shades of gray (which makes the extralegal dual survival of Katniss and Peeta a political problem). I know when the Games are over. Then I can go about my business for another year without a thought for the tributes who didn't make it.

I'd like to think that my answer to "What would I have done?" would be like Katniss's, who volunteers to substitute when her younger sister's name comes up in the lottery. The more plausible self-portrait, however, is in a chilling scene where the aristocrats, feasting in what amounts to their luxury boxes, are casually wagering on who will win while the adolescents are engaged in lethal combat.

This "plausible self-portrait" brings to the surface a memory from March 5, 1961.

I'm at a "Meditation for Lent in Words and Music" put on by a Presbyterian student group at Oxford. It is based on a set of poems, *The Witnesses*, by Clive Sansom.[5] The poet has composed speeches for various witnesses of the passion—Nicodemus, the owner of the donkey Jesus borrowed for his entry into Jerusalem, a dove seller, Caiaphas, Pilate, Judas, the centurion, and so on.

Never have I seen so vividly expressed the truth that had I been there, I'd have crucified Jesus. In the weakness of Pilate, the indecision of Nicodemus, the greediness of the dove seller, I'm looking into a mirror.

The Hunger Games makes the reality of Good Friday, and its challenge to me, more vivid than does Gibson's *The Passion of the Christ*.

Ally McBeal and Advent

The Fox TV show *Ally McBeal*, about a fictional Boston law firm, isn't where I'd expect to find an Advent lesson, but that's what I got when I tuned in on December 1, 1997.[6]

The episode opens with young lawyer Ally decorating a Christmas tree. Her roommate says it's still way too early. Ally replies that she likes to get the full benefit of the season.

This is a clue that the show will be about Advent, but the two interwoven stories that follow seem, until nearly the end, hardly promising material. A transgender woman is arrested on a charge of prostitution. There's legal wrangling over the right of a nephew to speak, in a funeral eulogy, about his late uncle's prejudice. An Advent lesson?

Stephanie has a record of two prior arrests. Ally, assigned to the case as a public defender, recommends plea bargaining for a short jail term but then has another idea: an insanity defense. She explains to Stephanie that it's a legal maneuver only. "I don't think you're crazy."

The puzzle of identity, the mystery of who any of us is, isn't treated in the show as it too often is by religious folk—solvable with a few biblical proof texts or a cultural conformity test. That Stephanie is confused about some things is acknowledged, but only in full recognition that we are all confused about things. Ally's relationship with Stephanie—honest, intimate, funny, respectful—comes close to the spontaneously generous way Jesus would have dealt with Stephanie.

The solution to Stephanie's plight isn't in the law. Ally believes that what Stephanie needs is a regular job. She persuades the district attorney to give it a try. Ally then offers to hire Stephanie to work in the computer section of her law office.

In an entirely unselfconscious imitation of the good Samaritan, Ally says that Stephanie's pay can be taken out of her salary. Others in the office welcome Stephanie with joshing and warmth, without a trace of solemn rectitude. All is well.

The parallel story is worthy of *Saturday Night Live*. The recently deceased uncle of the law firm's boss was a white member of a predominantly Black church, but he couldn't stand short people. His dying wish was that his nephew would tell the truth about him, especially about his peculiar prejudice. The Black pastor of the congregation seeks an injunction against such a travesty of funeral decorum. The judge, after hearing arguments about free speech and political correctness, denies the injunction.

The nephew, having won the right to tell the whole truth in the eulogy, leaves out the part about his uncle's prejudice. He returns to his seat in the nave. Suddenly the choir, front and center, beneath the cross of Jesus, begins singing, "We don't want any short people around here!" Soon everybody in the church, including the pastor, joins in, laughing the way the uncle wanted them to.

The uncle is not the only one who dies. All is well with Stephanie, but not for long. Ally gets a late-night phone call from the police. She goes to the street where Stephanie used to walk. Stephanie couldn't stay away from the old haunts. A customer, discovering she was physically male, slashed Stephanie in a fit of rage. Ally has to identify the body, because Stephanie's upright parents have refused to come.

Stephanie had told Ally that she was always sure to have fresh makeup on, the way some people are always sure to have clean underwear: "In case I die, I want to be presentable."

The episode ends with Ally carefully applying lipstick to Stephanie's corpse. I've never before seen such a powerful replay of the woman bathing Jesus's feet with her tears and wiping them with her hair.

This episode of *Ally McBeal* shows Advent, doesn't just tell about it. Advent is the unexpected ("Come, thou long-expected Jesus," yes, but the Jesus who came wasn't what was expected). My problem with Advent is that I've grown accustomed to it. This TV show sneaks up on me, painfully, joyfully.

Advent, which was once new, became new again. No way would I have predicted that within the hour after Ally's trimming of the tree I would hear a choir's hilarious song at the end of a funeral and watch Ally apply makeup in a morgue. Faith, hope, and love really do abide, even in the face of death. Saint Paul told me so. Ally McBeal showed me.

The Task at Hand

I issue a plea to other Christians who, like me, encounter the grace of God in these unlikely places and who want to encourage others to do the same: write letters to the editor, essays, articles, books, poems, dramas, screenplays; compose, draw, choreograph, sculpt; give lectures, lead discussion groups, teach classes, go on talk shows, blog; subscribe to the *Christian Century*, support councils of churches and seminaries—whatever it takes, whatever you can do.

You may be denounced. After I published something along these lines in a newspaper, a reader wrote telling me to enjoy my "ride on the hell-bound train." Don't flinch. Our claim on the tradition is second to none.

IN A WORD

I encounter the blindsiding grace of God when a drama—on TV, on the big screen, on the stage, on the page—catches me unsuspecting.

Grace On Board the Starship *Enterprise*

"I have myriad dialogue partners, many dead, some still alive." I wrote this in the prologue. It doesn't exhaust the category.

I also said my memories mix, mingle, ricochet, syncopate. But my memories aren't just of what has already been. They're also of conversations with dialogue partners who have yet to be.

I remember forward, taking a cue from the White Queen in *Through the Looking-Glass*: "It's a poor sort of memory that only works backwards."[1]

My immersion in *Star Trek: The Next Generation*, which aired in 1987–94 (and which I continue to watch in its forty-eight-DVD format), is almost religious in its persistence and tenacity. I have traveled in imagination to the twenty-fourth century, where I see and hear Captain Jean-Luc Picard and his crew of the starship *Enterprise* as they explore strange new worlds and spend time with some of the 1,754 civilizations they encounter.

The portrayal of Capt. Picard's life—three and a half centuries hence—has been for the imaginations of Earthlings in my time what Edwin Hubble discovered about the universe: expansion at an accelerating rate. To boldly go where no one has gone before is giddy, exhilarating, a bit scary, and quite irresistible.

We've had foretastes: the first to fly solo across the Atlantic, the first to scale Everest, the first to set foot on the moon, the first to crack the DNA code. But these are still close in, baby steps when set against Picard's exploration of distant star systems, his discovery of new life and new civilizations, his interaction with the android Cdr. Data. What would it be like to be Capt. Picard, I wonder—to see what he sees, know what he knows, doubt what he doubts, puzzle through (or even muddle through) what perplexes him, fear what he fears, love what he loves.

If *Star Trek: The Next Generation* time-warps me forward, some twenty years before the show's first episode I had a premonition of its expansion of my imagination, though it is only now, more than two decades after the conclusion of the television series, that the parallel has surfaced into consciousness.

The Most Room to Move Around

Early in my story I told about the historian Peter Brown, whose way of investigating the past—or better, of listening to the past—shaped my own view of how to make sense of what has come before.

In his great *Augustine of Hippo: A Biography*, after he has led me through the myriad philosophical and religious and even psychological twists and turns of the saint's youth and early adulthood, Brown offers this explanation for Augustine's conversion to Christianity: it gave him the most room to move around. Augustine realized that his "'true philosophy' was also the religion of a universal church." The message: "the 'highest pitch' of wisdom was available to any moderately educated and serious mind."[2]

Even now, half a century after I read it, I can recall the electrifying sensation: "Yes, that's it! The appeal of the Christian tradition to me is precisely its roominess, its encouragement of exploration." I didn't yet have Picard's words, but I can see that what Saint Augustine found, and I want, is the opportunity—indeed, the incentive—to go boldly, to seek out new life and new civilizations. Church for me is a place where I needn't hide, live a lie, pretend, kid myself, or check my mind at the door. I add curiosity to faith, hope, and love.

The other options Augustine tried had appealed to him initially because they claimed to offer clear, clipped, final answers. In each case Augustine came to see they were cramped, ultimately lifeless. As one of my mentors, George A. Buttrick, who was preacher to the university at Harvard, used to say, "The trouble with dead certainties is just that—they're dead."

If the Christian church is still around in Capt. Picard's time, I'm sure Augustine's will be a name familiar to him. Even if the church is only a historical memory, I suspect Augustine will not have faded from awareness—Picard might celebrate Augustine's two thousandth birthday on November 13, 2354 (Stardate 31865.75)— because Augustine's influence on Western culture is so profound in so many dimensions.

I look to Augustine not as an infallible guide—to do so would contradict his own exploratory instincts—but as an exemplar of a way of being Christian that is congruent with John Henry Newman's aphorism that I noted in encounter 2 as part of what has shaped my perspective: "'To live is to change, and to be perfect is to have changed often."

In another place Newman went further than Augustine likely would have, when he said that "what holds in all matters of fact" is "that there never was a rule without its exceptions."[3] Augustine, especially toward the end of his life, became more sure of himself—and on occasion a menace to other people. Newman's "never without exceptions" would have been a salutary caution. I value room to move around in what Augustine—or at least the later Augustine—would probably have declared off-limits . . . but we're in an expanding universe.

"Room to move around in." If I were asked to condense into five words what I think it is to be Christian now and in the age of *Star Trek*, these five would be the ones. The kind of Christian I have become has pushed boundaries, been wary of restrictions, resisted premature closure, held suspect certainties that exclude people unlike me.

As I noted in encounter 1, one flavor of Christianity inspires its adherents to take God out there into the world where God supposedly isn't, while another flavor, equally traditional and authentic—more traditional, in my estimation—inspires its adherents to be alert to what God is doing out there in the world where God already is. Some Christians, taking a cue from Capt. Picard, want to explore God's world, not conquer the world for God. I cast my lot with the explorers.

Familiar Ground

My memories of these encounters tell me that the grace of God I have met in so many ways in the past and present can also be found when the church has disappeared. *Star Trek: The Next Generation* is virtually bereft of any overtly Christian reference. Yet I, *as a Christian*, feel very much at home there.

Of course, I haven't *really* visited the twenty-fourth century. Time travel, even if it were theoretically possible, isn't at my disposal. But just as my imagination can take me fully into the town of Skotoprigonyevsk of *The Brothers Karamazov*, so can it make Capt. Picard's limitless horizons realistically vivid to me. From the twenty-fourth century I see my own time at a slant.

But memory lingers for a moment in the 1870s at Skotoprigonyevsk, where I also feel very much at home, before catapulting ahead again to the 2360s. From my hero Alyosha Karamazov I learn, as from Augustine and Picard, the meaning of "room to move around in"—of "walls opening out."

Alyosha's mentor and friend, the monk and elder Zosima, has died the day before. In the room where the body lies, Alyosha is praying while listening to another monk read the story in John 2 about Jesus at the wedding feast in Cana, where he turned water into wine.

Alyosha dozes and perceives the festive scene of joy and hospitality. "But what's this? what's this?" he asks of what he's seeing. "Why are the walls of the room opening out?" They are opening to encompass where Alyosha is. Father Zosima leaves his coffin, extends his hand, and raises Alyosha from his knees.

When Alyosha whispers, "I'm afraid . . . I don't dare to look" at Jesus, Zosima tells him not to be afraid. "Awful is his greatness before us, terrible is his loftiness, yet he is boundlessly merciful, he became like us out of love, and he is rejoicing with us, transforming water into wine, that the joy of the guests may not end. He is waiting for new guests, he is ceaselessly calling new guests, now and unto ages of ages."

After coming to from this reverie, Alyosha goes out into the starlit night, yearning for "freedom, space, vastness." He falls to the earth, weeping with joy. "It was as if threads from all those innumerable worlds of God all came together in his soul, and it was trembling all over, 'touching other worlds.'"[4]

This section of part 3, book 7, chapter 4 (called "Cana of Galilee") of *The Brothers Karamazov* will be read at my funeral.

Now I jump five hundred years ahead.

The twenty-fourth century I go to is the one conjured by *Star Trek*'s creator, Gene Roddenberry. (He died in 1991, halfway through the run of *The Next Generation*, but the subsequent writers made an effort to stay true to his vision.) As with any imagining of the future, it is both a reflection of and goad for its own time.

Roddenberry, who like Lewis Carroll's White Queen could believe "as many as six impossible things before breakfast,"[5] had no use for religion. His portrayal of the twenty-fourth century is bereft of Christianity, except in a vestigial, antiquarian way. In the whole series, the word "church" appears only twice: once, church and knickknacks are in the same category;[6] once, when the *Enterprise* has time-traveled to nineteenth-century San Francisco, the crew's boarding-house proprietress mentions having been in a church play as a child.[7]

The *Enterprise* neither takes nor finds the gospel as we are accustomed to hearing it.

Given current trends in American religious identity (the fastest growing category are "Nones," people with no religious affiliation), Roddenberry's prediction doesn't appear all that far-fetched. But over and over again, as I encounter Picard and his crew, I feel on familiar ground. The church isn't still around, but the culture, the folkways, the relationships portrayed on the *Enterprise* are shot through with the substance of the faith—the grace of God—as I have come to understand it.

Nearly every flash of grace that I have recounted in this book has its parallel in one or more places in Picard's world. Here are particularly striking ones.

Our Stories, and Things We Do Not Understand

Lieutenant Worf, chief of security, is a Klingon. When he was young, his parents were killed. Sergey Rozhenko, an officer of the Federation starship that answers the distress call, and his wife, Helena, take Worf in and raise him. Worf's Klingon warrior heritage, intensified by the high status of his ancestors in the Klingon Empire, is in tension with his formation in a human family. (As evidence of *Star Trek's* cultural clout, the Klingon language has been studied to such an extent that both the Bible and several Shakespeare plays have been translated into it.)[8]

Worf understands the power and function of stories—their complexity, their ambiguity, their open-endedness—in much the same way as I do those of the Bible. He says this of the legends of his people: "These are our stories. They tell us who we are." But when asked whether the stories are true, he turns the question inside out: "I have studied them all of my life, and find new truths in them every time."[9]

Worf is sympathetic to my way of reading the Bible. He would also second my motion in favor of Francis P. Church's "Is There a Santa Claus?" editorial, which highlights "all the wonders there are unseen and unseeable in the world."[10] Worf puts it directly and simply: "There are things we do not understand, yet they exist nonetheless."[11]

The Galactic Challenge of Ecumenism

Never in my sojourns in the twenty-fourth century do I hear the term "ecumenism." Even without the word, though, the reality is there. Ecumenism is a bigger challenge in the twenty-fourth century than in ours—Capt. Picard and his crew are dealing not just with the whole inhabited world, but with myriad inhabited *worlds*.

The United Federation of Planets faces unity issues similar to those faced in the Christian church.

The planet Kesprytt III, to which the *Enterprise* has come on January 9, 2370, has applied for membership in the Federation.[12] It turns out the planet's name papers over a rift.

Picard is hesitant, but the ship's physician, Dr. Beverly Crusher, says it's not a matter of admitting half the planet and excluding the other half. The Kes, who are three-quarters of the population, want in. The other quarter, the Prytt, don't want anything to do with anyone from outside. (This sounds remarkably like the principle of separation adhered to by some Christians—"complete separation from those who deny the faith,"[13] including Christians who do not agree with them 100 percent.)

But this is unprecedented, because only unified worlds have previously been admitted to the Federation—having overcome their differences, they were prepared to join something larger.

The *Enterprise* crew gets caught in the Kes-Prytt crossfire. The Kes say of the Prytt that they have no regard for civilized discourse, so trying to communicate with them is pointless. When asked, "How long has it been since your last diplomatic contact?," the Kes ambassador replies, "Almost a century." Ship's Counselor Deanna Troi then suggests that the other side "may have changed over the years." (The discovery of such "change over the years" on both sides is the backstory of Catholic-Protestant relations in the twentieth century, at the beginning of which they weren't talking to each other at all.)

There are among the Prytt some who favor friendly relations with the Kes (like the ecumenically minded Catholics who, prior to the Second Vatican Council, were ostracized), so suspicions of conspiracy are everywhere. When the Kes and Prytt are finally in the same room, they demur, saying they don't have authority to speak to the other side.

The conflict is not resolved. The *Enterprise* report states that the Kes are not ready for Federation membership.

I suggest that Capt. Picard give a parting gift to the Kes and the Prytt—a copy of the book by my friend and mentor Robert S. Bilheimer: *Breakthrough: The Emergence of the Ecumenical Tradition*.[14] All three of the nouns in the title have to work in sync: Tradition, Emergence, Breakthrough. If the Kes and the Prytt take the book's story to heart, maybe Kesprytt III will make a more compelling case next time.

"Everyone Wants to Be Normal"

In the most emotionally wrenching encounter I ever see the *Enterprise* have, Commander William Riker, the starship's First Officer, comes up against a reality he could not have expected.[15]

On March 8, 2368, Cdr. Riker joins Soren, from the planet J'naii, in the search for a missing shuttlecraft. When Riker uses a gendered pronoun, he is corrected by Soren: "We use a pronoun that is neutral."

This opens the way for Soren to tell Riker that the J'naii have evolved from a two-sex species to an androgynous one. Riker is puzzled by no gender, Soren by division into two sexes.

But Soren does understand. She (the pronoun, it turns out, is appropriate) is one of a small minority of the J'naii who experience themselves as gendered. She falls in love with Riker. This precipitates a monumental crisis with the J'naii officials.

At the judicial proceeding, Soren speaks with words familiar to me from gay people in our time: "It is not unnatural. I am not sick because I feel this way. I do not need to be helped. I do not need to be cured."

What follows qualifies as tragic.

Cdr. Riker pleads for permission to take Soren with him back to the *Enterprise*. One of the J'naii officials counters: "You see, Commander, on this world everyone wants to be normal."

And Soren capitulates. She says to Riker, "I had these terrible urges, and that is why I reached out to you."

This moment has two effects on me. First, I am grateful to have lived to see same-sex marriage legalized in the United States; as I noted in encounter 13, it happened faster than I (and many—maybe most—others) expected. But it also reminds me that for too long I thought of myself as "the norm," what God intended people to be. I wish I could tell those J'naii officials how misguided is the dogma that "everyone wants to be normal" if "normal" excludes people unlike them.

"Space and Time and Thought Aren't Separate"

On June 12, 2363, a character appears whose challenge to the imagination disturbs, if not dogma, then at least strongly held belief.[16]

The guest on the *Enterprise* is called the Traveler. He is initially disregarded because he is assistant to a Starfleet scientist who has come to enhance the warp drive. The scientist gets all the attention. The assistant gives a clue that he's mysterious when he says that humans can't pronounce his name.

Before long, the starship is not just across the galaxy, but three galaxies away, and not long after that, in a region of space that has never been charted (for sure, "where no one has gone before"). The Starfleet scientist is as baffled as everyone else. It's the sixteen-year-old Ensign Wesley Crusher who intuits what the Traveler knows that accounts for what happened: "Space and time and thought aren't the separate things they appear to be."

Of course, the most fundamental recalibrator of imagination in the twentieth century was Einstein's demonstration that "space and time aren't the separate things they appear to be." Who's to say that by the twenty-fourth century, thought won't be added to the list?

In any case, Capt. Picard and the entire crew have to reconfigure and refocus their thoughts to get the *Enterprise* back to where it started from, across the universe. In a very real sense they were, are, and will be where and when they imagine themselves. The line in reality between material and ideas is blurred. Picard instructs the crew: "We must begin controlling our thoughts."

Before their return to familiar territory, some *Enterprise* crew members experience visions and dreams. Capt. Picard encounters his long-dead mother, who asks perhaps the most profound question ever posed to him: "Out here? At what you say is the end of the universe? Or do you see this as the beginning of it?"

Picard's mother's query is a commentary on the lines from T. S. Eliot that I quoted in encounter 22, lines that I said have served me, for the past sixty years, as the clearest chart of my experience:

> We shall not cease from exploration
> And the end of all our exploring
> Will be to arrive where we started
> And know the place for the first time.[17]

Or, in the words of a famous hymn, "'Tis grace has brought me safe thus far, and grace will lead me home."

"Beyond What We Understand Now as Reality"

In 1988 Stephen Hawking, at the conclusion of his best seller *A Brief History of Time*, wrote, perhaps ironically, "If we discover a complete theory . . . it would be the ultimate triumph of human reason—for then we should know the mind of God." He considered deleting the sentence, but "had I done so, the sales might have been halved."[18]

I might expect that any echo in the twenty-fourth century of theologies from the twenty-first would be something like Hawking's notion of "the mind of God," but the *Enterprise* crew don't talk in these terms. I suspect that even if they pondered Hawking's (perhaps tongue-in-cheek) suggestion, their skepticism would result from suspicion of any claim to having a "complete" theory. The continual discovery of new life and new civilizations means that some hitherto unknown part of reality is still out there.

And Picard himself as much as says this.[19] The *Enterprise* is caught in a void that it turns out is overseen by an entity that wants to study human reaction to death. Lieutenant Commander Data asks the captain, "What is death?" Picard answers with a both/and: some say it's changing into another form for eternity, some say it's "our blinking into nothingness."

Data is unsatisfied with this sidestep. "Which do you believe, sir?"

Picard takes a middle path: "I believe that our existence must be more than either of these philosophies, . . . that our existence is part of a reality beyond what we understand now as reality."

Beyond what we understand now as reality—his "now" is the twenty-fourth century. In the realms of philosophy—even, I venture to say, of theology—he is an explorer, endlessly curious.

And Data, who has elicited from Picard a taking of the fork in the road, a salute to the both/and of John Stuart Mill's essays on Bentham and Coleridge, is in fact—right there on the bridge of the *Enterprise*—the most striking of all the "new life" that is the focus of the starship's mission.

Data is an android who works closely with humans and is fascinated by them. He shares our curiosity and our powers of reasoning (which he can carry out at a speed that leaves us in the dust), but feelings are, when I first meet him, entirely outside the range of his capacities.

But his longing to understand human feeling—even to "get" jokes and to be able to tell them in a way that draws genuine laughter so he can "join in"—persists and grows.[20] The longing undergoes setback only when, thanks to an emotion chip inserted into his system, the feelings that humans learn, gradually, to sort through and deal with, hit him all at once with tsunami force. "Although I understand, in technical terms, how life is formed, there is still a part of the process which eludes me."[21]

Data: "You See Things with the Wonder of a Child"

But, as always, there is a flip side. "You [Data] see things with the wonder of a child," says the hologram of the chief of security, Lieutenant Tasha Yar, prepared as a "last testament" for the crew should she die, which has happened: "and that makes you more human than any of us."[22]

I have already made a judgment, one that would elicit a rejoinder from some of the people I meet in *The Next Generation*. I have used "he" and "him" when referring to Data.

Dr. Katherine Pulaski, who serves for a season as ship's doctor, gets off on the wrong foot immediately. She calls Data Da(h)ta. "What's the difference?" Data's profound rejoinder: "One is my name, the other is not." Dr. Pulaski's response, what she intends as a rhetorical question to end the conversation, is a hint of an awareness that will dawn on her eventually: "Is this possible? With all of your neural nets, algorithms, and heuristics, is there some combination that makes up a circuit for bruised feelings?"[23]

Later on, still skeptical, she cannot understand why the captain and other crewmates use the personal pronoun.[24] Picard implicitly chides the doctor for speaking as if Data were absent. "Cdr. Data knows precisely what he is doing"—what *he* is doing, not what *it* is doing.

There comes a time when Starfleet admirals above Picard's pay grade insist that Data, who only looks human, be turned over to them for study and possible replication.[25] The captain balks: "We, too, are machines, just machines of a different type."

Picard precipitates a judicial ruling that Data is a sentient being whose release to the authorities would be tantamount to enslaving him. "Starfleet was founded to seek out new life." The decision will not only determine Data's status but also "reveal the kind of a people we are."

The judge doesn't have the luxury of suspending judgment. "Does Data have a soul? I don't know that he has. I don't know that I have. But I have got to give him the freedom to explore that question himself."

The conundrum that Data presents to his contemporaries—does he fit on a continuum that includes humans? is there a difference only in degree or decisively in kind?—is one that we in the early twenty-first century are confronting rapidly. I suspect that a Cdr. Data will not have to wait until the twenty-fourth century to appear on the scene.

Anne Foerst, quoted in encounters 21 and 23, wrote a doctoral dissertation on artificial intelligence and theology, and worked for a number of years in the AI lab at MIT. She has said that "everyone there was seeking meaning, in awe of creating a robot. We gain respect for the human system, because it's so difficult to reproduce it. When you try to rebuild yourself, you ask, 'Who am I?'"[26]

There is a nagging anxiety in many quarters these days, vividly reinforced by wildly popular motion pictures, that beings possessed of artificial intelligence will, by the end of this century—and maybe even sooner—become capable of learning, organizing, conspiring, and taking over. After all, if we "rebuild ourselves," to use Foerst's image, we might be expected to replicate some of the more horrific things we humans have done to one another.

However, barring the androids relegating us to evolutionary history as we *Homo sapiens* did to the Neanderthals, I suspect that even if a Cdr. Data comes along well before Capt. Picard's era, the questions will be as lively then as they are portrayed as being in his time, as imagined by *The Next Generation*.

Feelings are part of the mystery, but there is more.

Data: The Value of Failure

Do I have power to control my life, my destiny? Picard answers, "That kind of control is an illusion."[27]

If Data always knows the answer, does he lack the capacity for failure? When he asks Dr. Pulaski if there is something to be said for losing, she replies, "We humans learn more often from a failure or a mistake than we do from an easy success."[28] Picard carries this even further in a remark to Data on another occasion: "It is possible to commit no mistakes and still lose. That is not a weakness. That is life."[29] Picard might have added the words of Erasmus's character Folly, quoted in encounter 16: we need to "make mistakes together or individually, . . . [and] wisely overlook things."

Does it make any sense to say that Cdr. Data is "made in the image of God"? The answer many Christians would give—"Of course not"—is much too quick.

Evolution has blurred the line separating the human from what came before. While the claim that a soul is infused into us and is restricted to *Homo sapiens* takes care of the problem, there is no way to verify it. Certainly the notion of a soul that survives apart from the body is widespread, but it doesn't mesh neatly with "the resurrection of the body," and it has fueled a longstanding disparagement of embodiment as inessential to human identity.

Data's yearning to be human is where *Star Trek: The Next Generation* most directly informs my own theological perspective.

Data: "Shakespeare Enjoyed Mixing Opposites"

Picard, who loves the greatest of English dramatists, says to Data that Shakespeare is the best guide to what it means to be human. "But you must discover it through your own performance, not by imitating others."[30]

At another point, when Data is trying to be a credible Ebenezer Scrooge in a rendition of Dickens's *A Christmas Carol*, he says to Picard, "I am attempting to use performance to create emotional awareness. I believe if I can learn to duplicate the fear of Ebenezer Scrooge, I will be one step closer to truly understanding humanity." Picard responds that when Data "created" emotional awareness instead of imitating other actors, "you were already one step closer to understanding humanity."[31]

Data creates a program on the *Enterprise* holodeck for a performance of *The Tempest*.[32] He is mystified by the character Prospero,
but recognizes that there is something tragic.

This provides Picard the opening for what I think says as much
about him as about the Bard: "Yes, but there's a certain expec-
tancy too, a hopefulness about the future. You see, Shakespeare
enjoyed mixing opposites. The past and the future, hope and despair." *Mixing opposites*, not prematurely opting for one or the
other—like the Psalms, like Saint Benedict in his Rule, like Bentham and Coleridge.

Harold Bloom wrote a book in which he claimed, with evidence
to support the argument, that Shakespeare invented the notion of
"the human" as we, his heirs, understand it.[33] Augustine deserves
some of the credit, and Dante too, but for complexity and nuance,
nothing matches Shakespeare.

Picard's wisdom is condensed in the direction "You must discover it through your own performance." It's like Benjamin Britten's observation noted in encounter 25, "Music does not exist in
a vacuum, it does not exist until it is performed, and performance
imposes conditions." I believe that human nature, the human
condition, doesn't exist until it is performed, and performance
imposes conditions.

In the course of *The Next Generation*, Lt. Cdr. Data performs
human nature—just as we all do, all the time.

IN A WORD

I encounter God's timeless grace when I visit the
twenty-fourth century and, *as a Christian*, feel right
at home.

timeless

Part Nine

A Spirituality for
the Long Haul

Grace in the Overlap of "Spiritual" and "Religious"

History, science, art, imagination—all these realms and others besides are occasions for encounters with God's grace. Along the way in this story I have introduced many conversation partners who have been agents, direct or indirect, of that grace for me.

I have needed help navigating between the spiritual and the religious.

When I was in my twenties it would not have occurred to me to say I was spiritual but not religious. In recent decades, however, this distinction has become a staple of conversation, even of scholarly analysis. "SBNR" marks territory in the sociological landscape.[1]

I understand and respect those who wish to identify themselves thus. I can interpret the terms in a way that makes me want to make the claim for myself. When religion gets squeezed into narrow dogmas and moralizing straitjackets, when churches get defensive, "institutional religion" deserves the suspicion, even contempt, directed at it.

But I am both spiritual and religious. Three guides help me understand how this can be so.

First Guide: Robert Bilheimer—
"A Desire That I Simply Recognize"

First is Robert Bilheimer, my predecessor at the Collegeville Institute for Ecumenical and Cultural Research, and before that an official of both the World Council of Churches and the National Council of Churches of Christ in the USA. In other words, Bob Bilheimer was a denizen of the institutional church.

He recognized that lurking in the depths of the often unwieldy, creaking, deteriorating ship that is the church is the original impulse, the "spiritual" that people are referring to when they say they are "spiritual but not religious." Though he knew that the church can hamper what he considered the most pressing of all needs—"a spirituality for the long haul"—he believed also that without the church, this very spirituality would slip its moorings.[2]

But a spirituality for the long haul demands close attention to the present.

I have a conversation with Bob when he is in his late seventies. "I have always lived for and into the future," he says. He is superb at woodcraft. "I made a good deck so that in the years to come it would last and serve well. Now I am making the deck as good as I can because that's what I'm supposed to do right now. It is a *desire* that I simply recognize. It is not an intellectual construct, or the result of analytical thinking."

Bob, a master of intellectual constructs and analytical thinking, is amazed to find himself anchored by desire and curious about how this could be (the way Saint Augustine was). In the conversation that day I am overwhelmed and enticed by Bob's linking of curiosity and serenity.

Second Guide: Thomas F. Stransky, CSP—
"A Matter-of-Factness"

Second is Father Thomas Stransky, a Paulist priest who worked in the Vatican at the Secretariat for Promoting Christian Unity when it was founded by Pope Saint John XXIII (and whose aphorism about ecumenism—"something which, if we had a better name for, we would have more of"—I quoted in encounter 14). Tom, like Bob Bilheimer, was a denizen of the institutional church.

I'll never forget Tom's saying that he has a certain lighthearted-ness about the church. "The sense of common humanity leads me not to expect too much of authority. I believe in it, but my lower expectations mean that I do not have to get up every morning and ask, 'Whom am I going to get mad at today?' Is this cynicism? No. It is a matter-of-factness."[3] For Tom, spirituality pries the need for control out of him.

Bob Bilheimer and Tom Stransky, friends of mine, teach me to see the overlap of "spiritual" and "religious."

Third Guide: Bieke Vandekerckhove— "Beautiful, Intense, Grand, Whimsical, and Mysterious"

My third guide, whom I never met, is Bieke Vandekerckhove, a Belgian, whose book *The Taste of Silence* hit me with the force of revelation—the best sort, confirming what I already knew but didn't know I knew.[4] I had already seen the world in many colors. She makes the spiritual spectrum visible and palpable all the way into the infrared and ultraviolet.

At age nineteen Bieke was diagnosed with amyotrophic lateral sclerosis (ALS), commonly known as Lou Gehrig's disease. Doctors gave her two to five years to live. The condition went into remission. She lived another twenty-seven years, hampered by disabilities, requiring help from many, including her husband.

During that entire time, the distinct likelihood of relapse and death was ever present. She wrote her book letter by letter, using a computer program that could detect where on the keyboard her eye was focused. She died in 2015.

There is not a shred of sentimentality in *The Taste of Silence*, no wallowing in self-pity. When her world comes undone with the

ALS diagnosis, Bieke quickly discovers that the Christianity she has inherited is inadequate, in fact worse than useless.

But she doesn't leave it at that. Responding to some sort of inexplicable hunch—"it went totally against my routine and against everything that until then had been familiar to me"—she decides to spend time (a year initially) in a Benedictine monastery—not exactly a rebuke of institutional religion![5]

And here is the surprise she finds.

"I came upon the treasures of Christianity through a strange door," she writes. "A little back door, actually. Half decayed, hidden under a thick layer of dust, barely known and noticed. But on the inside, jumping with life." Monasteries. "This is no faith of rules and merits. Neither is it a faith of dogmas that must be accepted as truths. Here I discovered a faith of lived experience and inwardness, preserved throughout the centuries and passed on."[6]

"Barely known and noticed" these days, yes—though getting a lot more attention now than when I was growing up. But "preserved throughout the centuries"—and that preservation requires an institution. Of course institutional religion can stifle spirituality, but it can also nourish and sustain it, especially when the institution is treated with a certain lighthearted matter-of-factness. "Institutionalization" is not necessarily a crime against the spirit.

Bieke's story demonstrates, over and over again, the way spirituality and religion get synchronized in the paradox classically stated by Polonius in *Hamlet*: "by indirections find directions out."[7]

She initially "came upon the treasures of Christianity through . . . a little back door"—an image that evokes scientific breakthroughs as described by cosmologist Brian Greene, quoted in encounter 24: "Everybody's looking at a problem one way, and you come at it from the back."[8]

Then Bieke comes upon those treasures again through what she'd not have dreamed was a door to them at all: Zen Buddhism. She calls Benedictine spirituality and Zen Buddhism "the two lungs through which I breathe."[9]

One of her Zen teachers points to Moses as an instance of the ideal of the bodhisattva, who, out of compassion, pulls back from stepping over into nirvana in order to bring along those farther back. Moses asks God to blot him out of the book of life if the Israelite people are going to be destroyed because of their unfaithfulness. "My first contact with Zen," Bieke says, "led me right away to the core of the religion in which, as a Westerner, I had been brought up."[10]

The Benedictine nuns; the Zen practitioners; and her illness. Yes, her illness too: Bieke credits her confrontation with her mortality, her disabilities, her anguish, with fusing her religion and spirituality.

She quickly forestalls any easy notion that God made her sick in order to bless her. If you don't grasp the fragility of language, she writes, "you arrive at gruesome notions. The illness, or losing a child, etc., could be 'a mercy,' 'a blessing,' or whatever. Nonsense! Please let's not force it into the straitjacket of intellectual thought."[11]

The nun who is her spiritual guide at the monastery asks Bieke, every time they talk, "What do you long for?" Bieke is initially baffled—"as if you have something left to desire when everything is being taken from you!" Eventually she discovers that "it is longing, period. It is incomplete. It is open, to everything and everybody. . . . Sometimes it's there, mostly not. Then there's nothing to do but wait and wrestle."[12]

In 1989 I am part of a group in which we are asked to respond to "What am I waiting for?" As I think about it, I realize I am *content* to be waiting, but wasn't always so. I know something of Bieke's "eventually."

For much of my life I've not been willing to wait, to let go. There is a lot of the Texan "Go get 'em" spirit in me, and mostly I'm glad of that, but carried to an extreme, such a spirit can push the God of surprise, the God of grace, over the horizon. Like Bieke, I have to learn the virtue of simply waiting without obsessively wondering "What for?"

I come back, as so often, to Keats's negative capability: when one "is capable of being in uncertainties, mysteries, doubts, without any irritable reaching after fact and reason."[13] It's not just reaching that needs to be avoided—it's *irritable* reaching.

And what, for Bieke, comes after the waiting and wrestling? "Pushing through all possible ideas *about* reality to reality itself. And that reality is infinitely more beautiful, intense, grand, whimsical, and mysterious than the mental images within which we mostly live it and experience it."

The resolution: following her diagnosis, "when I saw everything as it were for the last time, it appeared as if I saw everything for the first time."[14]

"Beautiful, intense, grand, whimsical, and mysterious." These—especially whimsy—are qualities of spirituality as I know it too. But also of religion as I know it and as Bieke knew it. She knew as well, and so do I, that life and spirituality and religion can be dark, cruel. "Not everything is love." There are both "potentiality and difficulty."[15]

Waiting might not eventuate in a happy conclusion.

It's 2000. I'm back in Egypt on the trip where the heron put me in mind of "rereading all the sources." We're at Aswan, looking at the Unfinished Obelisk.

It would have stood 137 feet tall and weighed 1,168 tons, far taller and heavier than any other. But fissures began to appear, and with each crack in the granite the size of the obelisk was reduced. This kept happening. When the quarriers discovered a fissure near the obelisk's center, they abandoned the scheme.

As I stand looking at the supine obelisk in the withering Egyptian heat, I have a jumble of thoughts, mostly about what it would have been like for the designers and workers to realize years—decades?—into the project that it *wasn't going to work*. There are lessons aplenty lurking here, about pride and its comeuppance, about tyranny and the allure of glory, about the vanity of human wishes, but there is also something appealing about the boldness, even the recklessness of the striving. "Potentiality and difficulty." What they did, I conclude, was worth it.

"Beautiful, intense, grand, whimsical, and mysterious." This is a pretty good summary of why I go to church. Of course, the reality seldom lives up to the ideal. Sermons can be boring (though sometimes electrifying); liturgy, rote (though sometimes breathtaking). There's frequently a gap between what's enacted on Sunday—the Eucharist that unites us—and the divisiveness we're all part of the rest of the week (though sometimes the intimate connection between love and justice is evident in what we do).

Church, like much else in life, is both "potentiality and difficulty." I don't doubt for a minute the sincerity and integrity of those who find the "difficulty" a barrier to their encounter with the grace of God. Church can even be a hindrance not simply to spirituality: my dad used to urge people not to let church get in the way of their religion.

I choose to focus on the "potentiality." Church is certainly my formation, as I noted at the beginning of this book. But more. It has been, and still is, a capacious, alluring, and challenging arena. It's a place where I can explore, with others—most compellingly in our singing hymns together, both the classic ones from the era of Watts and Wesley and recent ones, such as "Sing a New Church" by my friend Delores Dufner, OSB: "Shape a circle ever wider and a people ever free." That's potentiality!

IN A WORD

I encounter the bighearted grace of God when Bob Bilheimer, Tom Stransky, and Bieke Vandekerckhove show me that with a certain lightheartedness I can find a spirituality for the long haul through the little back door of religion.

bighearted

Grace in a Culture of Trust, Not Fear

For Bieke Vandekerckhove, life at the intersection of Christianity and Buddhism is intense and illuminating. It is part of a larger picture.

Arnold J. Toynbee speculated that historians in the future, writing about the twentieth century, will judge the dialogues between Buddhists and Christians more significant than the conflict between democracy and communism.[1]

There will be other contenders for those historians' attention, of course. When I googled "most significant event of twentieth century," World War II was the clear winner, with scientific developments, whether the Wright brothers or making an atomic bomb or landing on the moon, clustered in second place; the Russian Revolution had a few votes; cinema was on the list; a particularly thought-provoking suggestion was the invention of fertilizer. But Toynbee has a point.

As a purely astonishing fact, it's hard to top the cultural tenacity of monasticism, which has existed for 2,500 years in the Buddhist tradition, and 1,700 years in the Christian. When Buddhist and Christian monastics get together, time both stands still and explodes. Millennia meet. Monastic Interreligious Dialogue, an organization that traces its roots to the Catholic Church's opening to the world at the Second Vatican Council, is like a particle accelerator, in which forces interact to reveal primordial conditions, some fundamental features of human nature and human community.

Monastic folks are impatient with theory. Practice is the beginning, middle, and end of living and knowing both Benedictine and Buddhist. Practice as the key was as revolutionary in fifth-century BCE India and fourth-century Egypt as in twenty-first-century America. From one perspective, monasticism is supremely countercultural. Taking a long view, however, everything else is countercultural, monasticism being the one more or less constant through the whole story.

"All Our Truths Need Bungee Cords"

The staying power of monasticism, its spirituality for the long haul, illustrates the force of the seismic shift in John Henry Newman's sensibility I noted in encounter 2—from horror of change to reveling in it. The key is in the conclusion of Saint Benedict's Rule, where he calls it a "little rule that we have written for beginners."[2]

As I once heard Abbot Jerome Theisen, OSB, say: "We're in process, in movement. Monasticism has been so varied through the centuries. We don't have it all nicely packaged." It is said that when Sister Remberta of Saint Benedict's Monastery in Saint Joseph, Minnesota, was asked at her sixtieth jubilee of monastic profession what she prays for, she answered, "Perseverance."

The encounter with Buddhist monastics has been the latest in a long series of occasions for Benedictines to move from one stage of beginning to another, from fearing the new to embracing it. Benedictines are capable of rootedness and far-ranging adventure at the same time. In one of his poems, my friend, and founder of the Collegeville Institute for Ecumenical and Cultural Research, Kilian McDonnell, OSB, gives a snapshot of this ironic ability: "All our truths need bungee cords."[3]

Some Christians assume that if they engage in conversation with someone from another tradition, they won't learn anything new, or at least anything significant. Benedictines don't think this way.

Adherents of the Rule, who are always at the beginning, expect to learn new things from just about everybody, even from others who are more novice than they. After all, Benedict instructs the abbot to call the whole community for counsel because "the Lord often reveals what is better to the younger."[4]

The Benedictine doesn't just expect to learn new things as in "new information" or "new facts." The Benedictine expects to learn new things about God, and new ways to think about things both old and new about God.

Benedictines are not afraid to seek God in the company of folks who don't talk about God at all, because they know that God isn't just in talk. Sometimes talk is the very last place I should look for God.

A recent memory underscores the theological power of silence.

The Eloquence of Emma's Silence

It's March 24, 2018. I'm watching the March for Our Lives in Washington, DC. The event is invented by student leaders from Marjory Stoneman Douglas High School in Parkland, Florida, where on Valentine's Day seventeen students were massacred.

Emma González speaks for two minutes. She names the victims, making them real. With each name, she says, "Never," listing things that the deceased will now never do again—"My friend Carmen would never complain to me about piano practice," and so on.

Then she goes silent.

The crowd is uneasy, and periodically breaks the quiet. I squirm with all of them. Nevertheless, she persists.

When her phone sounds, she speaks again, saying that since she came on the stage, six minutes and twenty seconds have passed— the time it took the shooter to write "never" to seventeen lives.[5]

Her silence rivets me. It's a master lesson in the art of "show, don't tell." It makes palpable the terror experienced by the victims and the survivors—a tenth of an hour that seemed an eternity. It highlights by contrast the meaning of the student movement's hashtag, #NeverAgain. It makes incontrovertible the void in the lives of the families of the victims, reminding me of the father who said he now has to visit the cemetery to have a conversation with his daughter.

González's litany of "nevers" resonates with one of the most searing moments in all literature. King Lear cradles the dead Cordelia in his arms, and wails, "Oh, thou'lt come no more, / Never, never, never, never, never."[6]

Her hush echoes what Simon and Garfunkel knew a half century earlier: "People writing songs that voices never share / And no one dared / Disturb the sound of silence."

González's hush puts me in mind of Ecclesiastes 3:7—there is "a time to keep silence"—and Jesus's silence before Pilate (Matt. 27:14). She evokes the grace of God without using any specifically theological language at all.

I have learned from Benedictines, and from Emma González too (though she might not put it this way), that the Christian tradition is a language school, not a dictionary, and that much authentic Christian testimony doesn't employ direct God-talk.

My theology is affected more deeply by the Benedictine tradition than by anything else.

In 1976 I became one of the first Protestant oblates of Saint John's Abbey in Collegeville, Minnesota (there are now about a hundred of us). By becoming an oblate, I say I will seek to integrate the spirit of Saint Benedict into my daily life. I've lived among Benedictine men and women for a long time, and never cease being amazed at their humor, resiliency, holy irreverence, and gift for tenacious friendship. I hope I have internalized at least a bit the wisdom I hear from my friend (and fellow Texan) Father Columba Stewart, OSB, when I ask him how he accounts for the monastic "long view" in the work he does digitizing manuscripts as executive director of the Hill Museum and Manuscript Library: "I don't need to rush. At the same time I need to do it. Yet I don't have to finish it."[7]

The fact that monasticism antedates almost all the major splits in church history is part of its appeal for me. Benedict can be claimed as Our Holy Father by far more than those who have "OSB" after their names, and even than the increasing numbers of oblates. The monastery, additionally, has much wisdom to offer the still divided churches on what seeking God together entails and promises. When I knock at the monastery's door, I'm not asked for credentials. "Come in and eat and pray with us."

Practice, Practice, Practice

To seek God after the monastic manner of life is truly to seek; it's not just digging around in what one already knows. Practice, practice, practice. If "worship and work" ever goes stale as the Benedictine motto, they might adopt or adapt a remark by legendary golfer Gary Player: "The more I practice, the luckier I get."

In 1996 I am asked by Monastic Interreligious Dialogue to be the interface between fifty monastics—men and women, half of them Christian and half of them Buddhist (including the Dalai Lama)—and a hundred observers, at the Gethsemani Encounter (at the monastery in Kentucky made famous by Thomas Merton).[8] It is a weeklong joint exploration of spiritual traditions and life, where papers are read and, more important, prayers are prayed, and meditations meditated, and silence kept, and pilgrimages walked through the cemetery, and trees planted.

Fundamental to the whole enterprise is the recognition that all—even the most venerable—are beginners. There is more reason to listen than to speak, and sometimes there is more reason for silence all around than for speaking or listening. It sounds self-contradictory, but amid all the talk there is a dialogue of silence.

One of my responsibilities is to meet with the observers and gather their questions to relay to the monastic participants.

Among the dozens of questions is this one, in which I hear the rumblings of cross-cultural tectonic plates: "How are good karma and bad karma and the mitigation of bad karma similar to and different from virtue and sin and forgiveness?" I suppose the fundamentalist answers would be, from the Christian side, that talk of karma is sin, and from the Buddhist side, that being burdened by the notion of sin is the consequence of bad karma.

That sort of question, intriguing as it is, remains at a theoretical level. The observers instinctively know that the whole point of the Gethsemani Encounter is to go deeper, into experience. They ask: "What is the *practical* difference between the Buddhist focus on self-perfection and the Christian aim to grow in likeness to Christ?" And, to take the shadow side: "In the name of religion much suffering has been inflicted on humanity. How do you deal with the legacy of harm your tradition has done?"

The most intimate questions cut through all abstractions and get to the heart of the matter.

"We would like to hear from the dialoguers' *personal* experience," the observers say. "What do you do when you pray, and how does it feel?" "Did you have a moment at which the experience 'clicked,' when you realized 'this is it'?" And the fundamental question of interreligious dialogue: "Has there been a moment when you realized you were hitting common ground with the experience of people in other religions, when you could say to the other, 'I feel my prayer is meeting your prayer'?" All this points to the paradox that as distinctions blur, experience comes into focus.

The Gethsemani Encounter highlights, italicizes, boldfaces a truth I have come to understand through many years of close association with monastic women and men: monastic culture really is a culture; it is about formation of whole persons; it is about recognition and realization more than it is about argument and logic. It is the discovery of the difference between having it all and having everything; stability that is the precondition for growth; obedience that doesn't reduce one's self to the vanishing point but rather brings one's self into sharp focus; community that allows individuality to flourish. There is clear recognition that all are beginners.

The crucial reality for a monastery is the story of the people who have formed the community, both in previous generations and now. It is essential to build a tradition not of rules but of behaviors.

When Buddhist and Christian monastics meet, they practice their life. Memories evoked in both communities—memories that extend back for centuries—are reminders that a distinction between "spiritual life" and "life" is artificial. The basic question is not "What do you say?" but "What do you mean?," and "What do you mean?" quickly leads to "How do you live?"

No greater spiritual worth resides inherently in scholarship than in woodworking or kitchen service. As Abbot Jerome once said to another abbot, "I'll trade you three theologians for one plumber." Visitors to a monastery who expect to find a bunch of holy people doing spiritual things are disoriented. The Rule's "No one will be excused from kitchen service" can be read as meaning that drudgery is an equal-opportunity employer. What it really signifies is that no one should be excluded from an arena where God can be found.

Jean Leclercq, in his classic book about the Benedictine tradition, *The Love of Learning and the Desire for God*, says that "if the great ideas of the past are to remain young and vital, each generation must, in turn, think them through and rediscover them in their pristine newness."[9] Dialogue with Buddhists has provided for Benedictines—all Christians, really—an effective means for that thinking through and rediscovery.

A Way Out of Our Cultural and Spiritual Doldrums

Benedictines are credited with saving civilization in the Middle Ages by patiently copying manuscripts. The stage has been set for their work and that of their Buddhist sisters and brothers in my time by the relentless encounter of customs and religions and languages and worldviews, in the face of which many people are afraid and respond by losing heart or becoming defensive, even shrill. I'm counting on monastics to help save civilization in the twenty-first century by showing us a way out of our cultural and spiritual doldrums through their example of a culture of trust, not fear.

Heading the list of fresh insights from Monastic Interreligious Dialogue, as I wrote in encounter 19, is the way Buddhists notice how positive Benedict is about human nature and its prospects.

I learn this as a consequence of a hunch I have at the Gethsemani Encounter.

As I listen to presentations by two of the Christians, I think, "If just a few terms were changed, these talks could be given by any of the Buddhists here." The next step: I propose to Monastic Interreligious Dialogue that they commission a book of Buddhist reflections on the Rule of Saint Benedict.

They say yes and ask me to edit it.

In the interview that begins encounter 1 above, following publication of *Benedict's Dharma: Buddhists Reflect on the Rule of Saint Benedict,* I am asked, "What did you learn along the way?"[10]

"First," I say, "I learned that Buddhist calendars are as packed as Christian ones; it took two years to get the four Buddhist writers and me together for two days! Second," I add, "the Buddhists highlighted Benedict's positive view of human nature. Third," I continue, "I was reminded that there are as many Buddhisms as there are Christianities—which is to say, the reality is Buddhists and Christians, not abstractions like 'Buddhism' and 'Christianity.'" I conclude with, "Fourth, I was blessed by the largeness of many spirits: authors, editors, colleagues of all sorts."

Neither the Buddha nor Benedict was gloomy, and Buddhists help to illuminate the ancient and tenacious—though often submerged—Christian understanding that my fundamental nature is the image of God, which I can trust more than I fear my devilishness. Benedict, like the Buddha, wants me to wake up.

IN A WORD

I encounter the sustaining grace of God when I learn from Buddhist and Christian monastics what they've been practicing for centuries: trust is more solidly grounded than fear.

sustaining

Grace in an Ancient Prayer

Openness, expansiveness, and curiosity—the substance of trust, the antidote to fear—undergird the practice of Buddhist and Christian monastics. They shine through a very old prayer.

The Unity Book of Prayers was published in 1969. Like many a person who is periodically asked to "lead us in prayer," I snap up such anthologies. The prayer that stunned and dazzled me, and has never grown stale no matter how often I have used it, is one by Saint Gregory of Nazianzus (325–91 CE), quoted below.[1]

When in 1999 I read a newspaper article about that year's Pulitzer Prize in Music to Melinda Wagner, whom I had taught in junior high Sunday school at the Swarthmore Presbyterian Church, I suggested to the board chair of the Collegeville Institute that if they wanted to mark my retirement, nothing would please me more than to commission Wagner to set Saint Gregory's prayer to music. At my retirement party in 2004 the combined choirs of the College of Saint Benedict and Saint John's University gave the premiere performance of *From a Book of Early Prayers*.[2]

Every scholar knows that around the next corner some discovery will complicate a pure and unencumbered reaction to a thing of mystery and beauty. There is doubt in some learned circles about Gregory's authorship of these verses. In one sense it does not really matter, since the text glorifies God regardless of who wrote it (*Hamlet* is *Hamlet* whether Shakespeare wrote it or not).

However, I am grateful to Professor John Anthony McGuckin, the acknowledged master of Gregory studies, for his response to my query.[3]

"Byzantine rhetorical schools set students the graduating task of composing a piece 'in the style of Gregory the Theologian,' so there are many pastiches in the chaos of the present poetic edition," but "the poem in question is not in any sense obviously 'medieval,'" McGuckin wrote to me. "I would give my guess that it is very probably by him."

Once upon a time the term "Christian" meant wider horizons, a larger heart, minds set free, room to move around. The fourth century was preeminently that "once upon a time." Cappadocia, where Gregory lived, was its epicenter.

Hymn to God (Hymnus ad Deum)

O God above all things
(what other name describes you?),
what words can sing your praises?

No word at all denotes you.
What mind can probe your secret?
No mind at all can grasp you.

Alone beyond the power of speech,
all we can speak of springs from you;
alone beyond the power of thought,
all we can think of stems from you.

All things proclaim you—
things that can speak, things that cannot.

All things revere you—
things that have reason, things that have not.

The whole world's longing
and pain mingle about you.

All things breathe you a prayer,
a silent hymn of your own composing.

There is no reference to Christ in Gregory's poem, a silence that
has fueled suspicion about its authenticity.

The Radical Nature of the Incarnation

From the moment I first read it, however, the poem has been for
me a standard of Christian identity, because it underscores the
radical nature of the Incarnation. This "God above all names," unnameable and ungraspable, is the God who came into the world.
"What a friend we have in Jesus," yes, but this friend is beyond
name, beyond thought, beyond speech.

And even more startling, this friend is one about whom, as he
says in Luke 19:40, "the stones would shout out" were his disciples
to remain silent. This Gospel passage is usually read as if Jesus's
remark is intended to put the Pharisees in their place. But the sting
of the rebuke is felt especially by the disciples. Jesus seems to be
saying that the proclamation of the truth does not depend on the
efforts and voices of his followers. "All things proclaim you—things
that can speak, things that cannot."

There are certainly situations in which a close and friendly Jesus
is required, one who softly and tenderly calls, who tarries with us in
the garden, who is with us as he was with Mary and Martha in their
sorrow at the death of their brother Lazarus. But there are occasions
when what is required is much better represented by the grand, even
forbidding icon of the Christ Pantocrator, "Ruler of All," so characteristic of Orthodox churches—and of the world's largest tapestry, by
Graham Sutherland, in Coventry Cathedral, beneath which Benjamin
Britten's *War Requiem*, discussed in encounter 25, was premiered.

The late Susan B. Snyder, professor of English at Swarthmore, with whom I cotaught a course on religion and literature, said, after reading *The Ironic Christian's Companion*,[4] "I'm still not persuaded, but I am prepared to say that 'There is no God, and Patrick knows his ways.'" I felt closer spiritually to her than I do to many people who profess the lordship of Christ—that is, the God Sue didn't know is more like the God I do know than is the God some Christians know, or at least appear to me to know. I would have liked for Sue, who fought terrible depression, to know she could trust God, but I did not think the way to point her to that trust was to tell her she needed a personal relationship with Jesus Christ.

The Eastern Christian tradition puts equal emphasis on both sides of its favorite epigram about the Incarnation: he became what we are in order that we might become what he is.[5] When Christ isn't really God, my being made in the image of God isn't all that big a deal. When Christ isn't really human, growing into the stature of Christ is a detour.

We in the West have tilted too far in the direction of Jesus being like us. Christ (it's a title, not Jesus's surname), the second person of the Trinity, "the firstborn of all creation," through whom "all things have been created" (Col. 1:15–16), is a corrective to the "man for others" image which can become parochial. The second person of the Trinity can too easily be used to bash the third, the Spirit, as when the recovery of the mystical tradition, especially by women, is treated with suspicion.

So, the first thing about Saint Gregory's prayer that gets my attention is what it says about Christ without mentioning Christ at all. It jolts me out of the too-easy chumminess with Jesus that bedevils American Christianity.

The Stones Will Do Just as Well

The second attention grabber is the dismantling of the wall between us humans and the rest of creation, a wall whose permeability I noted already in encounter 23. It has taken the threat of global catastrophe to force on our consciousness the interrelatedness of all things.

When in 1959 I preached the sermon noted in encounter 19, the havoc lurking in human dominion over the creation was something hardly anybody thought about, though just three years later Rachel Carson's *Silent Spring* would launch the environmental movement. Saint Gregory's prayer reminds me that the problem is not just unawareness, but goes deeper—to a misperception about the grounds for God's special regard for human beings.

Implicit in the prayer is a distinction: Gregory has the means—speech—for saying what can't be said, but all things, including those without speech and reason, proclaim and revere God. What I can do that they can't doesn't set me over against everything else but simply makes me a mouthpiece for "all things" that breathe a prayer that is of God's own composing—that is, their prayer is no less of God's composing than is mine.

And this follows from the claim that God became a human being. In an interchange of letters following our joint appearance on a panel, memoirist Patricia Hampl wrote this to me: "I happen to think that this metaphor (the Incarnation) is the greatest offering Christianity has to make to world culture. In it, poetry is rescued, and so is the life of every creature."[6]

Yes, the life of every creature. The disciples thought shouting hosanna was a big deal, but Jesus said the stones would do just as well.

And if "no mind at all can grasp" God, the possession of reason and speech doesn't give me significant advantage over other things when it comes to probing "God's secret." I can and should be grateful for my human capacities, but they are no big deal in the overall scheme of things.

As I noted in encounter 1, the Nicene Creed, spoken by countless Christians every week, illustrates this point. The creed calls God "Maker of heaven and earth, and of all things, visible and invisible." Delete the comma after "things," and there is an implied fundamental distinction between the kinds of things that are visible and the kinds that are invisible. Include the comma, and "all things" are of the same fundamental kind; the distinction between visible and invisible is secondary. Emily Dickinson got it: "I noticed," she wrote, "that the 'Supernatural,' was only the Natural, disclosed."[7]

There is here a convergence between Christian spirituality and that of Zen—Bieke Vandekerckhove, whose impact on me I related in encounter 29, marvels at "the Zen perspective that *everything* will be saved, even already *is* saved, including the last pebble."[8]

"Chronological Snobbery"

As I study the past I am in one way or another engaged in an assault on what C. S. Lewis called "'chronological snobbery,' the uncritical acceptance of the intellectual climate common to our own age and the assumption that whatever has gone out of date is on that account discredited."[9] Jaroslav Pelikan put it this way, in words I heard him say more than once: "I carry a brief for the dead."

Yes, being later doesn't make us better. But there is a flip side. If I have no warrant for thinking myself a cut above those who have gone before, I have every right to think of myself in the game right alongside them. "Chronological regret" is ruled out too.

There is a perfectly understandable—if nonetheless indefensible—prejudice in favor of our own time, though not necessarily in a positive sense. The "snobbery" is as likely to be expressed as "things have never been so bad" as it is "we're better than they were."

We might assume it was easy for Saint Gregory to pile up these glorious phrases about God because he was not confronted with the moral and intellectual challenges we have to face. We might imagine him in splendid isolation, uninterruptedly thinking high thoughts, undistractedly contemplating—living, in effect, in a dream world. He seems not only long ago, but also in a galaxy far, far away.

No way. Gregory's Cappadocia was noisy, crowded, and complicated. It would seem very familiar to us. Gregory's personal and professional ups and downs, ins and outs—his church was once raided by theological opponents who wounded him and killed a visiting bishop—make it clear that understanding God as portrayed in the poem was for Gregory not so much an inheritance as an accomplishment.

Gregory longed for a peaceful life of solitude and prayer, and now and then managed to get it. Most of the time he was in the thick of things. As priest and bishop he saw, daily, the "whole world's longing and pain." Hope is grounded in the paradox that all that longing and pain mingles about the God above all things.

Hope at a Graveyard Picnic

It's 1993. A Collegeville Institute consultation has just ended. It is called "Christian Hope Found Outside the Church."

It concludes in a way probably unique in the annals of ecumenical discussion—with a picnic on a grave. A Catholic priest, Father Joe Kremer, had been a member of the group in its earlier years. He died of AIDS the previous November. We knew of his illness. We had been astonished and blessed by his vitality, his stubbornness, his humor, his grace in the face of it. We realize that saying goodbye to Joe with song, prayer, laughter, and food at his grave in Saint Cloud is exactly what we have to do. We demonstrate that we are engaged in a study of Christian hope, not just of what makes us hopeful.

And in Saint Gregory's prayer, it's a blessing that it is God who is the focus of the longing and pain.

"My thoughts are not your thoughts, nor are your ways my ways, says the LORD" (Isa. 55:8). I used to think this was about the content of the thoughts—God is simply smarter than I am.

But the prayer of Saint Gregory suggests a different way to read the verse.

It's about how the mind of God works, not about what's in the mind of God. If all my loves, hates, fears, needs—all my thoughts and ways—were to congregate simultaneously around me, I would drown.

Saint Gregory's prayer does not pretend to tell me how the mind of God doesn't drown, but only that it doesn't. Perhaps the clue is that the prayer is of God's own composing. As Handel so poignantly scores it, quoting Isaiah 53:3, the Messiah was "a man of sorrows and acquainted with grief."

IN A WORD

I encounter the interrupting grace of God when I'm jolted out of a too-chumminess with Jesus.

interrupting

Grace in the Groundswell's Bell
over the Ebbing Sea's Roar

Keeping spirituality and religion together, or at least in sync, was no easier in Gregory's fourth-century Cappadocia than in subsequent centuries and different places. However, the sites of conflict or convergence change over time. So do the images in which the relationship is encoded.

After visiting fourth-century Cappadocia, I find myself in nineteenth-century England. Starting this final encounter of my story with Matthew Arnold is one of the neatest ironies of my life. As I noted in encounter 2, my first intellectual act on arriving at college was to write nine pages "refuting" him. Now he is a guide.

In his 1867 poem "Dover Beach," Arnold, cited in encounter 7 with an image for shifts in the way we read the Bible ("We are not driven off our ground; our ground itself changes with us"), conjures another figure of change: the sea, dark and foreboding.[1]

Many cultural pundits among his contemporaries were celebrating humanity's release from the shackles of religious tradition. Arnold was convinced traditional religion was irretrievable, but for him this was occasion for regret and sorrow, not rejoicing. Treasure had been lost.

> The sea of faith
> Was once, too, at the full, and round earth's shore
> Lay like the folds of a bright girdle furl'd;
> But now I only hear
> Its melancholy, long, withdrawing roar,
> Retreating to the breath
> Of the night-wind down the vast edges drear
> And naked shingles of the world.

The poem concludes with a picture of such stark gloom that it might be taken as a prophecy of the twentieth century, the most violent the world has yet known:

> And we are here as on a darkling plain
> Swept with confused alarms of struggle and flight,
> Where ignorant armies clash by night.

There is still a lot of faith around, a century and a half after Arnold registered its retreat. There is widespread suspicion, though, reinforced by the current decline in religious identity, that Arnold was basically right: faith is in ebb tide, and culture and politics are counterpointed against that melancholy, long, withdrawing roar.

But the sea has depths beneath the tides.

In 1922 T. S. Eliot portrayed in *The Waste Land* a world drained of all color, all vitality; there is only dryness, a desolation at least as hopeless as that of Arnold's darkling plain:

> A heap of broken images, where the sun beats,
> And the dead tree gives no shelter, the cricket no
>   relief,
> And the dry stone no sound of water.[2]

"The deep sea swell" appears in *The Waste Land*, but in a section called "Death by Water."

It is in 1941, after Eliot became a Christian, that water, in "The Dry Salvages," the third of his *Four Quartets*, becomes an image of life and hope, as the motion of the sea brings not death but stability, a reference point in the mist of space and time:

> And under the oppression of the silent fog
> The tolling bell
> Measures time not our time, rung by the unhurried
> Ground swell, . . .
> . . . .
> And the ground swell, that is and was from the
>   beginning,
> Clangs
> The bell.[3]

My Christian confidence—notice I do not say "certainty"—in the future is based on this: I hear the groundswell's bell pealing over the ebbing sea's roar.

The bell sounds in many places. Here are three in my time.

Groundswell 1: Mother Teresa's "Where Is My Faith?"

In the first instance it might seem that the roar drowns out the peal.

The world was stunned to learn, a few years after her death in 1997, that Mother Teresa of Kolkata (now Saint Teresa), Nobel Peace laureate and founder of the Missionaries of Charity, who serve the poorest of the poor, spent virtually her entire life spiritually dry and distanced from God.

"Where is my faith?" she writes. "Even deep down . . . there is nothing but emptiness and darkness." She prays, "If there be God—please forgive me. When I try to raise my thoughts to heaven, there is such convicting emptiness that those very thoughts return like sharp knives and hurt my very soul." She declares forthrightly:

"I have no faith. Repulsed, empty, no faith, no love, no zeal." Then, perhaps the most searing question: "What do I labor for? If there be no God, there can be no soul. If there be no soul then, Jesus, you also are not true."[4]

When I read critics who say it just shows how hypocritical Christians can be, I know they are wrong. They misunderstand how doubt and faith are twins. They fail to see that Saint Teresa's life and work are the groundswell's bell pealing over the ebbing sea's roar in her spiritual struggles.

The deep Jewish roots of Christianity are evident in Saint Teresa's quandary.

It is characteristic of the honesty of Jewish theology that it considers what purpose God could have had in permitting the denial of God. Among the *Hasidic Sayings* compiled by Martin Buber, which I read in high school, there is one I find especially haunting.

"To what end can the denial of God have been created?" The answer is not abstract or theoretical. "If someone comes to you and asks for help, you shall not turn them off with pious words, saying, 'Have faith and take your troubles to God!' You shall act as though there were no God, as though there were only one person in all the world who could help this one—only yourself."[5]

Saint Teresa was certainly not the first saintly Christian to experience such a dark night of the soul, though her night lasted far longer than most. She makes clear the reassuring yet terrifying truth in Eliot's calling the groundswell "unhurried." She demonstrates the crucial distinction between nonreligious people who flat-out disbelieve in God and religious people who feel that God has forsaken them. The feeling of lack is part of the experience of God. Sometimes God will come to me only if I do not call on God.

Groundswell 2: The Civil Rights Movement

The second instance of the groundswell is the role of Christian churches in the American civil rights movement of the twentieth century.

It has always struck me as ironic that the people I know who have the most tenacious faith in the goodness of God are those who have far more reason than I do to doubt it. The story of Black people in America is shot through with exclusion, brutality, derision, murder, often perpetrated by Christians and justified in theological terms.

I occasionally feel trapped, but it's a temporary inability to spin out of a circle of behavior or thought, to "take time off." This is entirely different from the pain of people who, because of a structural, genuinely inescapable reality like racism, cannot take any time off.

However, despite what would have been good reasons for African Americans to jettison the faith in the fight for liberation, nearly every picture I see of the civil rights struggle has in the foreground people in clerical garb and church buildings in the background. In the written record of the movement, sermons and prayers abound. And of course, there is the music.

I suspect that any anthology of major documents from the twentieth century that might be in libraries centuries from now will include "Letter from Birmingham City Jail" by the Rev. Dr. Martin Luther King Jr.[6] I know of no clearer pealing of the groundswell's bell in my lifetime than in Dr. King's challenge to his white ministerial colleagues.

His voice reverberates with biblical images and themes: "Injustice anywhere is a threat to justice everywhere. We are caught in an inescapable network of mutuality, tied in a single garment of destiny. Whatever affects one directly, affects all indirectly." Urgency and patience (sometimes the groundswell is unhurried) are intertwined: those who are marching and sitting in "have acted in the faith that right defeated is stronger than evil triumphant."

In an image that calls to mind both Arnold and Eliot, King hopes that "the deep fog of misunderstanding will be lifted from our fear-drenched communities."

In Saint Teresa I hear the groundswell's bell ringing in an unexpected minor key. The civil rights movement demonstrates the bell's outlasting what King called "the forces of social stagnation."

Groundswell 3: Concern for "Sister Mother Earth"

The recent history of concern for the environment shows a third way the bell can awaken people from their dogmatic slumbers.

Not so long ago, people alarmed by the ecological devastation humans are wreaking on the planet blamed Christians, who worship a God who told them to "be fruitful and multiply, and fill the earth and subdue it; and have dominion . . . over every living thing that moves upon the earth" (Gen. 1:28). Christians were certainly not the only culprits, but many churches were oblivious to the ecological crisis, or at least dismissed it as a political cause with little religious import.

Then, in a surprising development that attracted widespread media attention, a number of conservative evangelical leaders, some of whom I had come to know in my work at the Collegeville Institute for Ecumenical and Cultural Research, announced that God's concern for all of creation mandates that Christians actively engage in environmental protection.[7]

The sea of faith in the churches had been ebbing. But just as parts of the Bible that seem to condone slavery had eventually been drowned out by recognition that we are all made in God's image, so was the Bible's granting humans "dominion" subordinated to the groundswell's insistence, as Saint Francis put it, that God is to "be praised through our Sister Mother Earth, who sustains and governs us."[8]

What Andy Carlson Knew, and I Now Know

It's January 8, 2001. I'm at Andrew Carlson's funeral. The son of two friends of mine, Andy was well on his way to a PhD in comparative literature. He died in a freak accident while on vacation in Mexico.

The next day I write to his widow, Deb.

I hardly knew Andy.

That is, I hardly knew Andy until yesterday's service.

You, Deb, made him as vivid to me as some people I've known all my life.

What did I learn about Andy? Lots, but mainly this: Andy was so fully present to other people that they could be fully themselves in his presence without fear, without pretense, and with spontaneous delight.

All the great spiritual traditions are in one way or another trying to help us be ourselves in the way that apparently came naturally to Andy.

It's awful beyond telling, beyond imagining, that he is gone. It is a grace, one that may seem tiny now, one that in no way compensates for your loss, but a grace nonetheless, that you and, in part thanks to you, the rest of us have learned from him something about how to live without being cramped or stingy or selfish.

Maybe in my long life I've learned what Andy knew in his all-too-short one.

I hope I am fully present to other people. In 1983 I get a letter from a student, Liz La Porte, with a sentence that suggests I am at least on the way: "I really can't thank you enough for being my freedom fighter."

In eight decades I have come to realize that a Christian life lived with little certainty and with boundless curiosity is not a second-best option for those who just can't manage a no-loose-ends conviction and a no-second-thoughts commitment.

The best thing about being Christian is the excitement, the tension, the mystery, the clarity, the growth, and above all the delight that is woven through my days lived with a God whose grace can be trusted but not taken for granted. Saint Irenaeus, already in the second century, summed it up: "The glory of God is the human being fully alive and the life of the human being is the vision of God."[9]

Christian faith, as I know it, is an adventure in an ever-expanding universe. I hope that my story, as it draws to its end, is an occasion of grace for those who read it—that it broadens perspectives and enlarges territory—even explores strange new worlds—and loosens stiff spiritual joints so that movement can be free and spontaneous.

IN A WORD

I encounter the amazing (yes, finally) grace of God when I detect the groundswell's bell now, and three and a half centuries hence, and in ages long before, with an ear attuned to the unhurried and an eye not blocked by the silent fog.

amazing

Epilogue

Letter to Captain Picard

Encounter 29 recounts my immersion in *Star Trek: The Next Generation*. In the 127th episode, the crew of the starship *Enterprise* has time-warped back to nineteenth-century San Francisco, where they encounter Mark Twain. He surreptitiously transports back with them to the twenty-fourth century, and asks, "Where are we, and when?"[1] I understand something of his disorientation.

What to make of this odd thought that won't leave me alone?: I'm more at home with Captain Picard and his crew and the inhabitants of the civilizations they encounter than I am with many of my contemporaries—the ones who are usually called "Christian" in the headlines, who loudly trumpet their "for-sure" Christianity. They are strident, they draw sharp distinctions, they know with certainty what is good and what is evil. Since God belongs to them and they are God's bodyguards, they have sequestered God in the fortress church. Beyond the moat is error. The drawbridge is up.

I have studied, taught, and written about the Christian tradition for half a century. It was through seeing my own time at a slant from my "visits" to the twenty-fourth century that I came to understand just how central to my thought and being is the reality of God's grace.

As a token of thanks to Capt. Jean-Luc Picard, I send him this letter.

DEAR CAPTAIN PICARD,

In his ingenious 2016 book *Time Travel: A History* (one I suspect will be on Starfleet Academy reading lists), James Gleick says this: "If you were trapped in the past, how would you communicate with the future? In a general way, we are all trapped in the past and we are all communicating with the future, via books and epitaphs and time capsules and the rest. But we seldom need to message particular future people at specific future times."[2]

Seldom, but not never. At the conclusion of my story of encounters with the grace of God, I need to message a particular person, you, at a specific future time, the 2360s.

To get some sense of what it might be like for you to read this book three and a half centuries from now, I have picked up a volume from three and a half centuries ago that was also designed as an account of Christian identity and sensibility, the *Pensées* of Blaise Pascal (1623–62)—a book that is one of the intellectual glories of your beloved France.

350 Years Ago

Its contents are edited—he died at age thirty-nine (half what I've reached as I write this), before he could complete the treatise he had in mind. It has over nine hundred entries (with scholarly disputes as to how they should be ordered). My encounters, brief as they are, are overlong by contrast. I'm certainly not so foolish as to invite comparison between my style and substance and those of a celebrated master of elegant prose and philosophical depth. However, the equivalent time lapse between him and me and me and you is instructive.

There is much in the *Pensées* that seems familiar to me. First and foremost is its pattern of both/and instead of either/or: "a certain doubtful dimness from which our doubts cannot take away all the clearness, nor our own natural lights chase away all the darkness."[3] One might have expected Pascal, a mathematical genius of the first order, to gravitate toward certainty, toward no-loose-ends answers. But he found mathematics full of mystery, of infinities going in every direction. While he had high regard and respect for intellectual achievement, he was alert to the way pride insinuates itself and tricks the smart person into believing that others not so smart are inferior in their humanity.

Pascal's famous "wager"—if God is, believing will gain me infinite reward; if God isn't, believing won't lose me anything—is not nearly so crass as it is sometimes made out to be. It is grounded in profound meditation on the nature of the world and the elusive character of thought itself. However, it presupposes a sharp distinction between humanity and the rest of the biological world that has been called into serious question by developments since Pascal's time, especially by Darwin's theory of evolution.

Pascal's time, the middle of the seventeenth century, was one of much ferment in regard to religion.

The Thirty Years' War (1618–48), with a big component of Catholic-Protestant rivalry and mutual destruction, planted seeds of doubt. If, as the Peace of Westphalia decreed, a region's religion would be determined by that of its prince, metaphysical claims were subordinated to political ones. (The European Union of my own time—founded in 1993—would be as much a dream to Pascal as your United Federation of Planets—founded in 2161—is to me.)

There was, additionally, fierce doctrinal controversy within the Christian community. Pascal's other famous work, *Letters to a Provincial*, is a scathing and witty riposte to the Jesuits of his time. I suspect there were times Pascal was torn, as I sometimes am, between "Here I stand, I can do no other!"[4] and "Stop the world: I want to get off."[5]

Pascal was nineteen years old in 1642, the year Galileo died and Isaac Newton was born. Thought was trending at an accelerating rate away from the medieval comprehensive view that theology was the queen of the sciences. In England, Thomas Hobbes was declaring human life in the state of nature to be "solitary, poor, nasty, brutish, and short."[6] The church's silencing Galileo was a sign of desperate weakness. Newton's sense of himself as theologian (he wrote more on Scripture than he did on science) in retrospect looks quaint.

So, when I read the *Pensées*, I have a sense that twenty-first-century America isn't all that different from Pascal's seventeenth-century France—religious conflict and intellectual challenges to religion are the order of the day now too.

It seems that things are quite different in your time, Captain. You refer to periods of religious fighting in the distant past tense. I am distressed to read in one of your logs that there were nuclear winters on Earth in the twenty-first century,[7] and to hear Commander Data say that "In the early twenty-second century Earth was recovering from World War III"[8]—that would be in the time of my great-great-great-grandchildren—but there is no indication that that planet-wide conflagration had even a tinge of religious coloring.

Has Wesley Read the Book You Gave Him?

In terms of intellectual tradition, I suspect there will still be plenty of ferment, controversy, competition in your time, but it seems to me that you stand in a long line of thinkers like another great Frenchman, Montaigne, whom I cited in encounter 17, who was "more enchanted than alarmed by the bewildering variety of human practices."[9] There is a more recent philosopher from whom you yourself have learned, who is certainly part of this same tradition.

The young ensign Wesley Crusher is cramming for his Starfleet Academy exams. While traveling with him in a shuttlecraft you ask if he has read the book you gave him.[10] In a dodge I've sometimes employed when confronted with such a question, he replies, sheepishly, "Some of it."

He then goes on to explain that he doesn't expect William James to be on his exams. To which you respond, "The important things never will be. Anyone can be trained in the mechanics of piloting a starship. . . . Open your mind to the past—art, history, philosophy—and all this [by which you clearly mean the universe] may mean something."

You might have said to Wesley, and to countless others you met in your travels, words that often served as a transition in my father's sermons: "Come further now and see."

As you will have learned from what I said in encounter 17, William James is someone I read too. I doubt his *Varieties of Religious Experience* is the volume you gave Wesley—more likely it was his *Lectures on Pragmatism*—but James had deep insights into religion. He was more suspicious of religious institutions than I am; but for him, even if the Christian church is a bygone memory in your time, the reality of religious experience will be largely untouched. For James, "spiritual but not religious" is a shorthand definition of the fundamental human condition.

Leadership and Listening

Among your traits, Capt. Picard, the one that most resonates with my Christian sensibility is your understanding that the first requirement for successful leadership is listening—a commandment that accounts for the sustainability of the most persistent of Christian institutions: monasticism. The first word of the Rule of Saint Benedict is "Listen."[11] It's not just hearing, but really listening. If the church persists into the twenty-fourth century, I suspect monastic folks will have been at least partly responsible.

My friend David O'Fallon says that when he goes into potentially contentious meetings (he has worked for state agencies, so has gone to very few other kinds), he consciously chooses to view everyone in the room with compassion. He leaves aside, in his attitude, the very sharp, but in a sense abstract, fractious arguments that will fly through the air. He has taken full measure of the fact that the persons are what's real in that room. Because he's dealing with realities, not abstractions, he's on average more effective than he would be otherwise. He says he learned something about this from the Dalai Lama, who, as a good Buddhist, suspects that not even the persons are real!

Your compassion is like this. It helps account for your ability to see the humanity of the android, Cdr. Data, and for your success as a negotiator of truces in various sectors of the galaxy.

There are many technological marvels you take for granted that in my time I can hardly imagine. Warp drive, aided by the occasional wormhole, means you can cover mind-boggling distances. Transporters get you physically from orbit to a planet at the speed of light.

Lawrence Krauss, author of *The Physics of Star Trek*, has called into question the very possibility of either of these technologies, especially the transporter. He says that according to Heisenberg's uncertainty principle, there is no way to guarantee that the atoms constituting you, Picard on the *Enterprise*, will be accurately reconstituted into you, Picard on the ground.[12]

Krauss may well be right, though the history of physics has enough curious twists and turns to make me wonder.

What I Wish I Had: The Universal Translator

But while I would love to move at warp speed and transport to distant places instantaneously, there is another piece of your technology that I would like even more to have: the universal translator.

The most remarkable difference between your time and mine is the fact that everybody can talk to everybody—in all the new civilizations—and be understood. We have computer programs that make a stab at converting from one language to another, but the results are often comical. One of the biggest challenges of diplomacy is figuring out what the other side is really saying.

I find nearly all your encounters enlightening and provocative, often even reassuring. The one I love most is your time with the Tamarians.[13] The failure of the universal translator sets the stage for what I believe is the central point of contact between you and whatever might be left of the Christian tradition in your time.

Cdr. Data informs you that in each of the previous encounters with the Tamarians nothing bad happened, but there was no communication. You respond, "Communication is a matter of patience, imagination."

This is how the Tamarians talk to you: "Shaka, when the walls fell." "Lowani under two moons." "Darmok and Jalad at Tenagra." "Temba, his arms wide."

And for a long time, you have no idea what they're talking about.

With patience and imagination, you and your colleagues finally get it: the Tamarians converse by metaphors. Data realizes that they "communicate through narrative imagery—a reference to the individuals and places which appear in their mytho-historical accounts."

Counselor Deanna Troi proposes an analogy: "It's as if I were to say to you, 'Juliet on her balcony,'" and Dr. Beverly Crusher adds, "An image of romance." But then the problem: "If I didn't know who Juliet was or what she was doing on that balcony, the image alone wouldn't have any meaning."

In a confrontation that leads to both tragedy and breakthrough, an addition is made to the vocabulary: "Picard and Dathon at El-Adrel." It is your own retelling of the *Epic of Gilgamesh* that makes the connection.

As the *Enterprise* prepares to leave orbit, Cdr. Riker finds you reading. He notices the book is in Greek. "Oh," you say, "the Homeric Hymns—one of the root metaphors of our own culture." When he asks if it's for the next time you encounter the Tamarians, you reply, "More familiarity with our own mythology might help us relate to theirs. . . . Now the door is open between our peoples."

I think the staying power of the Christian tradition is in its root metaphors more than in its dogmas. My father said as much from the pulpit: "Through the centuries many attempts have been made to set forth the Christian vision in formal statements of faith and systems of theology. . . . But the languages of Christian faith most widely heard, grasped, and responded to are of a different kind. They are indirect languages, in which the presence and work of God is declared in connection with a person, a drama, and a community of faith." One of his sermons was titled "Isaiah, Jesus, Shakespeare, and Steinbeck."

Christian life is not a matter of detachedly viewing but of longingly gazing, not a matter of careful calculation but of breaking jars of expensive ointment, of recklessly selling a diversified portfolio in order to purchase a precious pearl; it is a matter of rejoicing over one lost sheep that is found more than over the ninety-nine that were always in the fold, of welcoming home prodigals with feasts, without asking what they have been up to. As my student quoted in encounter 1 said: Mary didn't write a book; she bore a child.

I respectfully suggest that you explore "Abraham, with knife raised"; "Moses, at the burning bush"; "Joshua, by the walls of Jericho"; "the woman of Endor, taking charge of King Saul"; "Isaiah, the coal at his lips"; "Jeremiah, burying a land deed in a clay jar"; "Job, sitting in the ashes"; "Mary, at the manger"; "the Syrophoenician woman, beating Jesus at his own game"; "Jesus, his arms wide;" "Peter, when the cock crowed"; "Paul, on the road to Damascus"; "Augustine, taken up from behind his own back where he had placed himself"; "Julian, holding the hazelnut"; "Pascal, with pen in hand"; "Mother Teresa, during the long dark night"; "Dr. King, in Birmingham Jail"; "Bieke Vandekerckhove, through the open little back door."

All best, Capt. Picard, and . . . God bless.

Patrick

Notes

Encounter 1: Grace in Formation

1. "An Interview with Patrick Henry," *Monastic Interreligious Dialogue Bulletin* 67 (October 2001), https://www.urbandharma.org/buca/BD1/bd1interview.pdf.

2. Weekly Article No. 219, in James M. Smallwood and Steven E. Gragert, eds., *Will Rogers' Weekly Articles, Vol. 2: The Coolidge Years, 1925–1927* (Stillwater, OK: Oklahoma State University Press, 1978); revised and printed on the Will Rogers Memorial Museum website, 2010, http://www.willrogers.com/writings.

3. Julius Lester, *Lovesong: Becoming a Jew* (New York: Henry Holt, 1988), 20.

4. "John Chrysostom: On the Birthday of our Savior Jesus Christ, a Sermon," trans. Bryson Sewell, 2013, http://www.tertullian.org/fathers/chrysostom_homily_2_on_christmas.htm. Though this homily is attributed to Chrysostom, Sewell says many scholars doubt its authenticity.

5. Saint John Chrysostom, *Homily on 1 Timothy 4:1–3*, in *Nicene and Post-Nicene Fathers*, series 1, vol. 13, ed. Philip Schaff et al., at https://en.wikisource.org/wiki/Nicene_and_Post-Nicene_Fathers:_Series_I/Volume_XIII/On_Timothy,_Titus,_and_Philemon/On_1_Timothy/1_Timothy_4:1-3 (with "hath" changed to "has," and "thine" to "yours").

Encounter 2: Grace in Perspective

This encounter adapts material that previously appeared in my book reviews "Traveling Mercies: Some Thoughts on Faith; By Anne Lamott; New York, Pantheon, 1999. 275 Pp. $23.00," *Theology Today* 56, no. 4 (January 2000): 608–12, doi:10.1177/004057360005600417; and "Amazing Grace: A Vocabulary of Faith; By Kathleen Norris; New York, Riverhead, 1998. 384 Pp. $12.95 (Pb)," *Theology Today* 56, no. 4 (January 2000): 608, doi:10.1177/004057360005600416. Used by permission.

1. A condensed translation, available at http://justus.anglican.org /resources/bio/263.html, of the account found in the Venerable Bede, *Ecclesiastical History of the English People*, II.13, trans. A. M. Sellar (London: George Bell and Sons, 1907), available at www.gutenberg .org/files/38326/38326-h/38326-h.html.

2. John Henry Newman, *Apologia pro Vita Sua* (1864; Eugene, OR: Wipf and Stock, 2017), 60.

3. John Henry Newman, *An Essay on the Development of Christian Doctrine*, 1.1.7 (1845; New York: Image Books, 1960), 63.

4. Matthew Arnold, "Culture and Anarchy" (1867–69), in *Matthew Arnold: Culture and Anarchy, and Other Writings*, ed. Stefan Collini (Cambridge: Cambridge University Press, 1993), 62.

5. Matthew Arnold, "The Study of Poetry," originally published as the introduction to T. H. Ward's anthology *The English Poets* (1880) and later in *Essays in Criticism*, Second Series (1888). Reprinted at https:// www.poetryfoundation.org/articles/69374/the-study-of-poetry.

6. Alisa Kasmir, *Hineni: In Imitation of Abraham* (Collegeville, MN: Liturgical Press, 2020), offers a fresh and innovative positive interpretation of Gen. 22, linking it to the practice of spiritual direction.

7. Anne Lamott, *Traveling Mercies: Some Thoughts on Faith* (New York: Pantheon, 1999), 27.

8. Kathleen Norris, *Amazing Grace: A Vocabulary of Faith* (New York: Riverhead Books, 1998), 11.

9. Lamott, *Traveling Mercies*, 10.

10. Norris, *Amazing Grace*, 4.

11. Lamott, *Traveling Mercies*, 8.

12. Lamott, 46–47.

13. Lamott, 52 (italics in original).

14. Norris, *Amazing Grace*, 6.

15. Norris, 63.

16. Norris, 8.

17. Lamott, *Traveling Mercies*, 72.

18. Mary Oliver, *What Do We Know: Poems and Prose Poems* (Cambridge, MA: Da Capo, 2002), 27–28.

Encounter 3: Grace in Balance

1. John Stuart Mill, "Bentham," in *Essays on Ethics, Religion and Society* (1830; Toronto: University of Toronto Press, 1969), 78, at http://oll-resources.s3.amazonaws.com/titles/241/0223.10.pdf.

2. John Stuart Mill, *Autobiography*, chapter 1, "Childhood and Early Education," in *The Harvard Classics*, vol. 25 (New York: P. F. Collier & Son, 1937), 7.

3. Mill, "Bentham," 83–84.

4. Mill, 90–91.

5. Mill, 92.

6. John Stuart Mill, "Coleridge," in *Essays on Ethics, Religion and Society*, 119.

7. Mill, *Autobiography*, chapter 5, "A Crisis in My Mental History. One Stage Onward," 86–89.

8. Mill, 94.

9. William Wordsworth, *Ode on Intimations of Immortality from Recollections of Early Childhood*, at https://poets.org/poem/ode-intimations-immortality-recollections-early-childhood.

Encounter 4: Grace in Dimensions

This encounter adapts material that previously appeared in my article "Images of God in Time and Space," *Theology Today* 61, no. 2 (July 2004): 202–12. Used by permission.

1. Stephen Hawking, *A Brief History of Time: From the Big Bang to Black Holes* (New York: Bantam, 1988), 136.

2. Quoted in Richard Corliss, "Over Easy" (review of *Continental Divide*), *Time*, September 14, 1981, 90.

3. Abraham Pais, *Niels Bohr's Times in Physics, Philosophy, and Polity* (Oxford: Oxford University Press, 1991), 29.

4. Ronald W. Clark, *Einstein: The Life and Times* (New York: Avon Books, 1972), 521.

5. Italo Calvino, *Cosmicomics* (New York: Harcourt, Brace, 1968).

6. Calvino, 36.

7. Albert Marden, quoted in K. C. Cole, "Escape from 3-D," *Discover*, July 1993, 52, http://discovermagazine.com/1993/jul/escapefrom3d237/.

8. Calvino, *Cosmicomics*, 43.

9. Calvino, 44.

Encounter 5: Grace in Surprise

This encounter adapts material that previously appeared in my article "'Master of the Stray Detail': Peter Brown and Historiography," *Religious Studies Review* 6, no. 2 (April 1980): 91–96. Used by permission.

1. Mark Twain, *Innocents Abroad* (1869), chapter 40, at https://www.gutenberg.org/files/3176/3176-h/3176-h.htm.

2. Peter Brown, *The Making of Late Antiquity* (Carl Newell Jackson Lectures) (Cambridge, MA: Harvard University Press, 1978), 1.

3. Brown, 7.

4. Peter Brown, *Religion and Society in the Age of Saint Augustine* (New York: Harper & Row, 1972), 12.

5. Cartoon by Peter Steiner, *New Yorker*, September 22, 1997, 72.

6. Letter No. 45, in *The Letters of John Keats 1814–1821*, vol. 1, ed. Hyder Edward Rollins (Cambridge, MA: Harvard University Press, 1958), 193.

7. Peter Brown, *Augustine of Hippo: A Biography* (Berkeley: University of California Press, 1969), 254–56.

8. Brown, *Religion and Society*, 15–17.

9. Brown, 19.

10. Brown, *Augustine of Hippo*, 156.

Encounter 6: Grace in Politics

1. Kurt Vonnegut, *Cat's Cradle* (New York: Holt, Rinehart and Winston, 1963), section 46.

2. "NCC Communication Commission Criticizes Reuters for Refusing to Sell Billboard Space to United Methodists," National Council of Churches News Service, October 27, 2003, http://www.ncccusa .org/news/03reutersbillboard.html. Responding to criticism, Reuters relented.

3. Garrison Keillor, "In Search of Lake Wobegon," *National Geographic*, December 2000, http://www.garrisonkeillor.com/national -geographic-in-search-of-lake-wobegon/.

4. Nick Coleman, "In God, er, the GOP we trust?; One prayer breakfast takes an almighty turn to the right," *Star Tribune* (Minneapolis), May 7, 2004, 3B.

Encounter 7: Grace in "Whatever"

1. Pius XII, *Divino afflante Spiritu*, http://w2.vatican.va/content/ pius-xii/en/encyclicals/documents/hf_p-xii_enc_30091943_divino-af-flante-spiritu.html.

2. For a nuanced appraisal of these two "originalisms," see Jaroslav Pelikan, *Interpreting the Bible and the Constitution*, a John W. Kluge Center Book (New Haven: Yale University Press, 2004).

3. Jaroslav Pelikan, *The Emergence of the Catholic Tradition (100–600)*, vol. 1 of *The Christian Tradition: A History of the Development of Doctrine* (Chicago: University of Chicago Press, 1971), 9.

4. Anthony Ugolnik, "Jacob's Ladder: Jaroslav Pelikan and the People of the Book," in Valerie Hotchkiss and Patrick Henry, eds., *Orthodoxy and Western Culture: A Collection of Essays Honoring Jaro-*

slav Pelikan on His Eightieth Birthday (Crestwood, NY: St. Vladimir's Seminary Press, 2005), 72–73.

5. Pope Saint Gregory I (the Great), *Moralia on Job* 4, available at http://faculty.georgetown.edu/jod/texts/moralia1.html.

6. Matthew Arnold, introduction to *Literature and Dogma: An Essay towards a Better Apprehension of the Bible*, 4th ed. (London: Smith, Elder, 1874), 8.

7. Augustine, *Confessions* 6.5, in *Confessions and Enchiridion*, ed. and trans. Albert C. Outler, The Library of Christian Classics, vol. 7 (Philadelphia: Westminster Press, 1955), 120.

Encounter 8: Grace in Opening Up and Broadening Out

This encounter adapts material that previously appeared in my book *New Directions in New Testament Study* (Philadelphia: Westminster Press, 1979; London: SCM Press, 1980). Used by permission.

1. Minneapolis: Fortress; Collegeville, MN: Liturgical Press, 1989.

2. Philadelphia: Westminster Press, 1977.

3. C. S. Lewis, *Letters to an American Lady*, ed. Clyde S. Kilby (Grand Rapids, MI: Eerdmans, 1967), 2.

Encounter 9: Grace in Verb Tenses

This encounter adapts material that previously appeared in my "Breaking Things Down, to Build," extended review of James L. Kugel, *The Bible as It Was*, *Harvard Divinity Bulletin* 28, no. 4 (1999): 23–24. Used by permission.

1. James L. Kugel, *The Bible As It Was* (Cambridge, MA: Belknap Press of Harvard University Press, 1997), 17–23.

2. Kugel, 566.

3. Harold Bloom, *The Anxiety of Influence: A Theory of Poetry*, 2nd ed. (New York: Oxford University Press, 1997).

4. *The Life of Teresa of Jesus: The Autobiography of St. Teresa of Ávila*, ed. and trans. E. Allison Peers (New York: Image Books, 1991), 143.

Encounter 10: Grace in Being *Left Behind* with *The Da Vinci Code*

1. "The 25 Most Influential Evangelicals in America," *Time*, February 7, 2005, http://content.time.com/time/specials/packages/article /0,28804,1993235_1993243_1993291,00.html.

2. Michelle Goldberg, "The Religious Right's Trojan Horse," *New York Times*, January 29, 2017.

3. The interview is reported at http://www.christianpost.com /news/michele-bachmann-rapture-of-the-church-is-coming-faster -than-anyone-can-see-god-will-punish-america-for-disobeying-his -word-137942/.

4. Cartoon by Mick Stevens, *New Yorker*, October 9, 1995, 90.

5. "The Greatest Story Ever Sold," *60 Minutes* interview, April 13, 2004, http://www.cbsnews.com/news/the-greatest-story-ever-sold/.

Encounter 11: Grace in Uncertainty

This encounter adapts material that previously appeared in my book *New Directions in New Testament Study* (Philadelphia: Westminster Press, 1979; London: SCM Press, 1980). Used by permission.

1. G. M. Young, quoted in W. D. Handcock's introduction to G. M. Young, *Victorian Essays* (London: Oxford University Press, 1962), 10.

2. Quoted in David O'Reilly, "Chaplain struggles with Catholic stance on female priests," Knight Ridder News Service, published in *Amarillo Globe-News*, January 11, 2001.

3. Rule of Benedict 73:8, in *RB 1980: The Rule of St. Benedict in Latin and English with Notes*, ed. Timothy Fry, OSB (Collegeville, MN: Liturgical Press, 1981), 297.

4. Tom Tickell, "Jesus's 80-year deadline," *The Guardian*, December 10, 1981, 1.

Encounter 12: Grace in the Digging

1. What follows about San Clemente is a weaving together of my own reminiscences of what I heard on a visit to the basilica in 1993

and what I have found at http://www.basilicasanclemente.com/eng/ and several tourist guide websites, all of it tested against the careful scholarship of Eileen Kane, "Contribution to a History of the Basilica of Saint Clement in Rome," *Studies: An Irish Quarterly Review* 73, no. 290 (Summer 1984), 117–45.

2. Adam Gopnik, "The Illiberal Imagination," *New Yorker*, March 20, 2017, 88. All subsequent quotes by Gopnik in encounter 12 are from this article.

Encounter 13: Grace in a Future That Ain't What It Used to Be

This encounter adapts material that previously appeared in my talk "Theological Reflections on Yogi Berra's 'The Future ain't what it used to be,'" plenary address to Covenant Network Conference, November 8, 2003, available at https://covnetpres.org/2003/11/822/.

1. *The Empire Strikes Back*, episode 5 of *Star Wars*, directed by Irvin Kershner, written by Leigh Brackett and Lawrence Kasdan, released May 17, 1980 (produced by Lucasfilm; distributed by Twentieth Century Fox).

2. Patrick Henry, *The Ironic Christian's Companion: Finding the Marks of God's Grace in the World* (New York: Riverhead Books, 1999), 30–31.

3. "Views about same-sex marriage among Catholics," from the 2014 Religious Landscape Study conducted by Pew Research Center, https://www.pewforum.org/religious-landscape-study/religious-tradition/catholic/views-about-same-sex-marriage/.

4. For an account of the "picnic battle," see https://www.senate.gov/artandhistory/history/minute/Witness_Bull_Run.htm.

5. Alexandra Alter, "Bible given fashion makeover to lure teen girls," Religion News Service, published in *Star Tribune* (Minneapolis), August 30, 2003. The following two quotes come from this story.

6. *Revolve: The Complete New Testament (Biblezines)* (Nashville: Thomas Nelson, 2003).

Encounter 14: Grace in Ecumenism

This encounter draws on material that previously appeared in my chapter "Ecumenism of the People," in *Twentieth-Century Global Christianity*, ed. Mary Farrell Bednarowski, Vol. 7 of *A People's History of Christianity* (Minneapolis: Fortress, 2008), 280–306. Used by permission.

1. Thomas Campbell, *Declaration and Address* (Washington, PA: Brown and Sample, 1809), 3, 6, available at https://community.logos .com/forums/p/37781/327063.aspx.

2. From Temple's sermon at his enthronement as archbishop, cited in F. A. Iremonger, *William Temple, Archbishop of Canterbury: His Life and Letters* (London: Oxford University Press, 1948), 387.

3. The report of the conference is available at http://collegevillein stitute.org/wp-content/uploads/2013/02/Ecumenism-Among-Us.pdf.

4. Quoted in Robert S. Bilheimer, *Breakthrough: The Emergence of the Ecumenical Tradition* (Grand Rapids, MI: Eerdmans; Geneva: WCC Publications, 1989), 4.

Encounter 15: Grace in the "Cannot"

This encounter draws on material that previously appeared in my article "Reconciling Memories: Building an Ecumenical Future," *Ecumenical Trends* 26, no. 4 (April 1997): 1–8. Used by permission.

1. Joan Chittister, *In Search of Belief* (Liguori, MO: Liguori/Triumph, 1999), 12.

2. Quoted in Esther Byle Bruland, *Regathering: The Church from "They" to "We"* (Grand Rapids, MI: Eerdmans, 1995), 100.

3. Margaret O'Gara, *The Ecumenical Gift Exchange* (Collegeville, MN: Michael Glazier/Liturgical Press, 1998), x.

4. F. M. Cornford, *Microcosmographia Academica: Being a Guide for the Young Academic Politician* (Cambridge: Bowes and Bowes, 1908), 15.

5. A remark made in a consultation at the Collegeville Institute for Ecumenical and Cultural Research.

Encounter 16: Grace in Reconciling Memories

This encounter draws on material that previously appeared in my article "Reconciling Memories: Building an Ecumenical Future," *Ecumenical Trends* 26, no. 4 (April 1997): 1–8. Used by permission.

1. In a personal letter from Chadwick to me postmarked May 14, 1996.

2. Erasmus, *The Praise of Folly*, trans. John P. Dolan, in *The Essential Erasmus* (New York: New American Library, 1964), 113.

3. Sidney T. Miller, "The Reasons for Some Legal Fictions," *Michigan Law Review* 8/8 (June 1910), 629.

4. Keith F. Nickle and Timothy F. Lull, eds., *A Common Calling: The Witness of Our Reformation Churches in North America Today* (Minneapolis: Augsburg Fortress, 1993), 49–50.

5. Nickle and Lull, 54.

6. Nelson Mandela, *Long Walk to Freedom: The Autobiography of Nelson Mandela* (Boston: Little, Brown, 1994), 22.

7. This story is told in Patrick Henry, "Images of the Church in the Second Nicene Council and in the *Libri Carolini*," in *Law, Church, and Society: Essays in Honor of Stephan Kuttner*, ed. Kenneth Pennington and Robert Somerville (Philadelphia: University of Pennsylvania Press, 1977), 237–52.

8. J. D. Mansi, ed., *Sacrorum conciliorum nova et amplissima collectio*, vol. 12 (Florence, 1766), 1031D.

9. Mansi, vol. 13 (Florence, 1767), 401D.

10. Mansi, vol. 13, 364B.

11. Text of the Joint Declaration is at http://www.vatican.va/roman _curia/pontifical_councils/chrstuni/documents/rc_pc_chrstuni_doc _31101999_cath-luth-joint-declaration_en.html.

12. The quotations in this paragraph are, respectively, from sec. 5,

para. 44 and para. 42 of the *1995 draft* of the Joint Declaration. The only text of that draft I have located on the Internet is in an Icelandic journal, *Gerðir kirkjuþings*, 1995, https://timarit.is/page/6491025#page /n113/mode/2up. The entire 1995 draft (in English) is at 101–18, the cited words themselves at 109. It's a pity that the rhetorical elixir of the paired "mutuallys" gets watered down in the approved 1999 text (5.40): "Therefore the Lutheran and the Catholic explications of justification are in their difference open to one another and do not destroy the consensus regarding the basic truths."

Encounter 17: Grace in Variety

1. https://www.pewresearch.org/fact-tank/2018/07/02/5-facts -about-episcopalians/; https://www.pewresearch.org/fact-tank/2018 /01/03/new-estimates-show-u-s-muslim-population-continues-to -grow/.

2. This statement about Buddhism was confirmed for me in an email from Professor Judith Simmer-Brown of Naropa University, who notes that "Los Angeles is the most diverse Buddhist city in the world."

3. Jane Kramer, "Me, Myself, and I: What made Michel de Montaigne the first modern man?," *New Yorker*, September 7, 2009, http:// www.newyorker.com/magazine/2009/09/07/me-myself-and-i.

4. Leonard Swidler and Paul Mojzes, eds., *Attitudes of Religions and Ideologies Toward the Outsider: The Other*, Religions in Dialogue, vol. 1 (Lewiston, NY: Edwin Mellen Press, 1990).

5. Anne Lamott, *Traveling Mercies: Some Thoughts on Faith* (New York: Pantheon, 1999), 235.

6. Yehezkel Landau, "An Interview with Krister Stendahl," *Harvard Divinity Bulletin* 35/1 (Winter 2007), https://bulletin.hds.harvard .edu/articles/winter2007/interview-krister-stendahl. Barbara Brown Taylor has an entire—and wonderful—book that takes its cue from Stendahl's remark: *Holy Envy: Finding God in the Faith of Others* (San Francisco: HarperOne, 2019).

7. In response to the question "What does diversity mean to me?," posed to members of the board of directors of the Collegeville Institute for Ecumenical and Cultural Research, February 2004.

Encounter 18: Grace in a Fugue

1. "The Greatest Story Ever Sold," *60 Minutes* interview, April 13, 2004, https://www.cbsnews.com/news/the-greatest-story-ever-sold/.

2. Cited in Patrick Henry, "A Minnesota Response," the final chapter of *Attitudes of Religions and Ideologies Toward the Outsider: The Other*, ed. Leonard Swidler and Paul Mojzes (Lewiston, NY: Edwin Mellen Press, 1990), 196.

3. In response to the question "What does diversity mean to me?," posed to members of the board of directors of the Collegeville Institute for Ecumenical and Cultural Research, February 2004.

Encounter 19: Grace in Finding an Old Sermon

1. Bruce Grierson, "The Age of U-Turns," *Time*, April 5, 2007.

2. *Groundhog Day*, directed by Harold Ramis, written by Danny Rubin and Harold Ramis, released February 4, 1993 (produced and distributed by Columbia Pictures).

3. *Star Trek: The Next Generation*, season 5, episode 18, "Cause and Effect," directed by Jonathan Frakes, written by Brannon Braga, aired March 21, 1992, distributed by Paramount Pictures (currently owned by ViacomCBS).

4. Patrick Henry, ed., *Benedict's Dharma: Buddhists Reflect on the Rule of Saint Benedict* (New York: Riverhead Books, 2001). The Buddhist contributors are Norman Fischer, Joseph Goldstein, Judith Simmer-Brown, and Yifa.

5. T. S. Eliot, "Little Gidding," section V, in *The Complete Poems and Plays 1909–1950* (New York: Harcourt, Brace, 1952), 145.

Encounter 20: Grace in Christian Autobiography

1. W. H. Auden, *The Age of Anxiety: A Baroque Eclogue*, ed. Alan Jacobs (1947; Princeton: Princeton University Press, 2011).

2. *The Life of Teresa of Jesus: The Autobiography of St. Teresa of Ávila*, ed. and trans. E. Allison Peers (New York: Image Books, 1991), 174.

3. C. S. Lewis, preface to *Surprised by Joy: The Shape of My Early Life* (New York: Harcourt, Brace, 1955), vii.

4. "Rowing," in *Selected Poems of Anne Sexton* (Boston: Houghton Mifflin Company, 2000), 229.

5. "Riding the Elevator into the Sky," *Selected Poems*, 231.

6. Augustine, *Confessions* 8.7.16, trans. Henry Chadwick (Oxford: Oxford University Press, 1991), 44.

7. *Teresa of Jesus*, 220.

8. *Teresa of Jesus*, 74.

9. *Teresa of Jesus*, 82.

10. *Teresa of Jesus*, 144.

11. Lewis, *Surprised by Joy*, 213–15.

12. *Teresa of Jesus*, 109.

Encounter 21: Grace in Science

1. List available at http://www.wmich.edu/mus-gened/mus170/bio graphy100.

2. To Émile Bernard, June 23, 1888, in *The Letters of Vincent van Gogh*, ed. Ronald de Leeuw, trans. Arnold Pomerans (New York: Penguin Books, 1997), 370. Italics (underlining) in original.

3. C. S. Lewis, "The Inner Ring," 1944 Memorial Lecture at King's College, University of London, available at http://www.lewissociety .org/innerring.php.

4. George Sylvester Viereck, "What Life Means to Einstein: An Interview," *Saturday Evening Post*, October 26, 1929, 117.

5. C. S. Lewis, *Out of the Silent Planet* (1938; New York: Scribner's Classics, 1996), 74.

6. This quotation, and others in this encounter, are from notes taken during the "Visiting Religious and Scientific Imaginations Afresh" project of the Collegeville Institute for Ecumenical and Cultural Research (2000–2002). The named participants have given permission to publish what they said.

7. See *Stanford Encyclopedia of Philosophy* (https://plato.stanford.edu/entries/condemnation), where the historical conundrums of the dispute are laid out.

Encounter 22: Grace in a Hazelnut

This encounter draws on material that previously appeared in my chapter "Analogy, Discovery, and Recognition in the Life of Science and the Life of Faith," in *Science and Faith: The Problem of the Human Being in Science and Theology, Proceedings of the International Conference, November 30–December 2, 2000*, ed. Natalia A. Pecherskaya and Greg Sandstrom (St. Petersburg: St. Petersburg School of Religion and Philosophy, 2001), 61–67. Used by permission.

1. Julian of Norwich, *Showings*, trans. Edmund Colledge, OSA, and James Walsh, SJ (Mahwah, NJ: Paulist Press, 1978), 130.

2. In *John Keats (The Oxford Authors)*, ed. Elizabeth Cook (Oxford: Oxford University Press, 1990), 32.

3. T. S. Eliot, "Little Gidding," section V, in *The Complete Poems and Plays 1909–1950* (New York: Harcourt, Brace, 1952), 145.

4. Angela Tilby, *Soul: God, Self, and the New Cosmology* (New York: Doubleday, 1992), 275, 125, 277.

5. Jaroslav Pelikan, *The Melody of Theology: A Philosophical Dictionary* (Cambridge, MA: Harvard University Press, 1988), 102.

Encounter 23: Grace on Darwin's Grave

1. There is uncertainty about whether these words were actually used. For a balanced account, see the website of the Oxford University

Museum of Natural History, where the "debate" was held on June 30, 1860: http://www.oum.ox.ac.uk/learning/htmls/debate.htm.

2. For the text of the statute, Public Acts, Chapter 27, House Bill No. 185, passed by the Sixty-Fourth General Assembly of the State of Tennessee on March 13, 1925, and signed by the governor eight days later, see http://www.famous-trials.com/scopesmonkey/2128-evolu tionstatutes.

3. *Inherit the Wind*, in *The Selected Plays of Jerome Lawrence and Robert E. Lee*, ed. Alan Woods (Columbus: Ohio State University Press, 1995), 69.

4. See Pope Pius XII's 1950 encyclical, *Humani generis*, 36, at http://www.vatican.va/content/pius-xii/en/encyclicals/documents /hf_p-xii_enc_12081950_humani-generis.html. The case has recently been made more forcefully by Pope Francis: https://www.usnews .com/news/articles/2014/10/28/pope-francis-comments-on-evolu tion-and-the-catholic-church.

5. https://creationmuseum.org/about/.

6. Anne Foerst, "Commander Data: A Candidate for Harvard Divinity School?," in *Religion in a Secular City: Essays in Honor of Harvey Cox*, ed. Arvind Sharma (Harrisburg, PA: Trinity Press International, 2001), 263.

7. *Star Trek: Picard*, season 1, episode 10, "Et in Arcadia Ego, Part 2," directed by Akiva Goldsman, written by Michael Chabon, aired March 26, 2020, on CBS Full Access.

8. The text of Dobzhansky's essay is available at https://www.pbs .org/wgbh/evolution/library/10/2/text_pop/l_102_01.html. The remark about his religious identity is in Michael Shermer and Frank J. Sulloway, "The Grand Old Man of Evolution: An Interview with Evolutionary Biologist Ernst Mayr," *Skeptic* 8, no. 1 (January 2000), 82, https://www.researchgate.net/publication/258332727_The_Grand _Old_Man_of_Evolution_An_Interview_with_Evolutionary_Biologist _Ernst_Mayr.

Encounter 24: Grace in *Scientific American*

1. See http://www.anglicannews.org/news/2012/11/archbishop-of
-canterbury-my-successor-needs-a-newspaper-in-one-hand-and
-a-bible-in-the-other.aspx, where Rowan Williams is quoted as using
an aphorism that is commonly credited to Karl Barth.

2. There is no agreement in the scientific or journalistic communities about spelling: Is it Neanderthal or Neandertal? *Scientific American* opts for the latter. I will otherwise stick with the more familiar
former.

3. Lydia Pyne, "Our Neanderthal Complex: What if our ancient
relatives did 'human' better?," *Nautilis*, October 16, 2014, http://nautil
.us/issue/18/genius/our-neanderthal-complex?.

4. For example, Origen, *On First Principles* 2.3.1, ed. G. W. Butter-
worth (New York: Harper Torchbooks, 1966), 83–84.

5. "The Future of String Theory—A Conversation with Brian
Greene," *Scientific American*, November 2003, 68–73.

6. Erasmus, *The Praise of Folly*, trans. John P. Dolan, in *The Essential Erasmus* (New York: New American Library, 1964), 113.

7. Augustine, *Confessions* 8.7.16, trans. Henry Chadwick (Oxford:
Oxford University Press, 1991), 44.

8. Personal conversation with author, 1994.

9. Gordon Bell and Jim Gemmell, "A Digital Life," *Scientific American*, March 2007, https://www.scientificamerican.com/article/a-dig
ital-life/.

10. Michael Shermer, "Can a Scientific Utopia Succeed?," *Scientific
American*, February 2014, https://www.scientificamerican.com/article
/can-a-scientific-utopia-succeed/.

Encounter 25: Grace in Coventry Cathedral and on the Hudson River

1. George Sylvester Viereck, "What Life Means to Einstein: An
Interview," *Saturday Evening Post*, October 26, 1929, 117.

2. Benjamin Britten, "On Receiving the First Aspen Award" (speech),

Aspen Amphitheatre, Aspen, Colorado, July 31, 1964, https://www.aspen musicfestival.com/benjamin-britten/.

3. "Flight 1549: A Routine Takeoff Turns Ugly," *60 Minutes* interview, February 8, 2009, http://www.cbsnews.com/news/flight-1549-a -routine-takeoff-turns-ugly/.

4. Gerald P. McNamara, "From Park Avenue to the Hudson: A Flight 1549 Diary," *Time*, February 24, 2009, http://content.time.com /time/nation/article/0,8599,1881311,00.html.

5. This phrase was used by one of my heroes, the late Senator Paul Wellstone, in a 1999 speech to the Sheet Metal Workers Union (and often in other settings as well); see Gary Cunningham, *Star Tribune* blog, September 22, 2010, https://www.startribune.com/we-all-do -better-when-we-all-do-better/103588254/.

6. Tim LaHaye and Jerry B. Jenkins, *Left Behind: A Novel of the Earth's Last Days*, Left Behind Series 1 (Carol Stream, IL: Tyndale, 1995), chapters 1–2.

Encounter 26: Grace in Art

This encounter draws on material that previously appeared in my article "Religion and Art: The Uneasy Alliance," *Religion in Life* 49, no. 4 (Winter 1980): 448–60. Used by permission.

1. Text of Eusebius's letter in Herman Hennephof, *Textus byzantini ad iconomachiam pertinentes*, no. 110 (Leiden: E. J. Brill, 1969), 42–44. I have imagined Constantia's remarks on the basis of the letter.

2. John Calvin, *Commentaries on the Last Four Books of Moses Arranged in the Form of a Harmony*, vol. 2 (Grand Rapids, MI: Eerdmans, 1950), 120, commenting on Deuteronomy 4:12.

3. John le Carré, *Our Game* (New York: Knopf, 1995), 250.

4. Hilary Thimmesh, OSB, *Marcel Breuer and the Committee of Twelve Plan a Church: A Monastic Memoir* (Collegeville, MN: Saint John's University Press, 2011).

5. Christopher Calderhead, *Illuminating the Word: The Making*

of The Saint John's Bible, 2nd ed. (Collegeville, MN: Liturgical Press, 2015).

6. In a letter to Max Born, March 3, 1947, in *The Born-Einstein Letters: Correspondence Between Albert Einstein and Max and Hedwig Born from 1916-1955, with Commentaries by Max Born* (London: Macmillan, 1971), 158. The German is "spukhafte Fernwirkung."

7. On entanglement, see Vlatko Vedral, "Living in a Quantum World," *Scientific American,* June 2011, https://www.scientificamer ican.com/article/living-in-a-quantum-world/.

8. Quoted in Thimmesh, *Marcel Breuer,* 20.

Encounter 27: Grace on a Baseball Diamond

This encounter draws on material that previously appeared in my article "'Field of Dreams' offers state's leaders a lesson: A story about hospitality pits the power of 'yes' against the forces of 'no,'" *Star Tribune* (Minneapolis), May 9, 2007, A17. Used by permission.

1. *Field of Dreams,* written and directed by Phil Alden Robinson, released May 5, 1989 (produced by Gordon Company; distributed by Universal Pictures).

Encounter 28: Grace Where I Don't Expect It

This encounter draws on material that previously appeared in my article "Television's Ally McBeal teaches true spirit of Advent this holiday season," *St. Cloud Times,* December 6, 1998, 11A. Used by permission.

1. *The Passion of the Christ,* directed by Mel Gibson, written by Benedict Fitzgerald and Mel Gibson, released February 25, 2004 (produced by Icon Productions; distributed by Newmarket Films).

2. *Spartacus,* directed by Stanley Kubrick, written by Dalton Trumbo, released October 6, 1960 (produced by Bryna Productions; distributed by Universal Pictures).

3. *The Hunger Games,* directed by Gary Ross, written by Gary

Ross, Suzanne Collins, and Billy Ray, released March 12, 2012 (produced and distributed by Lionsgate).

4. Nathaniel Philbrick, introduction to *A Night to Remember* by Walter Lord, 50th anniv. ed. (1955; repr., New York: Henry Holt, 2005), xiv.

5. Clive Sansom, *The Witnesses and Other Poems* (London: Methuen, 1956).

6. *Ally McBeal*, season 1, episode 10, "Boy to the World," directed by Thomas Schlamme, written by David E. Kelley, aired December 1, 1997, on Fox.

Encounter 29: Grace On Board the Starship *Enterprise*

1. Lewis Carroll, *Through the Looking-Glass and What Alice Found There* (1871), chapter 5, "Wool and Water."

2. Peter Brown, *Augustine of Hippo: A Biography* (Berkeley: University of California Press, 1969), 120.

3. John Henry Newman, "The Mission of Saint Benedict," *Atlantis*, January 1858, http://www.newmanreader.org/works/historical /volume2/benedictine/mission.html.

4. Fyodor Dostoevsky, *The Brothers Karamazov*, trans. Richard Pevear and Larissa Volokhonsky (New York: Vintage Classics, 1991), 359–63. The expression "touching other worlds" is Alyosha's recollection of something said earlier by Father Zosima, in chapter 3(g), "Of Prayer, Love, and the Touching of Other Worlds," 320.

5. Carroll, *Through the Looking-Glass*, chapter 5.

6. *Star Trek: The Next Generation* (abbreviated *TNG* in subsequent notes), season 4, episode 3, "Brothers," directed by Rob Bowman, written by Rick Berman, aired October 6, 1990, distributed by Paramount Pictures (currently owned by ViacomCBS). Note: initial distribution and current ownership apply to all episodes.

7. *TNG*, season 6, episode 1, "Time's Arrow: Part 2," directed by Les Landau, written by Jeri Taylor and Joe Menosky, aired September 19, 1992.

8. https://community.logos.com/cfs-filesystemfile...Files/.../3771
.Klingon-Bible.docx and https://www.kli.org/wiki/Klingon_Shake
speare_Restoration_Project.

9. *TNG*, season 6, episode 17, "Birthright, Part 2," directed by Dan
Curry, written by René Echevarria, aired February 27, 1993.

10. Francis P. Church, "Is There a Santa Claus?," *New York Sun*,
September 21, 1897. Discussed in encounter 1.

11. *TNG*, season 7, episode 18, "Eye of the Beholder," directed by
Cliff Bole, written by René Echevarria, aired February 26, 1994.

12. *TNG*, season 7, episode 8, "Attached," directed by Jonathan
Frakes, written by Nick Sagan, aired November 6, 1993.

13. Article 11, "Concerning Theological Error," of Central Baptist
Theological Seminary of Virginia Beach's Biblical Foundations Statement, *Catalog 2010–2012*, https://issuu.com/elehner/docs/cbts_cat
alog_2010-2012.

14. Robert S. Bilheimer, *Breakthrough: The Emergence of the Ecumenical Tradition* (Grand Rapids, MI: Eerdmans; Geneva: WCC
Publications, 1989).

15. *TNG*, season 5, episode 17, "The Outcast," directed by Robert
Scheerer, written by Jeri Taylor, aired March 14, 1992.

16. *TNG*, season 1, episode 5, "Where No One Has Gone Before,"
directed by Rob Bowman, written by Diane Duane and Michael
Reaves, aired October 24, 1987.

17. T. S. Eliot, "Little Gidding," section V, in *The Complete Poems
and Plays 1909–1950* (New York: Harcourt, Brace, 1952), 145.

18. Declan Fahy, *The New Celebrity Scientists: Out of the Lab and
Into the Limelight* (Lanham, MD: Rowman and Littlefield, 2015), 24.

19. *TNG*, season 2, episode 2, "Where Silence Has Lease," directed
by Winrich Kolbe, written by Jack B. Sowards, aired November 26,
1988.

20. *TNG*, season 2, episode 4, "The Outrageous Okona," directed
by Robert Becker, written by Burton Armus, Les Menchen, Lance
Dickson, and David Landsberg, aired December 10, 1988.

21. *TNG*, season 2, episode 1, "The Child," directed by Rob Bow-

man, written by Jaron Summers, Jon Povili, and Maurie Hurley, aired November 19, 1988.

22. *TNG*, season 1, episode 22, "Skin of Evil," directed by Joseph L. Scanlan, written by Joseph Stefano and Hannah Louise Shearer, aired April 23, 1988.

23. *TNG*, "The Child."

24. *TNG*, "Where Silence Has Lease."

25. *TNG*, season 2, episode 9, "The Measure of a Man," directed by Robert Scheerer, written by Melinda M. Snodgrass, aired February 11, 1989.

26. In the Collegeville Institute consultation on "Visiting Religious and Scientific Imaginations Afresh," referenced in encounter 21.

27. *TNG*, season 1, episode 25, "The Neutral Zone," directed by James L. Conway, written by Maurice Hurley, Deborah McIntyre, and Mona Clee, aired May 14, 1988.

28. *TNG*, season 2, episode 3, "Elementary, Dear Data," directed by Rob Bowman, written by Brian Alan Lane, aired December 3, 1988.

29. *TNG*, season 2, episode 21, "Peak Performance," directed by Robert Scheerer, written by David Kemper, aired July 8, 1989.

30. *TNG*, season 3, episode 10, "The Defector," directed by Robert Scheerer, written by Ronald D. Moore, aired January 1, 1990.

31. *TNG*, season 4, episode 13, "Devil's Due," directed by Tom Benko, written by Philip LaZebnik and William Douglas Lansford, aired February 2, 1991.

32. *TNG*, season 7, episode 23, "Emergence," directed by Cliff Bole, written by Joe Menosky and Brannon Braga, aired May 7, 1994.

33. Harold Bloom, *Shakespeare: The Invention of the Human* (New York: Riverhead Books, 1998).

Encounter 30: Grace in the Overlap of "Spiritual" and "Religious"

1. In *Belief without Borders: Inside the Minds of the Spiritual but not Religious* (New York: Oxford University Press, 2014), 238, Linda

A. Mercadante makes the counterintuitive but intriguing suggestion that "religion" is a broader, more inclusive category than "spirituality."

2. Robert S. Bilheimer, *A Spirituality for the Long Haul: Biblical Risk and Moral Stand* (Minneapolis: Augsburg Fortress, 1984).

3. Patrick Henry and Thomas F. Stransky, CSP, *God on Our Minds* (Philadelphia: Fortress; Collegeville, MN: Liturgical Press, 1982), 23.

4. Bieke Vandekerckhove, *The Taste of Silence: How I Came to Be at Home with Myself*, trans. Rudolf Van Puymbroek (Collegeville, MN: Liturgical Press, 2015).

5. Vandekerckhove, 41.

6. Vandekerckhove, 19.

7. *Hamlet*, act 2, scene 1.

8. "The Future of String Theory—A Conversation with Brian Greene," *Scientific American*, November 2003, 68–73.

9. Vandekerckhove, *The Taste of Silence*, xiv.

10. Vandekerckhove, 31.

11. Vandekerckhove, 45.

12. Vandekerckhove, 42.

13. Letter No. 45, in Hyder Edward Rollins, ed., *The Letters of John Keats 1814–1821*, vol. 1 (Cambridge, MA: Harvard University Press, 1958), 193.

14. Vandekerckhove, *The Taste of Silence*, 46. Italics in original.

15. Vandekerckhove, 144.

Encounter 31: Grace in a Culture of Trust, Not Fear

This encounter adapts material that previously appeared in my chapter "Meeting, Practice, and Memory: What Monastic Interreligious Dialogue Contributes to Monastic Culture," in *The Proceedings of the American Benedictine Academy Convention, August 12–15, 2004, St. Joseph, Minnesota* (New Series, Vol. 8), ed. Renée Branigan, OSB (Dickinson, North Dakota: King Speed Printing, 2004), 69–74. Used by permission.

This encounter also adapts material that previously appeared in my article "4 Minutes of Silence Spoke Louder than Words," *Star Tribune* (Minneapolis), March 27, 2018, A9. Used by permission.

1. This observation of Toynbee's is cited often, without specification. The closest I have come to finding an actual source is James L. Fredericks, "No Easy Answers: The Necessary Challenge of Interreligious Dialogue," *Commonweal* 137, no. 1 (January 15, 2010), 10–13 (also at https://www.commonwealmagazine.org/no-easy-answers), in which Fredericks recounts a conversation at Sophia University in Tokyo with Heinrich Dumoulin, a Jesuit scholar of Buddhism, who recounted the remark made during Toynbee's visit to Sophia in the 1950s.

2. Rule of Benedict 73:8, in *RB 1980: The Rule of St. Benedict in Latin and English with Notes*, ed. Timothy Fry, OSB (Collegeville, MN: Liturgical Press, 1981), 297.

3. Kilian McDonnell, "Then It Is Finished, Done?," in *Swift, Lord, You Are Not* (Collegeville, MN: Saint John's University Press, 2003), 26.

4. Rule of Benedict 3:3, in *RB 1980*, 179–80.

5. The speech is available at https://www.youtube.com/watch?v=u46HzTGVQhg.

6. Act 5, scene 3.

7. "A Conversation with 2019 Jefferson Lecturer Father Columba Stewart," Minnesota Humanities Center, October 3, 2019, https://mnhum.org/blog/a-conversation-with-2019-jefferson-lecturer-father-columba-stewart/.

8. Donald W. Mitchell and James Wiseman, OSB, eds., *The Gethsemani Encounter: A Dialogue on the Spiritual Life by Buddhist and Christian Monastics* (New York: Continuum, 1998).

9. Jean Leclercq, OSB, *The Love of Learning and the Desire for God: A Study of Monastic Culture*, trans. Catharine Misrahi (1961; repr., New York: Fordham University Press, 1982), 34.

10. "An Interview with Patrick Henry," *Monastic Interreligious Dialogue Bulletin* 67 (October 2001), https://www.urbandharma.org/buca /BD1/bd1interview.pdf.

Encounter 32: Grace in an Ancient Prayer

1. Gregory of Nazianzus, "Hymn to God," in *The Unity Book of Prayers* (London: Geoffrey Chapman, 1969), 17, adapted from *Early Christian Prayers*, ed. A. Hamman, trans. W. Mitchell (London: Longmans Green, 1961), 162. The poem is found in J.-P. Migne, *Patrologia Graeca*, vol. 37, cols. 507–8.

2. The score of "From a Book of Early Prayers," for SATB choir, a cappella, by Melinda Wagner, is available from Theodore Presser Company (Item Number: 312-41842).

3. His magisterial book is John McGuckin, *Saint Gregory of Nazianzus: An Intellectual Biography* (Crestwood, NY: St. Vladimir's Seminary Press, 2001).

4. Patrick Henry, *The Ironic Christian's Companion: Finding the Marks of God's Grace in the World* (New York: Riverhead Books, 1999).

5. Irenaeus, preface to book 5 of *Against Heresies*, in *The Ante-Nicene Fathers*, vol. 1, ed. A. Roberts and J. Donaldson (Grand Rapids, MI: Eerdmans, 1981), 526.

6. Patricia Hampl, letter to me, May 9, 1990.

7. Emily Dickinson, letter to Thomas Wentworth Higginson, February 1863, at http://archive.emilydickinson.org/correspondence /higginson/l280.html.

8. Bieke Vandekerckhove, *The Taste of Silence: How I Came to Be at Home with Myself*, trans. Rudolf Van Puymbroek (Collegeville, MN: Liturgical Press, 2015), 29. Italics in original.

9. C. S. Lewis, *Surprised by Joy: The Shape of My Early Life* (New York: Harcourt, Brace, 1955), 207.

Encounter 33:
Grace in the Groundswell's Bell over the Ebbing Sea's Roar

This encounter adapts material that previously appeared in my chapter "The Ground Swell's Bell Over the Ebbing Sea's Roar," in *For the Sake of the World: Choices for a Monastic Future, Proceedings of the American Benedictine Academy Convention, August 8–11, 1990,* ed. by Renée Branigan, OSB (Mott, North Dakota: Eido Printing, 1991), 11–20. Used by permission.

1. Matthew Arnold, "Dover Beach," in *The Portable Matthew Arnold,* ed. Lionel Trilling (New York: Viking, 1949), 166–67.

2. T. S. Eliot, "The Waste Land," lines 22–24, in *The Complete Poems and Plays 1909–1950* (New York: Harcourt, 1952), 38.

3. Eliot, "The Dry Salvages," in *The Complete Poems and Plays,* 131. The poems known as *Four Quartets* were published at different times and were first gathered together under that title in 1943.

4. Mother Teresa, *Come Be My Light: The Private Writings of the "Saint of Calcutta,"* ed. Brian Kolodiejchuk, MC (New York: Doubleday, 2007), 187.

5. Martin Buber, *Ten Rungs: Hasidic Sayings* (New York: Schocken Books, 1962), 85.

6. Text at http://www.thekingcenter.org/archive/document/letter-birmingham-city-jail-0#.

7. For the Evangelical Environmental Network, see http://www.creationcare.org/.

8. The prayer by Francis of Assisi known as the "Canticle of the Sun," or "Praise of the Creatures," is available at http://www.vatican.va/spirit/documents/spirit_20020210_lettera-fedeli-3_en.html.

9. *Against Heresies* 4.20.7, following the translation in *Catechism of the Catholic Church,* part 1, sect. 2, ch.1, art.1, para. 4, iii, 294, with "human being" substituted for "man."

Epilogue: Letter to Captain Picard

1. *Star Trek: The Next Generation* (abbreviated *TNG* in subsequent notes), season 6, episode 1, "Time's Arrow: Part 2," directed by Les Landau, written by Jeri Taylor and Joe Menosky, aired September 19, 1992, distributed by Paramount Pictures (currently owned by ViacomCBS). Note: initial distribution and current ownership apply to all episodes.

2. James Gleick, *Time Travel: A History* (New York: Pantheon Books, 2016), 299.

3. No. 392, in *Pascal's Pensées* (New York: Dutton, 1958), 106.

4. Words attributed to Martin Luther at the Diet of Worms (April 1521); they do not appear in the earliest transcripts.

5. Title of a 1966 film, directed by Philip Saville, written by Leslie Bricusse and Anthony Newley, released May 11, 1966 (produced and distributed by Warner Bros).

6. Thomas Hobbes, *Leviathan* (1651) 1.13.9, at https://www.guten berg.org/files/3207/3207-h/3207-h.htm#link2H_PART1.

7. *TNG*, season 5, episode 9, "A Matter of Time," directed by Paul Lynch, written by Rick Berman, aired November 16, 1991.

8. *TNG*, season 2, episode 18, "Up the Long Ladder," directed by Winrich Kolbe, written by Melinda M. Snodgrass, aired May 20, 1989.

9. Jane Kramer, "Me, Myself, and I: What made Michel de Montaigne the first modern man?," *New Yorker*, September 7, 2009, www .newyorker.com/magazine/2009/09/07/me-myself-and-i.

10. *TNG*, season 2, episode 17, "Samaritan Snare," directed by Les Landau, written by Robert McCullough, aired May 13, 1989.

11. Rule of Benedict, Prologue 1, in *RB 1980: The Rule of St. Benedict in Latin and English with Notes*, ed. Timothy Fry, OSB (Collegeville, MN: Liturgical Press, 1981), 157. The Latin is "Obsculta," 156.

12. Lawrence M. Krauss, *The Physics of Star Trek* (New York: Basic Books, 1995), 53–61, 65–83.

13. *TNG*, season 5, episode 2, "Darmok," directed by Winrich Kolbe, written by Joe Menosky and Philip LeZebnik, aired September 28, 1991.